Devil's Club

A Botanist's Journey Across the American Frontier

Trudie Behr Scott

Copyright

Devil's Club: A Botanist's Journey Across the American Frontier

© 2025 by Trudie Behr Scott. All rights reserved.

No part of this publication may be copied, reproduced, stored in a retrieval system, or transmitted in any form or by any means—electronic, mechanical, photocopying, recording, or otherwise—without the prior written consent of the author, except for brief excerpts used in reviews, academic references, or literary criticism.

This is a work of fiction.

Any resemblance to actual persons, living or dead, is purely coincidental unless otherwise stated. While inspired by real landscapes and historical contexts, the characters, events, and dialogues are products of the author's imagination.

Cover design by Trudie Behr Scott

Printed in the United States of America

First Printing: May 2025

KDP Printing

ISBN: 978-1-968619-18-3

Dedication

This book is a testament to the resilience and determination of all those who, like my mother, were born out of their time. Their dreams and aspirations often clashed with the expectations of their peers and their era. They embarked on a challenging journey to find a place where they could be acknowledged and respected for their individuality and choices.

Acknowledgments

I am indebted to and appreciate the following people:

Nick Bateman and his perceptive team believed in my book and edited it with grace and clarity.

My husband of forty-six years, Bruce Scott, encouraged me and supported the publication of this book.

My sage and nurturing professors at Stanford University, as well as Jerrico Writers in London, and the Mendocino Writers Conference.

My cheering friends who kept at me for many years to get it done: Stacey, Phila, Debbie, Ann, Catherine, and the Sister of My Heart.

My daughter-in-law, Lauren, who once thought they should change their name from Scott to Readers, and her children, who love to read—Izzie, Bruce, and Alice—fill my heart with love.

Michael Pincus, my lifetime mentor for all things who believes in me, and last but not least, The Bird Man of Point Reyes.

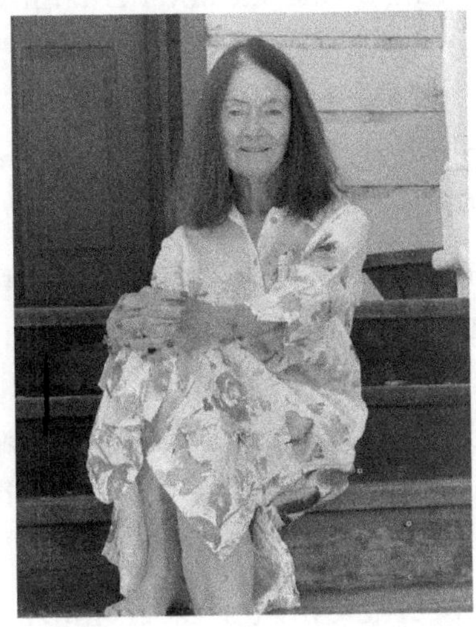

About the Author

Trudie Behr Scott is an author and passionate botanist living in a small coastal town in California, near a National Seashore. She resides in a historic schoolhouse with her husband, two dogs, and a lively community of wild birds that she lovingly feeds and gently tames. Her writing studio, tucked inside an old carriage house, offers a peaceful setting where she crafts her stories, often inspired by her deep connection to nature and the environment around her.

Trudie's journey as a writer began in an unexpected place. While attending law school, where she was the only woman in her class, she earned the Outstanding Student Award. It was this unique and formative experience that inspired her debut novel, *Devil's Club: A Botanist's Journey Across the American Frontier*. The story follows Rachael, a determined young woman who refuses to surrender her passion for botany despite the limitations of her time.

A significant part of Trudie's creative process involved firsthand research. During a spring break, she and her family traced the Oregon Trail by car, immersing themselves in its terrain and atmosphere. This journey, made all the more meaningful as she faced personal challenges with mobility, allowed her to authentically capture the essence of the trail for her novel.

Beyond writing, Trudie has spent years cultivating her understanding of nature, particularly through animal tracking and her deep rapport with wildlife. During a time of personal hardship, her quiet interactions with animals, including a fox and two jays, provided comfort, connection, and inspiration that shaped her creative vision.

With *Devil's Club*, Trudie invites readers into a world where nature, resilience, and self-discovery converge, echoing her own experiences of healing, adventure, and purpose rooted in the natural world.

Preface

There is a saying among writers that one is either a planner or a "pantser."

A planner outlines the plot of the entire book. A "pantser" flies by the seat of, well, their pants. But for me, I wrote this novel by walking miles on the trails outside of the Home of My Heart, my small house up on the coast. After finishing a scene, I would pull on my boots and jacket and head out. I would close my eyes, listen to the calming rhythm of the fingers of the waves caressing the sand, and allow my imagination to see the last scene. I could picture the people in the scene in my mind, where they stood, and how they felt. It's rather like staging a play with no script. Then, I let my imagination loose to answer the question of what should happen next. It rarely let me down.

The Oregon Trail had always been an interest of mine. I had a romantic view of it before I did research and drove the trail in a car. Then, I understood the true drama and hardship that those who traveled that trail faced, as well as the dangers they encountered—not only for themselves but also for their children. Hence, the shape of the story changed.

As time went on, I got to know and care about my characters as if they were family. I found myself riding in the wagon with Rachael. I saw what she saw and felt what she felt. I could feel the changes in her, even if I sometimes disagreed with them. The more I put her through, the more she fought back. I cried when I wrote several scenes and still cry when I reread them.

There is an intimacy about writing a novel that often goes unstated, but for me, that was one of the greatest pleasures. I invite you to read this book and come to know my family.

Introduction

The forest has always been a place of answers. In its stillness, we find reflection. In its growth, resilience. In *Devil's Club*, the forest is not just a setting—it is a living character, a keeper of memory, mystery, and quiet strength.

This is the story of Rachael, a young botanist shaped by the rhythms of the natural world and the loss of the man who taught her to see it. After her father's death, she is left not only with grief but with the tools he gave her—a love of plants, a deep reverence for the land, and an unspoken challenge: to follow her own path into the unknown.

Set in a time when women were rarely welcomed into scientific fields, *Devil's Club* is a journey through both wilderness and womanhood. Rachael's story unfolds among moss-laced trees and medicinal roots, where the lines between science and spirit, tradition and rebellion, begin to blur.

The plant for which this novel is named—*Devil's Club*—is thorned, powerful, and often misunderstood. Like the forest itself, it resists simple definitions. It wounds if handled carelessly but heals if approached with respect. In many ways, it is the perfect emblem of Rachael's world: wild, complex, and alive with hidden strength.

This book is a tribute to the knowledge that grows in silence, to the wisdom passed down through soil and spores, and to the courage it takes to step off the marked trail and follow the one only you can see.

More than a story, *Devil's Club* is an invitation to walk with the forest—to listen, to grieve, to grow—and to remember that nothing in nature, or in us, is wasted.

Table of Contents

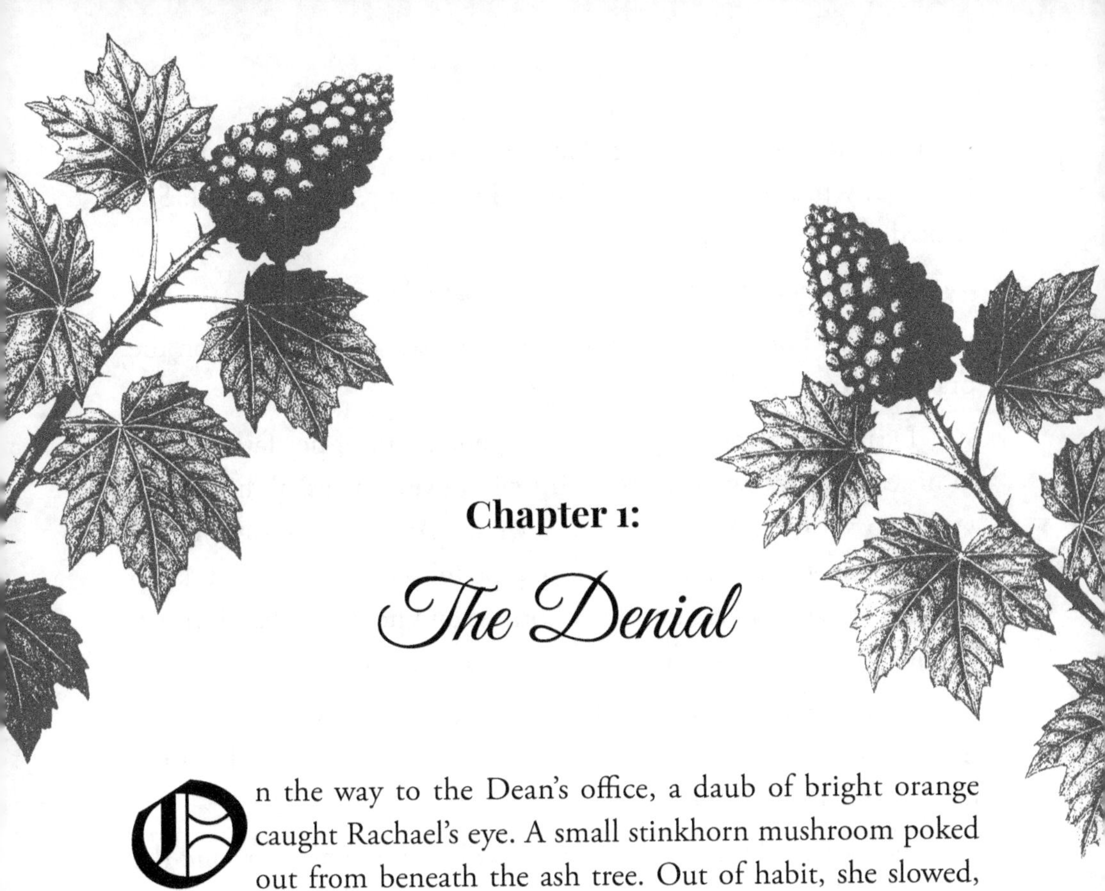

Chapter 1:

The Denial

On the way to the Dean's office, a daub of bright orange caught Rachael's eye. A small stinkhorn mushroom poked out from beneath the ash tree. Out of habit, she slowed, reached into a pocket of her black dress, and pulled out her talisman, a small penknife, a gift from her father. She knelt and gently lifted the mushroom with the back of the knife. It had been his favorite. Perhaps this find was a sign of good luck.

She stood and reached into her pocket for her collecting bag, but felt only the coarse material of her mourning dress; how she hated this dress. Bending down, Rachael tucked the mushroom back into the dirt. She would be late if she didn't hurry. There would be time to collect mushrooms later, after her acceptance into the Botany Department at New Geneva College.

Rachael's footsteps echoed as she climbed the familiar wooden stairs. The tight lace collar of her stiff mourning dress scratched the underside of her chin.

Harriet, a gray-haired woman with glasses, seated behind a desk stacked with papers, greeted her. Harriet gave her a frank but sympathetic nod, prompting Rachael to check her bun. No matter how many pins she used, her dense blonde hair tended to fall. She tucked an errant strand back into place.

"He's expecting you, dear," Harriet said. "Go right in."

Rachael nodded. Smoothing her skirt, she put her hand on the brass knob and pushed the door open.

Dean Frank rose to greet her. A gentleman of her father's age, in his early fifties, wore a tweed suit with a vest. As usual, his sleeves were too short, exposing his bony wrists. As he clasped her hand, Rachael inhaled the familiar scent of pipe tobacco, an aroma of damp autumn leaves and bergamot that both he and her father had favored. She just managed to quell the sob rising in her throat.

"There, there." He patted her shoulder. "I miss him, too. It'll never be the same without him. Please, sit down." He pulled out the chair across from his desk.

Rachael sat, folded her hands in her lap, and looked around the office. She had formed her first letters at this desk, her father gently guiding her hand as she held a fat pencil. She could almost feel his large, callused hand covering hers.

Clearing his throat, the Dean began, "First of all, Rachael, thank you for arranging to send your father's botany collection to the college. It was generous of him, and he will be an invaluable addition to our resources. I remember those Sunday lunches when you and your father would drag me away to show me your latest finds. I can see him now in his baggy pants and worn flannel shirt. You both loved to roam the woods together. He thought the world of you."

"I remember those luncheons, too. Especially the last one."

Rachael recalled her father sitting at the luncheon table, waving a letter from his friend Thomas, a revered botanist in Oregon. Thomas believed the Indians used a plant similar to Devil's Club and urged her father to travel west to find it. The Dean had dismissed it as "a fool's mission." She remembered how disappointed her father had been.

The Dean sighed. "With him passing so soon after your dear mother's death, I hope you consider me a benefactor and a mentor. I trust you know I have your best interests in mind." He smiled at her.

"Yes, which is why I knew you would support my application. I can't wait to begin."

"Let's talk about that." He shifted in his chair. "Your father adored you. But I warned him, as you grew older, that involving you in fieldwork, even with your talents, was, well…" He cleared his throat. "Not appropriate for a young lady to be out at all odd hours, in all kinds of weather." Two red spots bloomed on his cheeks. "Such work isn't conducive to raising a gentlewoman."

Rachael looked down at her hands in her lap and realized her nails were dirty. She had meant to wear gloves, but, as usual, she forgot. Rachael was not good at paying attention to such things. She tucked her feet under the chair, suddenly conscious that she hadn't changed her hobnailed boots for the more fashionable button-up kind. It was stuffy in here. Glancing at the closed window, she wished she could fling it open. She slipped her finger into her collar and tried to loosen it, but it only seemed tighter.

"I reminded him that if he didn't curtail your ramblings together, you would not have time to develop the, ah, well, the feminine qualities and skills that men desire in a woman."

"Dean Frank, my father, felt it was important for me to fulfill his legacy. I'm sure he must have discussed this with you. I'm more than willing to make the necessary sacrifices. I'm certain he would have wanted me to continue my study of botany here, at his alma mater." Her leg began to jiggle beneath the chair.

"If you'll just hear me out…"

The Dean looked directly at her. "I'm afraid your application has been denied."

She took a deep breath and pressed on. "But certainly, with all my experience, there must be a place here for me." Her voice rose. She felt her hand reach up to her neck again, tugging at the lace.

"The committee agreed that entering the program was not in your best interest. I'm afraid the decision was unanimous and final." He dropped his chin and looked over his glasses at her.

"You voted against me, too?" she asked, feeling heat rush into her face.

"Yes. I did."

Rachael leaped to her feet, fists clenched, ignoring his attempt to calm her.

"Can't I reapply? This time with your support? Certainly, as my father's closest friend, your vote against me was a mistake. My father would have expected you to advocate for me. I could organize the specimens in the lab and attend the lectures. You know how much I want to learn. There must be some way."

The Dean glanced over her head toward the closed door of his office.

"Is there no appeal, then? No chance at all?"

"No. I'm afraid not. The decision is final."

"Then I have nothing more to say, Dean Frank. I'll make other arrangements."

"Wait, Rachael, wait…"

But Rachael was already out the door.

Outside the building, she strode across the green lawn. How could it be that even Dean Frank had voted to deny her application? *Develop the feminine qualities that a man expects in a woman?* She was engaged to Richard, who understood her femininity well enough. Unlike her friend Mary, who sat around doing needlepoint and gossiping with the other girls, their hands covering their mouths in mock horror at a savory bit of news, Rachael could never fit in here. Never. She was a botanist.

She pulled the penknife from her pocket, turning it over and over.

She had last used it early in March when she and her father had collected a mushroom that grew only after a good soaking rain. She'd worn his old green sweater and her long "collecting skirt," which she had sewn herself, with multiple pockets for her tools: a small penknife, specimen bags, and a hand lens. She had knelt on the damp ground, fully aware her skirt was getting wet, but too absorbed in teasing the small, coral-colored mushroom from its place, a *Hygrocybe conica,* to care about a trivial discomfort like wet clothes.

What she wished she could forget was the sound of her father's strangled cry as he clutched his chest, gasped, and collapsed. She had run to get help, but he was gone by the time she returned. The doctor later told her he had likely died instantly. He meant to comfort her, but it didn't.

Not being accepted by Geneva insulted her father's memory and everything they had worked for together. What was she to do now? Sit alone in her parents' house during the required year of mourning, waiting patiently for Richard to marry her and take care of her for the rest of her life? Attend Mrs. Beckman's luncheons and listen to complaints about unreliable house servants or debates over where to find the best roast for Sunday supper?

An idea began to form. What about the letter from Thomas in Oregon, the one about Devil's Club, a plant not known on the East Coast? He claimed that every part of it could be used for medicinal purposes. The Indians were already using it and might be persuaded to share their knowledge. Its supposed power was legendary. If she could find it, bring back a specimen, and document its uses, she would be revered as a botanist.

She and her father had discussed going to Oregon, regardless of the Dean's opinion. They had even planned a route to Independence, Missouri, the jumping-off place for the wagons headed west.

Could she go alone and find the Devil's Club? She wasn't sure whether a single woman would be allowed to purchase a place on a wagon train or how much money she might need.

When her mother passed, her father had placed his estate in trust. She would speak to the family attorney. With the lawyer's advice and the proceeds from selling the house, she should have more than enough to fund the journey.

Looking up at a passing cloud, she sighed. The whole idea seemed like that cloud, drifting and insubstantial. A passing fancy, neither sensible nor practical. Just a far-fetched dream.

Still, she would talk to Richard tonight. He had supported her application after her father's passing. She believed he respected her for it and was even secretly pleased that she didn't spend her time idly gossiping with friends. Why, perhaps Richard could speak to the Dean on her behalf. Surely, he would be as angry as she was about her rejection, perhaps angry enough to intervene.

She walked across the green toward her family's house. Richard always wanted her to take a carriage, as most women her age feared scuffing their high-button boots, but she preferred to walk. She and her father had often wandered the woods together, speaking quietly about what they might find.

She would never have been rejected if he were still alive.

Clenching her fists, she then slowly unfolded each finger, just as her father had taught her when she was small and angry. At last, she reached the brick steps of her house, inserted the key into the lock, and turned it. For a moment, she imagined her penknife slipping beneath a leaf to dislodge a remnant of Devil's Club.

She saw herself taking it to the Dean and placing it triumphantly on his desk, the legendary plant in hand. But she shook her head, admonishing herself to stop dreaming impossible dreams.

Eager to release her too-tight bun, she raised her hands and raked her fingers through her hair until it fell loosely around her shoulders. The confining pins were scattered somewhere on the stairs, but she didn't care. She shook her head in relief and stepped into the vestibule.

Richard arrived later that night, as planned. He was dressed in the latest men's fashions: a coat with full sleeves and lapels and a shorter collar at the back of the neck. His trousers were long and tubular, accentuating his lanky frame. His brown hair was combed back in a wave over his forehead, and smelled, as always, of oil.

Seeing her swollen eyes, he asked, "Have you had a fight with Elizabeth? You know she can be petty at times."

"Oh, Richard, no, it's not that. I wanted tonight to be a celebration. I wanted to surprise you. I knew you'd be proud of me... But Richard," she gulped, "they rejected me. The decision was unanimous. I simply couldn't believe it. Surely you'll talk to the Dean on my behalf?"

Avoiding her eyes, he hesitated. "Well, darling, I don't think I can do that. Is this application so important? After all, we'll be married in a few months, and you'll have a household to run. Why would you want to pursue a degree in botany? Is it really so surprising that they turned you down?"

His perfectly waxed mustache twitched.

"Yes, the Dean knew I cataloged my father's collection. I expected to be accepted, and I thought you'd be proud of me. It never occurred to me that I didn't have your support."

He marched around the room and finally stopped, looming over her as she sat in her mother's chintz armchair.

"Actually, Rachael, I'm upset," he said, his voice tight. "Is this how you'd behave as my wife, no consideration for my thoughts or feelings on the matter?"

Looking down to avoid his florid face, she noticed his perfectly shined boots. She uncrossed her ankles and leaned back.

"I had hoped that after your father's death, you would give up meandering through the woods looking for plants."

Rachael's mouth tightened into a hard line, and her body stiffened. She looked up at him. Who was this man? Had he forgotten that he had once encouraged her to help her father?

"Is this what you think of me?" she burst out. "You, my father's friend, the one who sought to comfort me after Mother's death when my father was overwhelmed with grief. You were so warm and understanding. You encouraged me to help him. You said you respected how I cared for him. I thought you understood that botany wasn't a passing fancy. It was a passion. I..."

"I should have known better," he interrupted. "When you arrived at Mother's house for tea to plan the engagement party, wearing those horrible muddy boots, Mother reassured me afterwards that surely, in time, you'd become more interested in appropriate pursuits. You know, like your friend Elizabeth. She's learning to run a household. Those are the skills needed to support my career at the bank. Those are the skills of a reasonable wife."

As Richard gestured sharply, his hands cutting through the air between them, Rachael stood and walked several feet away.

"Why am I as tall as he is?" she wondered. She turned to look at her father's portrait on the wall. *How could we all have been so wrong about Richard? He encouraged my work. He was proud of me, or so I thought.*

Blood surged through her body. Her voice dropped in volume as she spoke through clenched teeth.

"That's what's expected of me? Managing housemaids and planning whether to serve pork roast or chicken? Do you not understand how devastated I am by this rejection? I deserved that place!" She stamped her foot, a childhood gesture of rage. It made a satisfying crack against the polished wood floor.

She continued before he could speak. "My father must have talked to you about my passion for botany. He was proud of my work."

"Actually," Richard replied coldly, "when I asked for your hand, he said he looked forward to seeing you safely settled as a wife. He thought marriage to me might bring some discipline into your life. You've always had a terrible temper, not your best quality."

Richard straightened as if trying to regain dominance. A wave of nausea rose in Rachael's throat. Her chin jutted forward.

"I don't believe you," she choked. "My father would never say such a thing. He admired my work."

Richard's nostrils flared. He shook his head, picked up his hat, and strode out the front door, shutting it carefully behind him.

Rachael went to the door, flung it open, and watched his figure retreat down the street. Then she slammed it shut, satisfied by the crash. Her mother's painting of her father, holding a giant Earthstar mushroom, fell from the wall.

Later that evening, a letter from Richard was delivered, ending their engagement.

After reading it, Rachael threw herself down on the velvet couch in the parlor, pounding her fists against a pillow in a fury at her own foolishness. She had misunderstood Richard entirely. She thought he accepted her, knew her. They had grown up together. Her father adored him and encouraged the match after her mother died. She had truly believed that Richard would support her ambitions as her father had.

But he and the Dean were the same.

How could I have been so wrong?

Rachael twisted the ring on her finger.

She was fortunate to have had a father who enjoyed teaching her and nurturing her passion. She would never believe he wanted her to marry and settle down, as Richard had claimed. What nonsense.

At that moment, Rachael made her decision: she would go to Oregon to find the Devil's Club and honor her father's memory. The Dean had ridiculed her father's belief in the plant's existence, and now, there was nothing left in Geneva to hold her back.

How unfortunate to be born a woman. If she were a man, she could simply go to Independence and join a wagon company without question. But as a single woman, she would face an entirely different set of challenges. *Proper* women did not travel alone. She could claim to be a widow, but even that might come with complications. She would have to wear black. Worse, men might see her as eligible, as someone to woo.

She was finished with all that.

Looking down at her left hand, she nodded and slipped off the diamond engagement ring. She would send it back to Richard through the post. That would settle the matter of her engagement and her single status.

She would buy herself a wedding ring tomorrow and consult her father's lawyer about selling the house.

Then, she would pretend she was married. It was as simple as that.

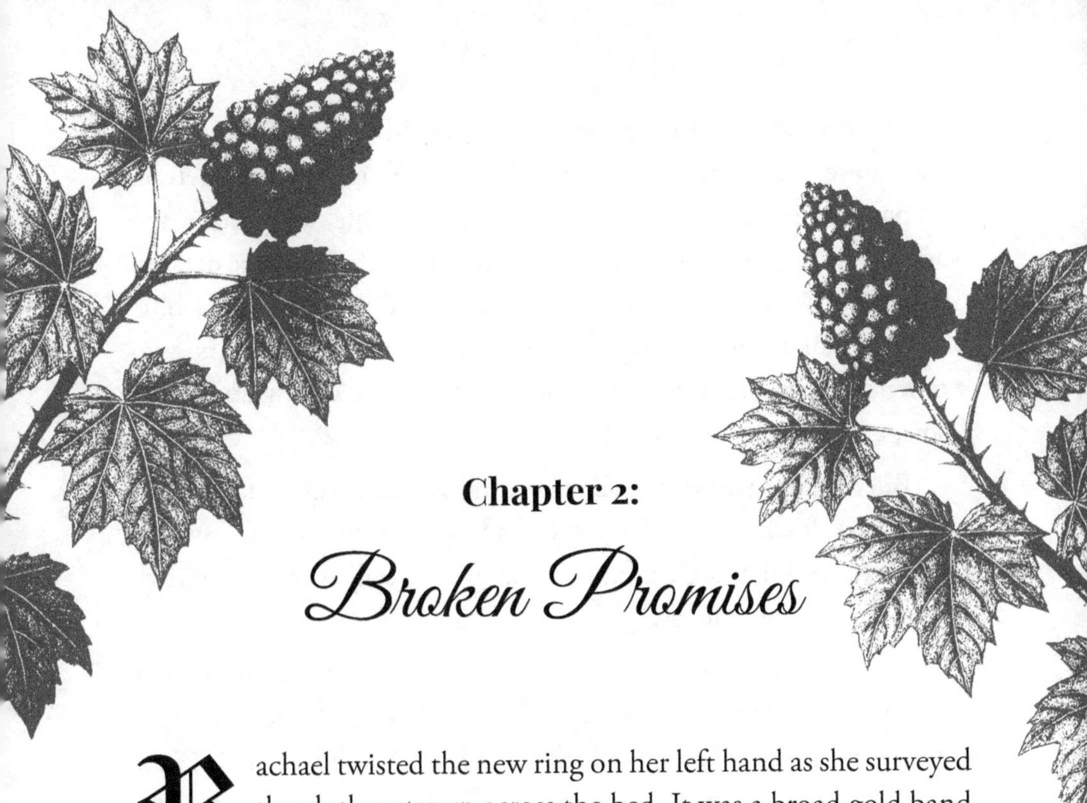

Chapter 2:

Broken Promises

Rachael twisted the new ring on her left hand as she surveyed the clothes strewn across the bed. It was a broad gold band she had purchased from a pawnbroker in the next town. He had given her a particular look but asked no questions—he wanted the business.

The clothes were another quandary. It had taken weeks to gather the items now laid out before her, and she needed to fit them all into a single satchel and the carpetbag she had recently purchased. Three hundred and forty dollars from the sale of the house were sewn into the hem of her wool traveling skirt. The rest she had deposited in the bank.

Rachael turned to the mirror, wondering whether she could pass for a married woman. At nineteen, she considered herself plain. Her face was oval with high cheekbones, a small nose, and almond-shaped hazel eyes. She liked her round, small mouth but was less fond of her long, curly blond hair, which always refused to stay neatly pinned in a bun. Tilting her head slightly, she reached up to grab a loose strand and attempted to tuck it back into place.

"So there," she said to her reflection.

She turned to examine the clothing again. She had visited the library to read everything she could about traveling the Oregon Trail. The pamphlets warned to take as little as possible, as space in the wagons was extremely limited. She allowed herself only three dresses: her favorite lavender one with the lace-trimmed bodice, a plain blue one, and a plain brown one. She also packed two underskirts, two woolen undershirts, three thick black woolen socks, sturdy leather boots, and her mother's shawl.

Burying her face in the shawl's softness, she caught a faint trace of lavender. Rachael closed her eyes and pictured her mother's warm brown eyes and the single dimple that appeared only when she smiled. She still missed her deeply.

Opening the bureau's bottom drawer, Rachael pulled out her collecting skirt. Hugging it to her chest, she hesitated, then placed it gently into her bag. How could she ever leave it behind? Who knew what she might discover on the journey?

She gazed out the window. It struck her as strange that she might never look upon this view again, never see the moonstruck backfields, never hear the scratch of the pine branch against her window, never feel the silky texture of her grandmother's quilt beneath her fingertips. How strange it was to leave everything she knew... and yet how thrilling.

Rachael opened the drawer of the large mahogany dresser once more. She retrieved her penknife and a small magnifying hand lens with a solid brass cover. Her fingers lingered over a folded letter tucked beneath her father's gifts.

Though it had arrived two months ago, the words still stung.

She and Richard had grown up together, yet he had ended their engagement in a letter written in his bold script: *Clear that you could never be happy with me... ending our engagement. Your ambitions could never fit into mine. That is what makes a successful marriage... I found your furor over being denied admission to the Botany department offensive and unladylike. It seemed more important to you than I am. Maybe it is.*

How different he was from the boy who had once caught tadpoles with her, laughing as they squished through the muddy banks of Brayer's Creek. He had seemed so tender after her mother died and then again after her father's passing. He had held and comforted her as she cried, whispering promises of everything they would share after marriage.

Everything but what she truly wanted: a greater understanding of botany.

Rachael closed her eyes, drew a deep breath, and tore the letter into small pieces. Her hands trembled as they pulled the words apart, letting the ink-stained scraps fall like ashes to the floor.

Rachael passed under the iron arch of the Washington Cemetery, following a small path to her parents' graves.

She wore her collecting skirt, which held everything she needed. She had come to say goodbye.

She and her father had visited her mother's grave every year on her birthday, cleaning the headstone and leaving a bouquet of calla lilies, her favorite flower. Rachael hadn't been back since her father's funeral. After watching the casket lowered into the earth and tossing in the first stone, which landed with a sharp clack, she fainted. Richard had caught her then, but now there was no Richard, no father, no mother.

As she approached the two graves beneath the large sycamore tree, her chest tightened. She reached into her pocket for a handkerchief. It was a relief to cry. She had held back the loneliness for months, and now the full weight of reality sat plainly before her.

Kneeling on the grass in front of the graves, she dabbed her closed eyes and took a long, steadying breath, then another. Her mother had taught her that trick when she was a child. Rachael could almost hear her gentle voice now, with its faint lilt: "Breathe, sweetheart. Breathe slowly. It will be all right."

Rachael reached into her collecting skirt and took out a small pouch containing ten calla lily bulbs. Then came her penknife, which she used to turn the soil and gently tap the white bulbs into the earth.

She moved to her mother's headstone and brushed away the dirt from the letters spelling *Emma Williams*.

"There," she said aloud, "you shall have your calla lilies in abundance for your birthday, even if I'm not here."

Next, she turned to her father's headstone and traced her fingers over the name *Arthur Williams*, feeling the deep, rough cuts of the newly carved letters. Though there was no dirt, she brushed the stone anyway, then sat down at the foot of the grave.

Reaching once more into her skirt, she removed a larger collecting bag and carefully pulled out a white Earthstar mushroom. Using the penknife again, she tucked it into the soil at the foot of the grave.

Brushing her hands clean with the empty pouches, Rachael sat down between the two graves. She felt calmer now, having performed these small rituals that felt right.

Looking at the stones, she began to speak.

"Well, Mother and Father, tomorrow I'm leaving New Geneva for Independence, Missouri, just as Father and I planned. From there, I'll book a seat on a wagon bound for Oregon. I'm going to find the Devil's Club that Thomas wrote about in his letter to you, Father. I've sent him a telegram to let him know I'm on my way. When I find that plant and document its uses, I'll bring it back and place it right on the Dean's desk."

Her voice grew firmer. "Father, I know you were right about that plant, and I intend to prove it. I'll be famous. And he'll regret voting against me."

Standing, Rachael turned to leave, then hesitated. Looking back at the graves, she felt tears prick at the corners of her eyes. She brushed them away with her sleeve.

"I will always love you. And you'll always be with me."

With that, Rachael turned once more and walked away.

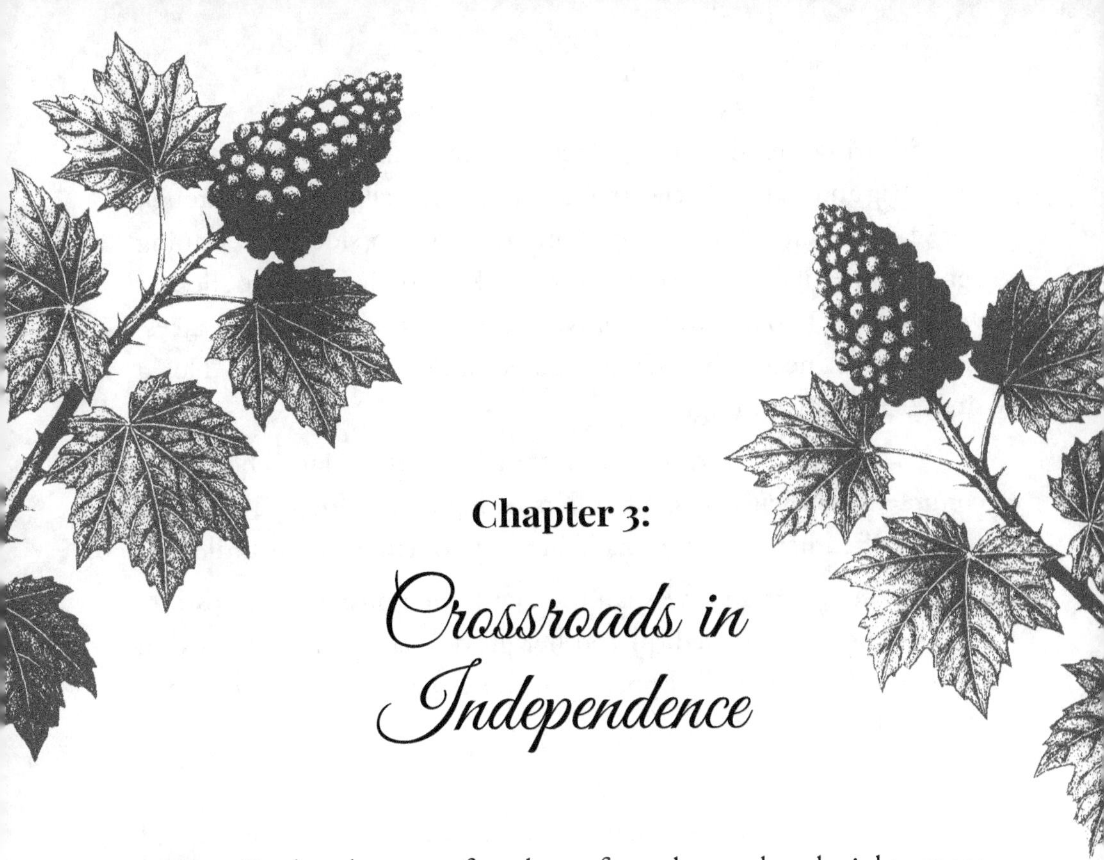

Chapter 3:

Crossroads in Independence

Tired and weary after days of coach travel and nights spent sleeping in gritty stage-stop rooms, Rachael finally arrived in Independence, Missouri, where she intended to purchase passage on one of the wagons heading to Oregon.

She looked around in amazement at the chaos: crowds of people, oxen, sheep, horses, and children of all sizes running pell-mell down the street. The combined smell of unwashed bodies and animals made her reach for her handkerchief to cover her nose and mouth.

Peering through the swirling dust, she squinted at the storefronts, trying to read their signs. She could just make out *Livery Stable, Hotel Bartlett, CLEAN ROOMS, Cheap Rates!,* and *Jenkins Mercantile Store.*

She had never imagined the town would be like this. It was so different from the small college town of Geneva, with its tidy brick houses and surrounding green hills. Independence was dusty, loud, and chaotic. Geneva had been clean and peaceful. Even the dirty stage stops along the journey hadn't prepared her for this rough-and-tumble frontier town.

Squaring her shoulders, Rachael stood taller and gripped her carpetbag and leather satchel in one hand. She walked briskly through the scattered crowd of men loitering on wooden sidewalks, leaning against buildings, or slouching on benches. Their feet were shod in worn brown boots, cowboy hats shaded their sun-darkened faces, and colorful neckerchiefs hung loosely around their necks. Not a single suited man in sight.

As she passed, several men muttered. She tried not to hear their comments or their occasional offers of help. She clutched her bags tighter, lifted her chin, and made her way to Jenkins Mercantile.

The shop entrance was jammed with men pushing and jostling one another. She paused, placed her gloved hand on the back of a man ahead of her, and slipped into the crowd, only to bump into another broad back.

"Excuse me," Rachael said.

At the sound of a woman's voice, the men turned. They jerked their heads toward her, surprised. Quickly, they parted to let her through. As she passed, Rachael scanned the shop but saw no other female shoppers and not a single female clerk.

A bead of sweat rolled down her back. She shifted the satchel containing some of her money to her front and wrapped her arms protectively around it.

"May I help you, ma'am?"

Rachael found herself looking at a bespectacled store clerk in his forties. His thinning brown hair was combed across his forehead. He wore a stiff, starched white shirt and black trousers. His fingers tapped the wooden counter, and his lips were drawn into a thin, unsmiling line.

She set her jaw and met his eyes.

"Yes, you can help me, sir. I'm here to buy passage for my husband and me on a wagon to Oregon. I was told at the livery station that this was the place to inquire."

"Well, ma'am," he said slowly, "that'd be right. Where's your husband?"

She drew a steady breath. "John isn't feeling well. He's resting in our room at the hotel. I thought I'd make the inquiry for both of us."

The clerk raised his eyebrows and looked her over skeptically. "Well, he should come in when he's feeling better."

"Sir," Rachael said, removing her left glove and extending her hand to show her ring, "I think I can handle this."

The clerk remained unmoved.

"Frankly, little lady, I'd feel more comfortable dealing with your husband. There are financial matters involved, things you might not understand. These passages can be a complicated business."

"Yes, I understand, but I'm sure I…"

"Hey, Joseph! Good to see you. Come over here. Maybe you can help this… Mrs., I'm far too busy to babysit."

A preacher in a clerical collar stepped forward, hand outstretched. Rachael stood stiffly, breathing hard. Her knuckles turned white as she tightened her grip on her bags.

"Hello, Mrs.," the preacher said gently. "Why don't we step outside and see if we can sort this out?"

He placed a guiding hand on her back, ushering her toward the door. Inside, the crowd of men parted again. Whispers and whistles followed her as she passed.

Rachael lifted her chin and tried to meet their eyes defiantly. But finally, she bowed her head and allowed Joseph to guide her outside onto the crowded sidewalk. More men stared. Those who hadn't witnessed the earlier scene were curious now.

"Perhaps a cup of tea at the hotel?" the minister asked.

Rachael could only nod.

That evening, Rachael sat on the iron-framed bed, contemplating the small hotel room she had rented. The only notable feature was a tattered blue-and-red cross-stitched quilt. It would have to suffice while she worked to secure her passage west.

She began pacing back and forth across the worn rag rug. Buying a place on a wagon from the mercantile store had been a failure. She saw that clearly now. Pretending that the mythical "John" was with her had been foolish. How could she produce a husband who didn't exist? She needed to be more creative.

She considered again the idea of claiming to be a widow, but that wouldn't work either. She didn't want to dress in black. And she certainly didn't want to be courted.

She paused at the dresser and picked up her penknife, turning it over in her hand. The familiar motion was comforting. It helped her think. What if she said her husband was already in Oregon, waiting for her? That he had sent money for her journey?

Rachael stopped and sat at the small desk. *Yes,* she thought, *that could work.* Her eyes lit up, and she smiled. They probably didn't like the idea of a woman having her own money, so she would simply say her husband had sent her just enough to join him.

The idea filled her with relief. As her father used to say, after a long day in the woods, she was "bone tired." It was time to say her prayers and go to bed. Tomorrow, she would put her plan into action. Reverend Joseph had invited her to church, his last words echoing in her mind: *"Come to the Lord's house tomorrow. The Lord will provide."*

She planned to take him at his word.

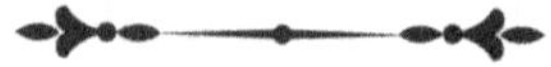

The next morning, Rachael pushed open the heavy door of the whitewashed clapboard church. She kept her eyes low and made her way to a pew near the back. Dressed in her lavender gown, she hoped to make a good impression on the small congregation.

Sitting down on the hard bench, she glanced across the room, searching for Reverend Joe. He hadn't yet arrived. To calm her nerves and steady her pounding heart, she opened the family Bible. Her mother had read to her from it every night before bed. As Rachael read a familiar passage, she could almost hear her mother's soothing voice.

Soon, the rhythmic cadence of the verses relaxed her. Her lips moved silently as she repeated the passage over and over. Her shoulders dropped. She had always appreciated the meditative quiet before service, and it seemed this congregation did as well.

Suddenly, the church door flew open.

Rachael wasn't the only one who jumped in her seat. She turned, startled, toward the source of the disruption.

A large man strode confidently down the aisle, dressed in a gray suit with a long jacket, checkered trousers, and a double-breasted vest. Grease slicked back his salt-and-pepper hair. His narrow face reminded Rachael of a ferret. The front pew groaned beneath his weight as he sat.

In his wake came Reverend Joe, accompanied by a second minister and a small, thin woman in a robin's egg blue dress. Two children followed behind her. The red-haired boy looked about five; his gangly, blonde sister, perhaps thirteen. The girl seemed not yet grown into her height, her hair slipping loose from pinned braids.

Rachael smiled in sympathy.

Reverend Joseph stepped up to the simple wooden pulpit and began the service. As Rachael mouthed the familiar prayers, she tried to keep her worries at bay, but they kept reasserting themselves.

Finally, the last *Amen* was spoken, and the Reverend invited the congregation to tea in the small rectory. The pews emptied from front to back, as was customary. Rachael kept her eyes on her prayer book as the others filed past. She felt the large man from an earlier glance in her direction and then looked away.

Someone to avoid, she thought, stealing a glance at his retreating figure. He had a predator's gait.

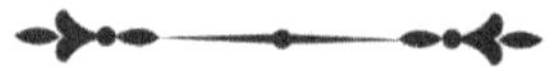

Inside the rectory, Rachael was pleasantly surprised by the sight of a pretty green china tea set arranged on a white linen-covered table. Behind it stood a stout older woman in a dark blue suit. As Rachael approached, the woman smiled brightly.

"I'm pleased to meet you, Mrs. Williams. I'm Reverend Joseph's wife, Martha. It's so nice to meet someone from New York. I come from upstate, too! Joe so enjoyed talking with you yesterday. I could hardly contain my excitement when I learned you were from Geneva. It's been ages since I spoke with someone from near my hometown. I must serve the tea now, but promise me we'll sit down later for a nice long chat."

"I'll look forward to it," Rachael replied warmly.

As Martha turned to serve the next parishioner, Rachael stepped aside and caught sight of the young blonde girl she had seen earlier in the service. The child was seated at a small table by the window, head bent, working furiously. Curious, Rachael stepped closer and peeked over her shoulder. The girl was sketching a flower, clearly a daylily.

"Why, that's very well done, child. You have talent. May I take a closer look?"

Startled by the stranger's voice, the girl hugged her sketchpad to her chest.

"I–I–It's n–not f–fin–ished," she stammered.

"That's quite all right. What's your name?"

The girl's braids swung over her shoulder as she turned toward Rachael. One braid had come unpinned.

"It looks like we both share the problem of very disobedient hair," Rachael said, mimicking the mock-stern tone of a grammar school teacher.

For that, she received a shy, slight smile.

"My n–name is S–S–Sara," the girl said softly.

"You know, Sara, I like to draw too. Flowers are my favorite. Give me a piece of paper, and I'll show you."

Sara turned the page in her sketchbook to hide her drawing, then handed the book and a small, chewed pencil to Rachael. Sitting beside her, Rachael quickly drew a calla lily and turned the sketch toward her.

Sara's eyes widened, her mouth forming a small "O" of delight.

Just then, Reverend Joe approached. "I see you've met my niece, Sara," he said, patting the child gently on the head.

Rachael resisted the urge to shudder. She had always disliked being patted on the head like a dog. Sara pulled away from his hand. Apparently, they shared more than unruly hair.

Taking Rachael gently by the elbow, Reverend Joe said, "It seems the Good Lord is watching over you, Mrs. Williams. There's someone I'd like you to meet."

Rachael stood, giving Sara a sympathetic smile as the Reverend guided her toward his fellow minister and a petite woman who was busy keeping her young son away from the molasses and sugar cookies.

"This is the woman I was telling you about, Robert. Her name is Rachael Williams, and she's looking for a place on a wagon to Oregon." He gestured toward the small woman. "And this is my sister, Ann."

"It is a pleasure to meet you," Rachael said with a polite smile.

Reverend Joseph continued, "Robert, you were concerned about the absence of a woman companion for Annie, who is once again blessed by the Lord with another child. I suggest that you consider including Mrs. Williams in your party. What do you think?"

The ministers exchanged looks. Ann glanced at her husband while Rachael took a moment to regard her prospective travel companions. Reverend Robert's suit was frayed around the collar, and Ann's dress, though beautifully patched, showed signs of careful mending.

"Well," Rachael said, clearing her throat, "I can pay my way and help with your children. I've already met your daughter, Sara—she seems quite shy, but she has an artistic gift."

"She has an affliction," her father said quietly, his chin dipping.

"Yes, I noticed," Rachael replied gently, "but it's a small thing." She pressed on quickly. "My husband, James, is already in Oregon. He sent me the money so I could join him. I can pay you fairly. I like children. I can help Sara with her art and keep your son out of mischief. I love to tell stories, and I know a great deal about plants and reptiles."

The Reverend and his wife stared at her in silence. *Perhaps knowledge of reptiles sounds strange for a woman*, Rachael thought. She quickly added, "Of course, I have no love for snakes."

Reverend Robert looked at Ann. She gave a subtle nod.

"Trust in the Lord, and the Lord will provide," declared Reverend Joseph, rocking back on his heels.

Reverend Robert continued, "One more person must approve this arrangement. The leader of our small company is the gentleman in the corner speaking to those young men. His name is Mr. Grey. He's recruiting hands to help with his sheep. We're already late in the season to begin our journey, and he's concerned about the pasture. Many flocks have already left. I'll bring him over to meet you, Mrs. Williams."

Rachael followed the Reverend's gaze, and her stomach dropped. It was the man she had silently nicknamed *the Ferret*.

She watched as Reverend Robert approached him. Mr. Grey bent his head to listen, his narrow face hardening. His lips pressed into a thin line. When he looked in Rachael's direction, his eyes grew sharp, and he frowned deeply. He shook off the Reverend's hand and began walking toward her, his gaze locked on hers.

Rachael stood taller and met his approach with steely resolve.

Mr. Ferret, she thought, *you've met your match.*

He stopped directly in front of her and looked her up and down with a measuring glare.

"Mrs. Williams," he drawled, "I hear you'd like to join our party and purchase a place on Reverend Godley's wagon."

Rachael nodded curtly, meeting his eyes. "Yes, that's correct, Mr… I'm sorry, I don't know your name."

"Mr. Grey," he replied. "I'm the wagon master."

"Yes, Mr. Grey, then. I have the money to pay for a seat, and the Reverend and his wife have agreed. Only you stand in my way."

Her mouth was set in a firm line.

Grey's narrow eyes gleamed with amusement. "How much are you planning to pay them?"

He watched her closely, clearly entertained by the question and her momentary hesitation.

"What do you think?"

He's baiting me, she realized. She dug her fingernails into her palms to keep her temper in check. Taking a deep breath, she met his eyes.

"We haven't discussed that yet, but I was thinking around one hundred dollars." She turned toward the Godleys, who still seemed frozen in place.

Reverend Godley gave a slow nod. "That will do nicely, Mrs. Williams."

Mr. Grey's eyes sharpened. "And my dear Mrs. Williams, how much will you pay me?"

"I wasn't aware I owed you anything."

"I'll charge you one hundred and fifty dollars. That covers food, bedding, and safety. Either you pay it, or this conversation is over. Your payment to the Godleys only covers your seat on their wagon."

"All right, Mr. Grey, if that's what it costs. I'll pay you. I'll give you a third now, a third when we reach Fort Laramie, and the remainder when we arrive in Oregon."

Mr. Grey peered into her eyes. "I must ask, where did you get this money?"

"Frankly, sir, that's none of your business."

"If it becomes my money, it becomes my business."

"Well then, it came from my husband in Oregon. He's done quite well in the shearing business and sent me the money for my passage. I plan to join him there."

"Really," Mr. Grey replied, his tone edged with skepticism. "And where in Oregon does he reside?"

Rachael hesitated for only a moment before answering, "Catsop Plains, sir."

"How interesting." His eyes narrowed. "I have a sheep ranch there. My wife and three children live on that ranch. Wouldn't it be something if they had met?"

"Yes," Rachael replied, her heart pounding. "That would be very interesting indeed."

Heat flushed her cheeks. *Of all the towns, how had she picked the very one Mr. Grey called home?* But the lie could not be undone. Steeling herself, she met his gaze and smiled faintly. After all, her passage was now arranged.

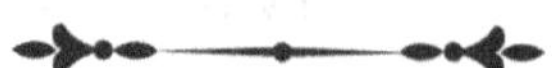

Rachael walked along the planked boardwalk toward the manse, gloved hands folded, hair neatly pinned, and her blue dress freshly pressed. She paused at the dusty window of Jenkins Mercantile, relieved to see a woman behind the till and no sign of the surly clerk she had faced the day before.

Men still loitered outside the shop, smoking and spitting tobacco into a metal bucket. She lifted her skirt to step around a glob that had missed the mark and shuddered. Ignoring the stares and whistles, she hurried past.

Soon, she would leave. Mr. Grey had sent a message: they would assemble in two days at a small house he had borrowed, twelve miles outside town. There, they would stitch tents, prepare canvas covers for the wagons, and take inventory before setting out.

This was one of Mr. Grey's ideas that she agreed with. Perhaps he wasn't entirely unpleasant. Her father had always emphasized the importance of being prepared.

So lost in thought was Rachael that she nearly passed the gate to the white clapboard house that served as the manse. She walked through a tiny garden filled with red geraniums, climbed the two porch steps, and was greeted at the blue-painted door by Reverend Joseph's wife.

The woman's stout frame and firm embrace surprised Rachael and brought sudden tears to her eyes. It had been so long since someone had hugged her. The woman smelled of pastry flour and a faint trace of rose water.

She smiled warmly. Her hostess wore a green delaine dress patterned with tiny blue flowers. Her gray eyes were crinkled with laugh lines, and the starch she had applied glistened visibly on her moist cheeks.

She turned and led Rachael to an alcove in a bay window, where tea had been laid out with the same green china set used at church. On the table sat plates of delicate butter sandwiches and generous slices of pound cake.

Rachael's mouth watered.

"Why, this certainly is a feast, Mrs. Mitchem."

"Goodness, child, call me Martha," she said warmly as she poured the tea and offered lemon slices and sugar. "We're not formal folks, and it's not every day I get to have tea with someone from New York. I'm homesick, I confess," she added, settling into a small chair that creaked under her weight.

Rachael joined her.

"Joseph told me you're meeting your husband in Oregon. You must miss him terribly," Martha said, her eyes searching Rachael's face. "How difficult it must be to be apart."

Rachael took a sip of tea, but it was too hot. She swallowed quickly to keep from burning her mouth. For some reason, lying to this warm, honest woman was especially difficult. Dishonesty was unfamiliar to her, but it was necessary. If she was going to make it to Oregon and find the Devil's Club, she couldn't let a scruple stand in her way. The alternative was returning to New York and begging Richard to take her back.

She set the teacup down, took a steadying breath, and began. "Yes, I do miss him. There was a great deal to do before I left—selling the house and most of our belongings."

Rachael tried to change the subject, even as she struggled to summon an image of her imaginary husband, John.

"Do you hear from him often? He must be worried about you making this trip alone."

"Yes, ma'am, I suppose he is," Rachael replied, a flush creeping across her face. She brushed her skirt, trying to steady her hands, and looked down at her boots.

Martha leaned forward, her tone more serious. "Are you ready for this journey? It isn't easy, and without family or a man to guard you…"

"Yes, I suppose so, but it can't be helped. I just need to get to Oregon and to him as soon as possible." She paused, then brightened slightly. "Actually, I do need some advice." Rachael looked up into Martha's kind face, relieved to steer the conversation away from dangerous territory.

"Do you know anything about a Mr. Grey? We had a bit of a set-to. I'm not sure what to make of him."

"Oh dear, I'm not surprised," Martha replied with a sniff. "Mr. Grey has a reputation as a good leader, but he's very rigid. This isn't his first trip to Oregon; he's gone twice before. Why, he wouldn't even let his wife take her mother's things." Martha's voice bristled. "A harsh man—but knowledgeable." Her teacup rattled slightly as she set it down with more force than necessary.

"I see," said Rachael. She'd best stay on his good side.

"Well, you'll have Ann and Reverend Robert with you. Robert says Mr. Grey is a preacher, too."

"Really?" Rachael blurted. *He* was the last person she'd have guessed to be a minister.

"Robert and Ann told me he's very worried about starting so late. He's concerned there won't be enough pasture for the sheep. Still, they reassured me he knows the trail well. His fellow travelers, however, may not be his first concern."

Rachael rubbed the back of her neck. *Had she made a mistake joining this group?*

"But I'm sure he's a good captain. Most wagon masters have never been on the trail, though they may claim they have. Not many know it and its dangers as well as he does. Ultimately, you'll be in good hands."

Rachael's shoulders relaxed. She would just have to trust him, even if she didn't like him.

Martha passed her a plate of pound cake and helped herself to a slice. A comfortable silence settled between them as they each lifted a moist bite of yellow cake to their lips.

Then Martha placed her plate down and sighed.

"Rachael, I confess—I had more than one reason for inviting you to tea."

"Why, Martha, what is it?"

"I'm concerned about Ann, my husband's sister. We're both worried about her. She's a sweet soul, but her pregnancies have been hard. The last one nearly took her. She was told she shouldn't get pregnant again."

Martha shook her head, her voice lowering.

"Her husband is so pleased about the baby, but I can't imagine her giving birth on this journey. Do you know anything about childbirth? If you're traveling with them, you'll be expected to help."

"Oh, Martha, I know very little. Little indeed," Rachael said, biting her lip.

Martha reached across the table and gently patted her hand. "I thought as much. I have something for you."

She picked up a small book with a green Morocco leather cover.

"This belonged to my mother. She was a midwife and the wisest woman I've ever known. This is her book on midwifery. She also had a deep interest in medicinal plants, and you'll find copious notes in the margins and on the flyleaves. I think she once hoped to write a book about the uses of these plants."

"Martha, I can't take this. Really—I can't. It was your mother's…"

"Child, it's no use to me. I'm past childbearing, and I don't know the scientific names of plants. My mother was proud of her work. She'd want you to have it. Please, take it, for Ann's sake."

Martha pressed the book into Rachael's hands.

"There may be other women on the journey who've borne children and know the general procedures, but I fear Ann will need someone who's studied and can help if things go wrong. That's why I'm giving you this book. Read it carefully. There's a whole section on difficult births. My mother attended more than a few."

"Oh, Martha… I don't know. This feels…well…" Rachael faltered.

"Joseph told me you studied botany with your father. That's unusual for a woman. It tells me you have a strong mind and that you can learn. You'll find what you need in this book."

"But studying plants is very different from helping a woman through childbirth, especially if it's dangerous for the mother or the baby. I…"

"I need your help. Truly, I do," Martha said firmly. "I love Ann, but she can be stubborn. She believes this pregnancy is a sign from God that their journey to convert lost souls is righteous. Between you and me, I can't understand why Robert would take her across the country in her condition. Joseph and I have tried to talk to them out of it, but nothing has worked. We need someone we can trust, someone strong and willing to learn."

Martha fixed her with a steady gaze.

"You'll promise me you'll study this book, won't you? You'll take care of Ann. Promise me, Rachael."

Rachael looked out the window at the garden full of bright red geraniums. Her stomach churned. This was a heavy responsibility. Studying botany in solitude was one thing; using it to treat people, especially in such dangerous, unpredictable circumstances, was something else entirely.

She wasn't a healer by nature. She was an observer. A scientist. Detached. What if she failed? What if she hurt Ann or the baby?

She had agreed to help Ann and her children by joining their wagon, but only as a companion. Not as a midwife.

Rachael opened the book in her lap and flipped through the pages. A detailed, beautifully sketched drawing of a yarrow plant caught her eye. She leaned closer, reading the margin note describing its uses.

Why had I never known this? she wondered.

Martha, sensing her growing interest, spoke softly. "See? This book was meant for you. Please, Rachael, there's no one else."

This was no ordinary book. It was a book of consequence. A resource she could learn from. She turned more pages, stopping at a section titled *Difficult Problems During a Birth*. The concise handwriting in the margins drew her in.

Yes, she thought. *I can do this.*

She was intelligent. She could study, learn, and apply what she read. And more than that, someone finally believed in her. Martha saw what the Dean had dismissed, what Richard had rejected.

Rachael met Martha's eyes.

"All right. Yes. I'll do everything I can. Thank you, Martha. I'll do my best to deserve your faith in me."

Martha's face broke into a relieved smile. She picked up her teacup and took a small sip. Rachael noticed a faint crack in the green porcelain.

Was this the right thing to do? The promise weighed heavily. She wanted to pull it back, to say no; it was too much to ask. But she couldn't.

She had given her word.

For a moment, she saw her father's face, his stern eyes fixed on hers as he once admonished her for breaking a promise.

"One's word is a sacred trust, a bond between the giver and receiver that, if broken, can never be made right."

She had been little then. She had broken a magnifying glass she had promised not to touch. She cried in shame until her father took her in his arms and forgave her. She could almost feel the scratchy texture of his tweed jacket against her cheek.

Suddenly, she was struck by a powerful realization: she didn't need to answer to anyone but herself. She *could* do what she felt was right. She *would*. She had the knowledge of botany and a new resource in the midwife's notes. She owed it to Ann and to herself to help as best she could.

A quiver of excitement ran through her.

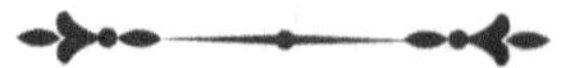

Rachael returned to her hotel with the green leather book clutched tightly in her hand. It was evening, and most of the men had retired to the saloon or to other places she preferred not to imagine. It was a relief to walk without their jeers and whistles trailing behind her.

As she passed the window of the mercantile store, she noticed only one customer at the counter, a woman. Rachael pushed open the door. The scent of wood, fabric, and flour greeted her. Inside, she saw stacked goods: coats, canvas, pots, pans, sacks of sugar and flour, leather bundles, and even a wagon wheel leaning against the far wall.

She couldn't help but overhear the conversation between the stout woman in a black dress and the store clerk.

"Well, Mrs. Dix, your young son isn't with you this evening."

"No, heaven be thanked," the woman replied with a sigh. "He found some other boys to run with. Camille was kind enough to keep an eye on him for a bit."

She lowered her voice, then added, "Just two more days now. Mr. Grey says we're to head to a small house in Westport, one his friend lent him. He wants to see how we do together as a company. We'll sew the tents and wagon covers. He's checking every item we're bringing. Says food is the most important thing."

Rachael perked up. *This woman must be part of the company.* Hearing her speak sent Rachael's thoughts racing back to her own preparations. She mentally inventoried the wool underskirts, shirts, three dresses, boots, warm socks, and her mother's shawl packed in her bag. *Too little? Too much?*

The clerk muttered something Rachael couldn't make out.

"Certainly," Mrs. Dix continued, "and please add six more yards of India rubber cloth, a gutta-percha bucket, some needles, and strong thread to my order. If you've got a tin bucket, I'd prefer it, but I've heard the latex from the gutta-percha tree works just as well."

"Indeed, it does," the clerk replied. "I'm afraid we're all out of tin buckets. Sold out months ago. Bit late in the season to be heading west."

"Can't be helped, I suppose," Mrs. Dix muttered, fingering the rubbery bucket. "Just add this."

Gutta-percha? Rachael thought. *What on earth is that?*

It was time to introduce herself.

She crossed the wooden floor to the counter and said gently, "I couldn't help overhearing that you're part of Mr. Grey's wagon train."

She offered a smile. "I'm going with you as well. My name is Rachael Williams. I heard the clerk call you Mrs. Dix?"

The older woman turned and looked Rachael over, her eyes scanning her from head to toe.

Do I have a stain on my dress? Rachael wondered, her face flushing with heat.

"I've arranged for a seat on the Godleys' wagon," she said quickly. "I'm to help manage the children and keep company with Ann. I'm pleased to meet another lady. I hope we can be friends." She extended her hand.

Mrs. Dix didn't take it.

Instead, she squinted at Rachael. "Yes, I've heard about you. You're some kind of plant finder, I'm told."

"Yes, I'm a botanist," Rachael replied, feeling the heat rise to her neck. Her temper stirred as well.

"Going to meet your husband in Oregon, aren't you?"

"My," Rachael said, forcing a calm tone, "news certainly travels fast."

The store clerk burst out laughing, her hand flying to her mouth. "Yes, faster than some men can spit… and they *can* spit fast—and far."

Rachael laughed with her. "Yes, I nearly got hit. It's disgusting."

Mrs. Dix grunted. "Don't know about a single woman on a wagon train. Might cause problems."

"But I'm not single, Mrs. Dix," Rachael said lightly. "I'm just not currently with my husband. I'm strong and capable. I'll give you nothing to worry about."

She forced a smile to her lips. She had expected challenges, but not this level of scrutiny. *Will all the women be like this?*

She clenched her teeth behind her smile. Right then and there, she made a quiet vow: no matter how hard the journey became, she would not complain. She would prove herself, her strength, her intelligence, and her worth.

She would read Martha's mother's book cover to cover, learn everything about midwifery and medicinal plants, and perhaps even dispense medicine on the trail.

Her jaw set with determination.

"My name is Mary Perkins," said the clerk, her brown eyes flicking between the two women. "Is there anything else I can do for you, Mrs. Dix? If you're finished, I can arrange delivery for tomorrow morning."

Rachael took a deep breath and lifted her chin.

"Good evening, then, Mrs. Dix," she said. "As I mentioned, I hope we can become friends."

Mrs. Dix merely snorted, turned away, and walked out the door without a word.

She'll be difficult, Rachael thought. *And it seems she dislikes me already.*

She left the mercantile, walking briskly through the darkness toward the sanctuary of her hotel room.

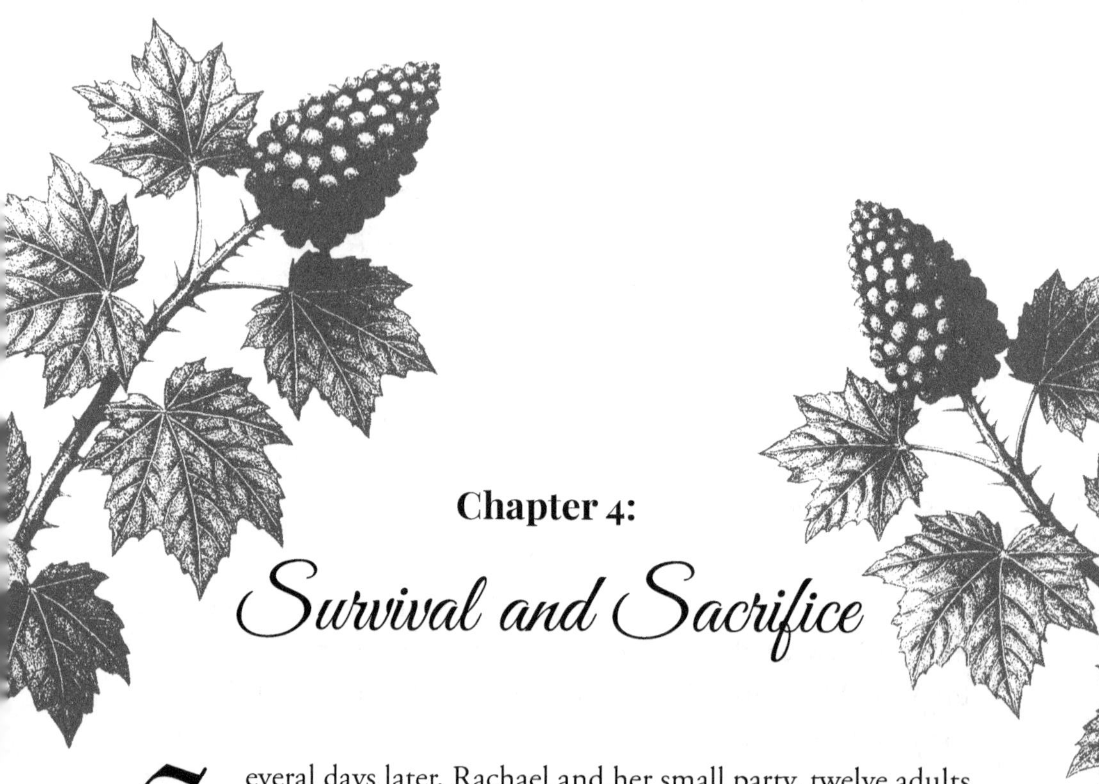

Chapter 4:
Survival and Sacrifice

Several days later, Rachael and her small party, twelve adults and six children, moved to Westport, twelve miles out of town, into a tiny house provided by a friend of Mr. Grey's. The house consisted of three rooms: one large room upstairs where the men were to sleep, and two rooms downstairs, one for the women and children, and another that served as both kitchen and workroom. Behind the house stood a one-hole privy.

It was here that Rachael first experienced the harsh realities of life on the trail and the importance of adequate provisions. That first night, there weren't enough plates for everyone. Mrs. Dix slept on a mattress she shared with her niece, Camille. The other women made do with a single quilt between them. It didn't seem right, especially since Rachael had paid Mr. Grey for bedding as part of her passage.

She slept very little that night. Mrs. Dix's loud, snorting snores echoed through the room, and Rachael woke with a headache and a sore hip. *The floor is hard enough—what will the ground in a tent feel like?* She wondered. Clearly, she needed another quilt.

She approached Hannah, Tom's wife, and asked if she might have an extra quilt Rachael could buy.

A dark braid coiled around her head. Hannah tilted it thoughtfully, then said, "It's old and a bit torn, but it'll do." She bent over her small trunk and pulled out a blue, cross-stitched quilt.

"I made this myself. The stitches aren't tight. I'm better with numbers than sewing. I used to keep the books for Tom's family store. We hope to open one of our own once we reach Oregon."

Rachael tucked that detail away for future reference. "Thank you, Hannah. Anything will help. I'm so stiff." She stretched, raising her arms above her head.

"I imagine we'll all get used to it," Hannah said, handing her the quilt. She flipped her long brown braid back over her shoulder. "Keep it. It's yours. I probably packed too many anyway."

Mrs. Dix, overhearing the exchange, grumbled, "Seems you'd have had the sense to bring enough bedding."

Hannah turned to her, meeting her gaze directly. "I don't mind sharing my quilts or whatever else someone might need. On this trip, we'll all have to help one another." She offered a firm smile.

"Hmph," was all Mrs. Dix replied.

During the days in Westport, the women worked together to sew the heavy canvas for the wagon coverings and the tents they would use on the trail. The canvas was thick and stiff. Even with thimbles, by the end of the first day, their fingers were sore and blistered from forcing needles through the unyielding fabric.

That evening, Rachael sought an opportunity to speak with Ann.

Had Martha told her about the promise? The question haunted her. If Ann didn't know, Rachael would have to broach it herself, and she needed to make it clear that her knowledge of childbirth was limited, confined mostly to the contents of Martha's mother's book.

Rachael observed Ann as the woman worked on the tents. Her face looked pale and drawn. Though she was the most skilled at sewing the tiny, precise stitches, she appeared distracted and withdrawn. Her head remained bowed, and she spoke little.

Rachael had little to say as well, concentrating hard on her stitches. She hated sewing.

The opportunity came after supper. Though they should have stayed to help with the dishes, Rachael noticed Ann slip quietly out the door. She followed, shawl in hand. Ann had forgotten it, and it made the perfect excuse.

Rachael caught up to her in the yard.

"Here, Ann, you forgot your shawl. We haven't had much time to talk in private. Could we talk now?"

Ann turned toward her, her expression unreadable. "Yes, of course. I've been meaning to speak with you privately. The room was hot and stuffy. I prefer being outside in the evening when the stars begin to appear; it brings me closer to our Lord."

She paused, then added, "Inside, there was too much tittle-tattle about people's lives. I find it trying, especially in this heat. Mrs. Dix heard from Camille that I'm pregnant and congratulated me on God's blessing. I'm sure she'll help me when the time comes. She doesn't seem one to make quick judgments."

Mrs. Dix doesn't make quick judgments? That hadn't been Rachael's experience. Why had the woman been so cold toward her from the start?

Ann's assumption that Mrs. Dix would help during the birth was... complicated. Best to tread carefully.

"Yes, dusk is beautiful," Rachael said, steering the conversation elsewhere. "Though my favorite time is early morning. Why don't we sit on the porch? It'll be more comfortable, and we can still see the stars."

They walked back and settled onto the large porch swing. For a while, neither spoke. They simply listened to the serenade of tree crickets. As the light faded, more stars emerged overhead.

"Sitting here reminds me of the swing we had at the manse," Ann said softly. "My first husband and I would sit on it every evening when the weather was fine and even when it wasn't. Life felt simpler then."

The swing creaked gently as it moved. Rachael found it difficult to picture Reverend Robert calmly sitting on a swing; he always seemed too busy giving orders.

"I had the pleasure of meeting your aunt in Independence," Rachael offered. "She invited me to tea. I greatly enjoyed her company. She's very concerned about you and about the birth."

"Yes," Ann said, folding her hands in her lap. "She told me she gave you her mother's book on midwifery. She hoped you'd look after me."

Rachael nodded. "Yes, and I agreed. But Ann, I want to be honest, I don't have any special knowledge. I've started reading your grandmother's book. I've learned about gestation and how long labor usually lasts. Just this afternoon, I read the section on early pregnancy ailments. Do you experience nausea in the mornings? I found a plant today that's recommended for it. I could—"

"I don't want it," Ann interrupted. "I don't need it. I'm praying to the Lord for help."

She kept her eyes on her feet. "Robert prayed, and God granted us this child. Don't worry, Robert says God will care for me. I believe He will, too. It took us five years to save for this journey. I see this child as a sign of God's grace."

Rachael didn't know how to respond. Clearly, Ann placed her faith firmly in her husband's beliefs.

A coyote howled nearby. A moment later, an answering yip-yip echoed in the distance.

"Such a plaintive call, isn't it?" Ann said. "So sad. It gives me shivers." She looked up from her lap, eyes unfocused, staring into the darkness.

"You don't think those beasts are close, do you?"

"No," Rachael replied calmly. "And I don't think we're in any danger. I like to think of the calls as communication. Maybe they're warning one another, 'Stay away, dangerous humans!'"

Ann gave a soft titter, but the sound didn't reach her eyes.

"So, Martha told me that Christopher's birth was a difficult one and that the doctor advised you not to have more children. Is that right?"

Rachael knew she was treading dangerous ground, but felt it was important for Ann to understand the risks. Perhaps then she would take the necessary precautions.

"Yes, the doctor said that," Ann replied evenly. "But God gave us this baby. And as Robert says, we must trust in the Lord. I do. His will be done."

Rachael noticed her own hands were clenched. She occasionally attended church with her mother and believed in some higher power; how else could nature be so precise and orderly? But she also believed firmly in free will. An idea occurred to her, a potential bridge between their views.

"I'm sure God will help, Ann. Isn't there a saying, 'God helps those who help themselves'? I'm sure you'll take care during this time. And I hope to help you do that."

Ann simply nodded.

Frustration caught in Rachael's throat. Was Ann so devout that she would begin a journey this dangerous without considering the risks to herself or her unborn child? Rachael found herself agreeing with Martha's concerns and wondering about Reverend Robert's sense. Was he not worried? Were they so certain of heaven that they dismissed earthly risks?

It would be harder than she thought to care for a woman who didn't think she needed care. But she had given her word. She had to find a way.

The screen door creaked open, and Hannah appeared.

"May I join you two?" she asked, settling on the swing between them. "What a beautiful night. The stars seem so much clearer out here." She glanced between them. "What were you two talking about?"

She reached back and tossed her braid over her shoulder, something Rachael had seen her do many times now.

Ann's hands cupped her belly. "We were talking about God's blessings. I'm fortunate. He has blessed me with another child."

Hannah glanced at her hands. "Well, congratulations, Ann. As for me, I sincerely hope God doesn't bless me until we get to Oregon. This trip is going to be hard enough as it is."

Ann stiffened. She planted her feet on the porch and brought the swing to a halt.

A coyote howled, this time closer. Rachael wished she could howl back.

Tension crackled in the air.

"Why, Hannah," Ann said sharply, "having children is our duty. The Bible tells us to bring forth a multitude to serve the Lord."

"Duty or not, I'd prefer to wait until Oregon," Hannah replied coolly.

Rachael felt caught between them, uncertain of where to stand. She hated this feeling, the tension, the unspoken judgments. She longed to say something to smooth things over, but nothing came to mind.

Why were women so difficult to understand?

Rising from the swing, she gave a polite goodnight and fled the house.

A few days later, the company moved about two miles out of town, establishing their first encampment in a shallow draw between two small hills. The men walked beside the oxen, pulling the wagons, while the women and children traveled on foot. Along the path, groves of plane trees and bushes heavy with chokecherries lined the way. The air was sweet with the scent of damp grass and thick banks of verbena thriving in the moist soil. A small creek murmured over smooth stones.

That evening, the group gathered by the cookfire to discuss which belongings were essential for comfort and safety and what could be left behind. All knew that Mr. Grey would soon be inspecting their wagons.

Rachael listened but said little. Hannah debated what to keep and finally decided to part with a heavy iron skillet and one of her quilts. Her husband, Tom, sorted through his toolbox, setting aside odd bits of hardware.

Reverend Robert and Ann declared they had packed wisely and would keep everything, including a small box of books.

Nearby, Mrs. Dix motioned to her son, Daniel, and her niece, Camille. They gathered by their wagon, heads bent together. Rachael overheard Mrs. Dix saying, "We paid for this trip, and I'll be needing everything I brought. How else am I supposed to set up a decent household?"

Feeling she had already packed the bare minimum, Rachael took some time to explore. Noticing what she thought was feverfew growing through the grasses, she wandered the camp's perimeter, peering into bushes and under trees to see what else she might find. She remained cautious of snakes, stepping carefully.

Eventually, she gathered a large bunch of verbena and feverfew, determined to dry some in her bag and place the rest in a cup on the back of the cook's wagon.

How exhilarating it was to finally be on her way. She imagined the others must feel it, too.

At midday, while waiting for Mr. Grey, Rachael filled her plate with beans and looked around for a place to eat. Small family groups were seated together: the Dixes with Camille and Henry, Hannah with Tom and Roy, and the Godleys, Ann, Robert, Christopher, and Sara.

Her shoulders tensed. She was suddenly reminded of those old school lunches, sitting alone while others clustered in groups. She had never found it easy to ask if she could join a table. On the rare occasions she had dared, the conversation usually stopped the moment she sat down. Would it be the same here?

Spotting a small tree stump up the slope, Rachael made her way there instead. From the small hillock, the view stretched over gently rolling hills. Tall grass swayed lightly in the breeze. She set her plate down on the ground, then pulled out her collecting bag and Martha's mother's book.

I don't need people, she told herself. *I'm used to being alone.* She would use her solitude wisely.

Opening the book, she began reading about the early stages of pregnancy. One passage described **Aralia nudicaulis L.**, a plant said to help strengthen the blood.

If only I had someone to share this with, she thought. *Would one of these women become my friend?* She had to admit, she hoped so.

Rachael's eyes swept over the family groups below. Since her father's death and the breakup with Richard, loneliness had become her quiet companion. When her eyes began to well, she ordered herself to stop.

Feeling sorry for yourself serves no purpose. It was a family rule.

She shook her head. *Nonsense. I don't need others. I have my brain and my own pursuits. Phooey to them.*

Once more, she imagined herself standing in a lecture hall, explaining her discovery of the Devil's Club. Her voice would be firm, her posture confident, and the men in the audience would gaze up at her with the respect she had earned.

She looked back down at the book and continued to read.

Mr. Grey returned from town in a wagon filled with supplies. Tied behind it was a small bay horse with a sidesaddle.

As the group gathered around, he remarked, "Some of the ladies may enjoy riding. My wife certainly did."

He added that later, he would observe each woman try a short ride just to ensure it was safe.

Not a bad idea, Rachael thought. She hadn't ridden in several years but had always enjoyed it. She looked forward to showing Mr. Grey her capabilities.

"But first," Mr. Grey said, interrupting her thoughts, "it's time to inspect the luggage each of you plans to carry. Most equipment has been unloaded, but I insist every wagon must be completely emptied."

Rachael's stomach tightened. The idea that this man, a relative stranger, would handle and inspect everyone's possessions struck her as intrusive, improper, even. His insistence that the wagons be completely emptied frustrated several members of the party.

Mrs. Dix was the most vocal. She complained loudly to her husband.

Even if some others agreed with her, they stayed silent. Mr. Grey ignored her outburst, which, Rachael had to admit, seemed wise, though his silence only escalated Mrs. Dix's fury.

Still, for once, Rachael found herself agreeing with Mrs. Dix.

The wagons were soon stripped bare, and all the trunks, crates, carpetbags, and personal items were stacked outside in neat rows, each family's belongings arranged in a distinct pile. The boxes contained carefully wrapped china, bundles of clothing, extra pots and pans, and even a tiny spinning wheel.

Mr. Grey instructed each group to stand behind their possessions as he began his inspection.

Rachael's body tensed. *What if he thinks I've brought too much?* She had packed light, deliberately so, but with Mr. Grey, nothing could be counted on. She was still smarting from the way he had baited her back at the church.

He started with the Evans family's modest pile. Their largest box contained tools for wagon maintenance: spare springs, metal for repairs, and fittings for the wagon tongues. Two small satchels of clothes and a pair of iron pots rounded out their belongings. Young Roy sat nearby, playing with rocks, completely unbothered by the activity.

"Well, Tom," Mr. Grey said, "I made a wise choice in our arrangement. I tested your knowledge and skill when you proposed maintaining the wagons in exchange for a discount."

A discount? Rachael blinked. She hadn't known anyone had negotiated different terms. But then, Hannah had lent her a quilt; perhaps she shouldn't pry. Still, it sparked a small knot of curiosity.

Mr. Grey pulled a hammer from the tool chest and twisted the head to test its security. "The condition of these tools shows me you understand what this journey demands. Frankly, I'm impressed."

"Thank you, sir," Tom replied, his expression unreadable.

Finally, Mr. Grey picked up a small rosebush cutting wrapped in burlap.

Rachael recognized it, and Hannah had shown it to her while looking for the quilt. She held her breath.

"This can't go, Tom," Mr. Grey said flatly. "It won't survive the heat. It'll die anyway. And we can't waste water."

Hannah stepped forward, her eyes glistening. "But Mr. Grey, it's just a small thing. I brought it to start my garden, just this and a few seeds. It means a lot to me. It's a cutting from my favorite bush at home. Its roots are wrapped in burlap. It needs very little water. I—"

"I'm sorry, Hannah," he interrupted without looking at her. He turned to Tom. "There's no room for plants."

He set the rosebush aside.

Tom put a quiet arm around Hannah's waist. Rachael felt a pang of sympathy as she watched Hannah blink back tears. *Something so small. A rosebush?*

She stepped forward before she could stop herself. "Mr. Grey, surely something this small can't make much difference in weight. I—"

"Did I ask for your opinion, Mrs. Williams?" he snapped, not turning to face her. "Do not offer it again."

"But Mr. Grey—" she started, but he was already walking away toward the Godleys' belongings.

Rachael muttered under her breath, "A rosebush, for heaven's sake."

Grey reached the Godleys' wagon and opened a neatly packed trunk holding the family's clothing. For two adults and two children, it was relatively modest. Still, he rummaged through the contents, shifting items around.

Rachael clenched her jaw. *Does he really think they're hiding something under a nightshirt?*

Mr. Grey inspected the Godleys' cooking pots and their collection of bedding quilts. He nodded in approval.

"Efficient and thrifty," he remarked.

Reverend Robert dipped his chin at the praise. Ann, already visibly pregnant, looked pale. *Perhaps Martha's mother's book contains a recipe for a blood-strengthening tea,* Rachael thought. Christopher and Sara were off playing quietly on the far side of the wagon.

Mr. Grey moved on to the Dixes' belongings: several household crates, boxes of china, and a large rocking chair that looked absurdly out of place on the open plain. He pushed most of the crates and the chair to one side without ceremony.

Mrs. Dix stepped forward, planting her hands on her hips. Her face was tight with fury.

"Now listen here, Mr. Grey. We're paying for this trip like everyone else. Charles and James will be helping with the sheep. Some of these items are priceless! That crate holds my late mother's Wedgwood butter dish. These things will furnish our new home in Oregon. Some of those linens and plates have been in my family for generations. Surely you can't expect us to abandon everything?"

Even Rachael could see her point. Couldn't Mrs. Dix at least consolidate the most precious items into a smaller crate? It seemed a rational compromise.

"My dear Mrs. Dix," Mr. Grey said, his tone growing colder, "I warned you that very few personal possessions are allowed on this trip." He pointed at the rocking chair. "This is completely impractical."

"That chair was my mother's and her mother's before her. I nursed James in it. A master craftsman built it. Surely—"

"These goods add too much weight for the oxen. What *we*, and I emphasize *we*, need is food. I've ridden this trail twice. I know what's required. You'll leave what I tell you to leave, or you and your family can walk back to Independence. The wagon belongs to me."

Walk back to Independence? That was five miles behind them! Rachael recalled Martha's warning about Grey's harshness, and after the rosebush incident, she didn't doubt his threats.

She bit her cuticle, debating whether to speak. *Should I suggest she consolidate her heirlooms into a smaller crate?* Her skin prickled. She hated bullies. What if Grey demanded she abandon her penknife or hand lens? She'd be lost, unable to identify plants from Martha's mother's book, unable to collect or preserve specimens.

Mrs. Dix's voice broke through her thoughts. "Charles! Charles, do something!"

Her husband stared at the ground, pawing at the dirt with his boot, looking like he might flee.

"Why, Betsy, perhaps—"

"You wouldn't, sir!" she cried, turning back to Grey. "You wouldn't dare make us walk back to Independence!"

Her hands fluttered in front of his face, her voice shrill.

Rachael's cheeks flushed. *Should I offer to carry one of her crates as my own?*

"Oh, yes, I would," Grey said, his voice like ice. "Make no doubt about it. I am the wagon master on this trip. I *will* be obeyed, and my decisions will *not* be questioned. If you can't accept that, there's no point in going further."

Rachael balked. *Such arrogance.* His words were harsh and tactless. He was a tyrant, a ruffian, really.

She glanced around and saw tension etched into every face.

Let the woman keep some of her precious belongings, she thought bitterly.

Overhead, a cloud passed in front of the sun, casting a shadow across the camp.

Mr. Grey, having finished with the Dix family's belongings, turned to Rachael's pile. Her modest collection, a large leather satchel and a carpetbag, now came under his scrutiny.

How embarrassing. It felt invasive and unnecessary, but Rachael said nothing, her body taut with anticipation.

"Well now, Mrs. Dix," he called over his shoulder, holding up Rachael's carpetbag, "this is what I call a sensible, small array of personal items. I wish everyone were as Spartan as Mrs. Williams."

There was a low rumble of thunder in the distance.

Mrs. Dix shot Rachael a glare.

Trying to deflect it, Rachael looked down at her belongings and offered, "Perhaps, Mr. Grey, since my load is small, the Dix family could be allowed a few more of their things? Maybe the rocking chair?"

"Are you questioning my judgment?" Mr. Grey snapped.

"Certainly not, but—"

"Then do not interfere."

He shot her a hard look and promptly dragged the rocking chair over to the rejected pile. Turning his back on them, he strode to the cook wagon to speak with Old Bill, the cook.

Rachael bit her lip, barely managing to stay silent.

The others scattered to re-pack their wagons. When no one was watching, Rachael quietly retrieved the small rose cutting from the ground, still wrapped in burlap, and tucked it into her satchel.

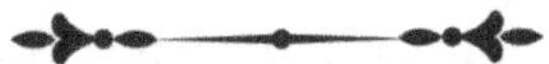

The next afternoon, Mr. Grey announced it was a good time to let the ladies try riding the horse. He had brought a small roan mare with a sidesaddle tied behind the supply wagon.

Mrs. Dix scoffed. "Ride? Absolutely not! Gallivanting on the back of some beast? Never."

Hannah declined, too, saying she needed to keep an eye on young Roy, who had a habit of wandering.

Mr. Grey grunted. "Let's hope that habit is broken soon."

That left only Camille and Rachael.

"Well then," he said, leading the mare forward, "which one of you ladies would like to go first?"

Rachael looked toward Camille, trying to judge whether the girl wanted the opportunity. Camille's expression was unreadable. Rachael hesitated. She'd never been particularly good at reading social cues, much better with botany, where patterns and growth were predictable.

She remembered how classmates had teased her for her social awkwardness. Some even said it was because she was an only child of doting, older parents. And now, those old feelings, self-consciousness, and hesitation resurfaced.

Camille didn't move.

Rachael, forcing herself to sound confident, said, "I'll go first if Camille doesn't want to. I haven't ridden in a while, but I used to ride a lot."

"I'm glad to hear you're so accomplished," Mr. Grey replied. His tone carried a note of challenge.

Is he mocking me? she wondered. *Let him.* She knew how to ride. That was all that mattered.

She took the reins, ignoring his expression, and focused on the task. Before mounting, she gently stroked the mare's nose. The horse lowered its head and nudged her for another pat, which she gave gladly.

Mr. Grey fussed with the saddle as she prepared to mount.

She gathered the reins in her left hand. When he offered his cupped hands, she placed her left foot in them, let him boost her, and swung her right leg over.

Now seated securely in the sidesaddle, she smoothed her skirts and adjusted her seat.

Mr. Grey raised his eyebrows and gave a smirking nod. She took it as a compliment.

He hadn't expected her to manage it, but she had.

"All set then," he said. "You haven't forgotten anything, have you?"

"I don't think so," Rachael replied, scanning her memory. "No, I'm quite certain. I'm ready."

"All right then," Mr. Grey said, "take her around in a small circle at a walk."

Rachael did as instructed, her confidence steadily increasing. She remembered how much she had loved the rhythm of a horse's feet and the comforting balance of the sidesaddle.

"Try a trot now."

She gently nudged the horse with her heels, and it broke into a smooth trot. For a moment, everything felt perfect until she realized something was off. She wasn't slipping, but the saddle was.

The saddle began to slide sideways. Without hesitation, Rachael pushed off and landed on her feet. The horse stopped obediently. Regaining her composure, she approached the mare slowly, speaking in low, calming tones as she retook the reins.

Nearby, she heard chuckles, Mr. Grey and Mrs. Dix's son, James.

"Haven't you always been taught to check your cinch before getting on, Mrs. Williams?" Mr. Grey said, barely disguising his amusement.

Rachael's nostrils flared. *So that's how it's going to be.* "Usually, when I've ridden," she snapped, "the grooms were responsible for making sure the cinch was tight."

The moment she said it, she regretted it.

"Well, there are no grooms here, as you can see," Mr. Grey replied coolly.

"No," Rachael said sharply. "And apparently, no gentlemen either. I'll remember that."

Mr. Grey and James stared at her, momentarily silenced.

She moved around to the horse's side and repositioned the saddle. Reaching beneath the mare's belly, she tightened the cinch firmly. Then, she looked squarely at Mr. Grey and gave the horse a small push, prompting it to shift. The mare exhaled loudly. Rachael reached again and pulled the cinch tighter.

"As you can see, Mr. Grey, I do know about cinches. Shall we try again?"

Without waiting for his response, Rachael ignored his offered hands and mounted using the stirrup. Once seated, she guided the mare into a smooth circle at a trot, then encouraged a gentle canter. With practiced ease, she performed a flying lead change, shifting her weight to prompt the horse to change leads, the front hooves striking the ground with grace.

She was proud, *enormously* proud, and dismounted with a crisp bow. Camille and Hannah clapped. Mrs. Dix scandalized, scowled at them both.

"What a disgusting display," she muttered. "Very unladylike."

Rachael paid her no mind.

Now, it was Camille's turn. Her cheeks were flushed crimson.

"I'm afraid I've got a headache from too much sun," she said, brushing her brow.

"If I choose to ride," Mrs. Dix added, "I'll do so later when it's cooler."

Mr. Miller, removing his hat, stepped forward. "Why, I'd be more than happy to watch her ride in the evening when it's cool."

Camille nodded quickly and retreated to the shade behind the Dix family's wagon.

Well, Rachael thought, *perhaps there is one gentleman in this group.* She gave Mr. Miller a small nod, handed the reins back to Mr. Grey, and turned to assist Camille.

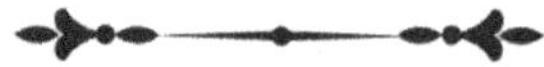

Later that afternoon, the entire party worked together to set up the tents for the first time. They erected the tent posts and ran a line from one end to the other. Then, they carefully laid the canvas over the top, pulling it down gently at the back.

The front of each tent had an opening closed with ties stitched into the canvas, which could be looped back as needed. The first time, they accidentally positioned the tent with the door facing the wrong way, but the mistake was quickly fixed.

Finally, they secured the sides by driving stakes through the hand-sewn ovals at the tent's bottom.

Although Mr. Grey insisted on checking the lines to ensure they were tight enough, Rachael and Camille still felt proud of their accomplishment. He explained that it was important for all the tents to open facing one another so the group could see and hear each other in case of trouble.

This bit of control annoyed Rachael, but, for once, she held her tongue.

There wasn't enough headroom to stand upright, so everyone had to crawl into their tents for the next step: laying down Indian Rubber blankets to guard against dampness from the ground. Next came the quilts and bundles of clothing repurposed as pillows. Once the bedding was down, there was hardly any room left in the nine-foot space.

That first night, Rachael couldn't help but gawk at the plush beauty of Mrs. Dix's maroon cross-stitched quilt. It was thick enough to pass for a mattress. Camille dragged it into the tent, clearly intended to be shared with her aunt. They had a second quilt to use as a cover and real pillows, no less. *No wonder they hadn't slept in the wagon,* Rachael thought with a flash of envy.

She laid her own thin quilt over the rubber sheet, then added the older, heavier quilt that Hannah had lent her. She placed a cloth over her satchel to use as a pillow. Next to her, Sara set up her bedding with quiet excitement.

"To be truthful," Rachael whispered to her, "so am I."

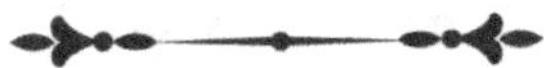

Across the camp, Charles, his son Henry, his stepson James, and young Christopher set up what would soon be known as the "Men's Tent." Christopher and Henry were so excitable that Reverend Robert eventually told them to sit outside and let the older men handle the work.

Ann and Robert arranged their sleeping space in one cramped corner of the wagon next to the box. Rachael wondered if Sara and Christopher would be lonely without their parents, but both children adapted with little complaint.

Mr. Miller let the young shepherds set up a tent for the three of them near the sheep pen. When the tent collapsed for the third time, he laughed and reassured them, "Don't worry. You'll get it next time."

Eventually, they did.

Tom and Hannah set up a separate tent with the help of their young son, Roy. Though Roy's "help" likely caused more delays than progress, Tom showed admirable patience with the boy's enthusiasm.

Mr. Grey erected his own snug tent next to the springboard wagon. Cookie, Old Bill, would sleep in the bed of that same wagon, surrounded by sacks of beans, sugar, and flour and his various pots and pans.

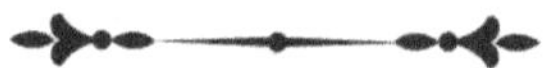

That night, Rachael sat awkwardly on a small barrel at suppertime, cornpone and beans balanced on her lap. Much to her surprise, Camille sat beside her on the same barrel.

"I've been meaning to thank you," Camille said, voice low. "For standing up to Mr. Grey earlier. When he was so harsh about my aunt's things, frankly, he scared me to death, so gruff and mean."

"I'm afraid your aunt doesn't care much for me," Rachael said. "Though I don't quite know what I've done."

Camille paused, fork halfway to her mouth. "I don't think it's really about you. It's just… You remind her of her older sister."

Rachael turned to face her. She noticed Camille did the same, almost in sync.

"My aunt has always believed that Mary, that's her sister, was too bold. She did things that, well, weren't considered proper for a decent young woman. You being a botanist reminds her of that. She doesn't believe women should have interests outside the home. It's not really you she dislikes; it's the idea of you."

Camille hesitated, then added, "For what it's worth, I disagree. I'd actually like to know more about what you do."

"Well, that's a nice thing to hear. I'd love to tell you—"

Camille took a bite of her food, and a strange expression crossed her face.

Rachael laughed. "Cookie isn't much of a cook, is he? These beans taste like mud, though I can't say I've ever eaten them."

Camille laughed, too. "I bet mud would taste better. And this cornpone? Harder than a rock. I make biscuits; maybe I can help him." She set down her plate with a grimace.

"Now *that's* a good idea if I ever heard one." Rachael followed suit, setting her plate aside.

She was surprised by how much she was enjoying Camille's company. There was something easy about the young woman. Beneath their shared laughter, a glimmer of friendship began to form, maybe even the possibility of shared purpose.

"Rachael, can I ask you a favor?"

"Of course."

"I know you're helping Ann on this trip, so could you ask her if Robert will be holding Sunday services? And if we observe the Sabbath as a day of rest?" Camille's tone became quieter. "I enjoy good service, but, between us, I heard in Independence that the companies that rested on the Sabbath fared better. Their animals lasted longer. It makes sense, doesn't it? Even the beasts need a day of rest."

She looked down at the ground.

Rachael felt her heart warm. Camille clearly cared about her aunt and uncle.

"We don't have much money left after preparing for this trip," Camille added. "If the oxen give out, I don't know what we'll do."

Rachael nodded, touched by Camille's quiet concern. There was more to this young woman than met the eye.

"I have my own reasons for wanting to go to Oregon," Camille said suddenly, glancing up. Her mouth twitched as if she were suppressing something deeper.

Rachael was intrigued but held back. She'd learned, often the hard way, that patience was more effective than pressing too soon. She remembered how often she'd blundered into conversations, her questions labeled "impertinent." The sting of high school laughter still echoed in her memory.

She bit her lip, collected her thoughts, and then said carefully, "Well, Camille, I imagine Reverend Robert won't make that decision. It'll be Mr. Grey."

Camille blinked. "Mr. Grey? A minister?"

Rachael chuckled. "I know. I couldn't believe it either. But Ann's aunt Martha told me. I was just as surprised."

Camille's eyes shifted toward the campfire, where Mr. Grey stood speaking with George Miller, the head drover.

"Oh. Well… I suppose I'll have to wait and see what he decides." She crossed her arms and held her stomach.

Rachael noted the expression on Camille's face when she looked at Mr. Grey. *Unease.* A decision settled in her mind.

"Would you like me to ask him?" she offered. "I'd be happy to. I'll even mention what you heard about the animals needing rest."

Camille's face lit up. On impulse, she reached over and squeezed Rachael's hand.

That small gesture sealed the bond for Rachael. This young woman was her friend. At least, she hoped so. She squeezed Camille's hand back and smiled. "I'll talk to him in the morning."

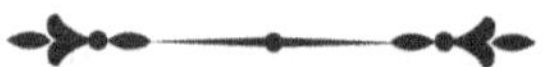

That evening, Mr. Grey addressed the group with his usual commanding tone.

"We'll be leaving *very* early in the morning," he announced. "We must avoid the worst heat of the day."

He looked around at the tired faces.

"You'll all learn quickly that you need to turn in right after supper. Most mornings, we'll eat a cold breakfast and move out. I'll tolerate no sluggishness."

He pointed toward the younger boys. "The sheep first, so boys," he said, nodding to Phillip and John, "you'll be up before anyone else. Mr. Miller, you'll oversee them."

"James," he added, with a steely glance, "I'll wake you myself."

He went on, "Our main meal will be at noon. We'll rest the animals briefly, then move on again. I expect us to cover a minimum of twelve to fifteen miles per day, more if possible. Remember: this is not a pleasure trip. There are dangers on the trail. I expect you'll come to understand that soon enough."

Rachael took Sara with her to wash their faces in the nearby stream, lending the child her small towel. Earlier that day, Rachael had braided Sara's hair, a simple, neat pattern that reminded her of when her own mother used to do the same for her.

It felt strange, at first, to tend to someone else's child in such a personal way. And yet, she had to admit, she liked it. Sara had beamed when she saw the results in the water's reflection.

Rachael couldn't help but notice how Ann seemed to pay little attention to her daughter. It puzzled her. Why such a distance?

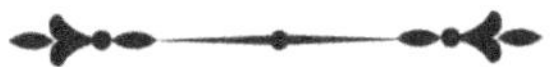

Later, Rachael and Sara crawled into the tent and settled onto their pallets. Camille and Mrs. Dix were already tucked into what Rachael would later come to think of as *their nest*, the soft maroon quilts and real pillows giving it an almost regal appearance.

"Good night, Camille. Good night, Mrs. Dix," Rachael offered softly.

"Good night," Camille replied.

Mrs. Dix gave a grunt in response.

Rachael pulled the quilt up under Sara's chin and gave her small hand a gentle pat. "Good night, Sara, honey. Sleep well."

"Y-y-you t-t-too," Sara stammered, her voice sleepy and sincere.

Rachael lay back on her own bedding, staring up at the dark canvas above her. Her thoughts ran wild. *Why does Ann keep her distance from Sara? What could Camille's real reason be for going to Oregon? Could she and Ann ever truly be friends? And what exactly would this journey demand of them all?*

Her mind spun with unanswered questions. But her body was spent.

Despite the muffled cacophony of Mrs. Dix's ragged snores, sleep came swiftly. She sank into it, deep and dreamless, until the faint light of early morning brushed against the edges of the tent.

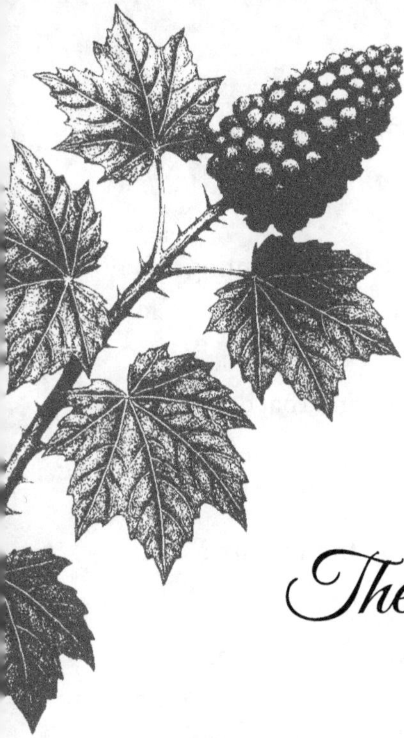

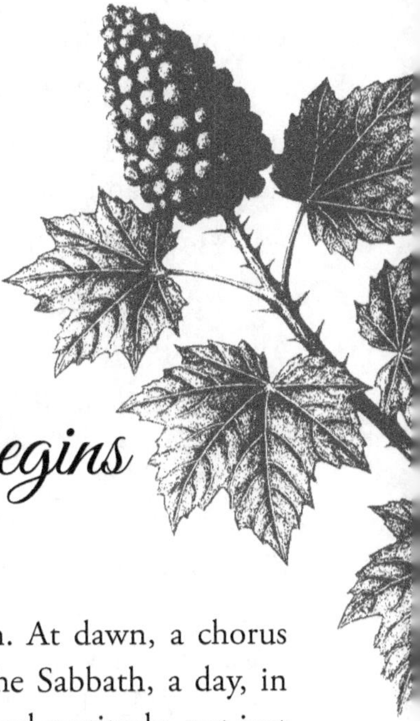

Chapter 5:
The Trail Begins

The light crept slowly across the plain. At dawn, a chorus of birds heralded the beginning of the Sabbath, a day, in Rachael's mind, meant for reflection and gratitude, not just a pause from hardship but a moment to contemplate the greater whole of life.

To Rachael, God revealed Himself in the natural world. In the elegant curve of a newborn fern frond. In the variety of leaf shapes, each with a purpose. And in the night sky, where sometimes, it seemed the stars hung so low she might reach out and touch them.

She crawled quietly around the sleeping women in the tent, pulled her shawl over her shoulders, and stepped outside into the cool morning. Out of habit, she made a small wish as she greeted the day.

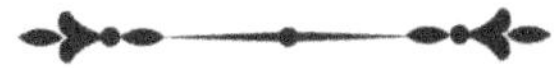

Mr. Grey was already by the fire, a tin cup of coffee in hand. When she approached, he offered it to her without a word. She took it, surprised, and sipped.

She didn't like confrontation, though it seemed to follow her on this journey. Then again, perhaps it wasn't her; perhaps it was Mr. Grey who invited it with his bristly manner.

"Mr. Grey," she began, "are we to observe the Sabbath during this journey? Will you be leading a service? And will it be, as expected, a day of rest and contemplation?"

He took back his cup and drank before answering. "That depends."

Rachael blinked. "Depends? On what, possibly, could it depend? The Lord *requires* it."

"Oh," he replied dryly, "so you've spoken to Him recently?"

"Mr. Grey!"

"I apologize." He sighed. "Let me explain. I will honor the Sabbath when I'm sure the company can make the required distances to reach Oregon before the weather turns. There may be days we must keep moving when a river rises or snow threatens the mountain passes. We left later than I'd hoped. Much later. It's vital that I get my sheep to Oregon."

He paused, then added, "But I'll try. I'm a man of faith, Mrs. Williams. I *will* try."

Rachael considered this. She noticed, for the first time, that he had a single dimple when he smiled. It softened his otherwise stern face. Perhaps he wasn't as harsh as she'd assumed. He was their leader, after all. And he had made this trip before.

Still, she'd promised Camille.

"But as Christians, our duty, God asks so little of us. Surely—"

Mr. Grey chuckled. Then, quickly said, "Forgive me. You just reminded me of my wife, Mary. She was the same way, adamant about keeping the Sabbath. Once, she wrote to Reverend Beeker in Philadelphia about it. Asked if we should stop for the Sabbath, even if the rest of the wagon train didn't."

"And what did he say?" Rachael asked, curious.

"He wrote back, 'If I were on a liner crossing the ocean, I wouldn't jump off on Saturday night.' That answer eased her mind. I hope it eases yours."

He looked into the distance.

"So, again, I say: it depends. But it matters to me, too."

Rachael nodded. "The woman at the mercantile in Independence said those who keep the Sabbath do it as much for their animals' sake as their own. That even beasts need rest."

"Mrs. Williams, are you an animal doctor now?" His tone was sharp. "You think I haven't thought of them? We all depend on them. That's why we stop at noon each day. They rest then. I've made this trip twice before."

She nodded again, slowly this time.

He's right, she thought. *I can explain that to Camille.* The logic was sound, even if she didn't like how it was delivered.

The rising sun now spilled fully over the chokeberry bushes, casting away the last of the shadows.

"All right, Mr. Grey. I'll hold you to your promise—to *try*. As our leader, I know you have difficult choices to make. I'll do what I can to accept them. God willing."

"God willing indeed, Mrs. Williams."

She glanced down at his tin cup. "Is there any more of that coffee?"

He refilled it without a word.

It was the first day on the trail. Anticipation buzzed through the camp. Everyone seemed eager to begin the expedition.

After a cold breakfast of bacon and hardtack, they were ready. The oxen stood harnessed in their oxbows. Even Bo, the sheepdog, dashed about with barely contained excitement as the sheep moved out. Riding behind the bleating herd were George Miller, the head drover, and the two hired boys, John and Phillip.

As the sheep disappeared down the trail, the small party let out a collective "Hurrah!" to mark their official start.

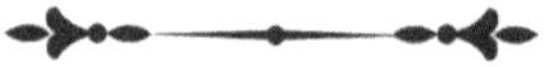

Mr. Grey led the column on his big, roan horse, followed by the Evans wagon. Mr. Evans walked beside the oxen while Hannah and Roy sat on the wagon seat. Next came the Dix family wagon, with Charles walking beside it and Mrs. Dix riding with Henry and Camille. James, Mrs. Dix's son, rode beside them on a borrowed horse.

Reverend Robert walked at the head of the Godley wagon, whip in hand. Inside sat Ann, with Sara and Rachael beside her, and Christopher perched on an overturned bucket in the back. The water buckets sloshed behind them, their rhythm comforting. The sound reminded Rachael of childhood baths, splashing her hands through the water to make waves. Without thinking, she reached over and squeezed Sara's hand gently.

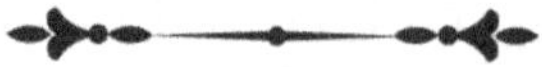

Two days later, before sunrise, Rachael hoisted herself onto the saddle of the small bay horse. Tired and sore from two days on the wagon's hard wooden bench, she had finally convinced Mr. Grey to let her ride.

Settling into the sidesaddle, she adjusted her skirt and took up the reins. The bay shifted sideways, responding to her weight. She nudged him gently, and he obeyed.

See, Little Red, she thought, patting his neck. *We're going to do just fine.*

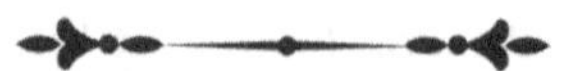

At daybreak, a mist hovered over the valley. The scent of last night's rain lingered in the air. At least the dust, so thick over the past few days it clung to skin, clothing, and even food, would be tamped down for now.

Mr. Grey appeared pleased with their progress, reporting they were averaging fifteen miles a day. Rachael made a mental note to ask how he calculated the distance.

The sheep and their tenders had already departed an hour earlier. The wagons, packed the night before, were ready. As usual, they had a cold breakfast. Mr. Grey always insisted on early starts.

Cookie, driving the springboard wagon, sat hunched on the seat, his gnarled hands tight on the reins. His lined face and thick white whiskers made him seem at least sixty. He rarely spoke beyond a grunt and kept mostly to himself. Rachael had noticed the small bottle he tucked beneath his seat and sipped from throughout the day. She doubted Mr. Grey knew about it.

Still, Cookie's cooking was tolerable, and Rachael hoped Camille might soon step in with her promised biscuits.

As was the custom, Mr. Grey sent the springboard wagon out first. It carried the tents, bedding, cookware, and provisions. The rest of the group readied their wagons.

Rachael rode alongside the Godleys' wagon, where Ann and the children sat. She spotted Christopher sitting on a folded blanket behind his mother. He caught her eye and waved. She waved back.

Leaning forward slightly, Rachael tapped her heels against the bay's sides and moved into pace beside the wagon. Reverend Robert walked near the oxen, whip in hand. He swung it more often than she liked. Rachael hated that whip but supposed it was necessary.

Eventually, she and her mount settled into a steady rhythm. Her body relaxed, the strain in her lower back easing. They passed through a lush valley carpeted with thick grass. Stands of oaks and other trees lined the distant slopes, though too far away to identify.

Rachael amused herself with a game she used to play with her mother, matching grass tones to watercolor paints. *Viridian? Sap green? Hooker's green?* She settled on a blend of Hooker's and Sap. It was peaceful, the quiet broken only by the creak of wagon wheels and the occasional cry of a meadowlark, its yellow feathers flashing among the tall grass.

Robert yelled and jumped out of the way as his wagon lurched. The oxen reared sideways, nearly overturning the entire wagon. Both Sara and her mother tumbled back into the bed of the wagon. He struggled to regain control, but the animals' eyes rolled wildly in alarm.

Then Rachael saw it: a colossal snake coiled on the side of the trail. Before she could even scream, Mr. Evans appeared, pulled his rifle from its sheath, and shot it. The sudden crack of the rifle was too much for the small bay horse. With a sharp snort, it bolted into a gallop, nearly unseating her.

Rachael yanked at the reins, sawing back and forth, but the horse only ran faster. Then reason took over. She stopped fighting and let him run. Fortunately, the trail ahead was flat and clear. Her hat had flown off the moment the horse bolted, and her braids whipped wildly behind her. And yet, she realized, *I'm not afraid.* In fact, she was smiling.

How exhilarating!

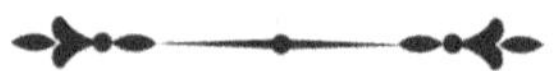

The bay crested a small hill and finally began to tire. Rachael slowed him into a canter, then a trot, and finally a walk. His sides heaved with exertion. She leaned forward, patting his lathered neck and murmuring softly. Then she laughed out loud.

"Well, at least now we're far away from that snake."

Behind her came the thunder of hooves and the sharp snap of reins. She turned and saw Mr. Grey, red-faced and hatless, riding hard to catch up. His horse skidded slightly on the dirt as he pulled up.

Rachael bit the inside of her cheek to stop herself from laughing. He looked thoroughly ridiculous.

Breathing hard, he dismounted.

"Well, here you are," he said between gasps. "I thought I'd find you flat on the ground or worse. And here you are, still seated. I'm impressed, Mrs. Williams. You're a better horsewoman than I expected."

"Indeed, Mr. Grey. I'm rather surprised myself. But I'm none the worse for it." She grinned. "Actually… I quite liked it." She reached down to smooth her horse's mane.

"Do me a favor," he said, wiping his brow with a red handkerchief, "don't make a habit of it."

She had half-expected a lecture for panicking the horse, for holding up the company, but Mr. Grey said nothing more. He simply turned his horse around and rode slowly back with her.

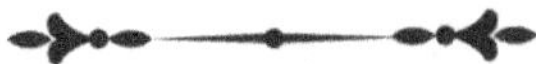

Later that day, when she dismounted, her dress caught on the saddle horn, and she twisted her ankle as she landed. She tried to act as if nothing was wrong, but Mr. Grey noticed her limp and pulled her aside.

"Let me see that ankle of yours. Walking on it will only make it worse."

Rachael bristled. She didn't want a fuss. She had been proud to impress him earlier. She didn't want that ruined by something as foolish as a sprain.

"It's nothing. Really."

"Sit down and let me look. I trained with a doctor, you know. I'm afraid you'll have to remove your boot."

She hesitated. "I can do it, thank you."

Rachael sat on a log and bent to unlace her boot. Despite her efforts, a cry of pain escaped as she pulled it off.

Mr. Grey knelt and cradled her ankle in one hand, gently pressing and testing with the other. Rachael bit her lip.

"Good. It's not broken. I knew it would hurt when the boot came off. Look here; it's swelling fast. You need to keep it elevated and stay off it as much as possible. Tomorrow, you'll need to ride in a wagon. I'll find someone to make room."

Her face flushed a deep red. He was still holding her ankle. His touch was surprisingly gentle, but the moment felt far too intimate. Her stomach fluttered. She tried to avoid his gaze. Her heart pounded in her chest, thudding in time with a single repeated thought: *Go away. Go away.*

"Wait here. I'll be back."

If she could have, she would have run. But here she was, bootless, embarrassed, and feeling vulnerable. He'd even propped her foot on another log.

Moments later, Mr. Grey returned with a strip of cloth. He knelt again and wrapped her ankle with surprising care, tight enough to support it but not so tight that it caused further pain. When he finished, he helped guide her foot back into her boot.

"Don't lace the boot. Tie the laces loosely so you don't trip. Try to walk on it as little as possible. Here, I've found a spare pole for you to lean on." Mr. Grey stood over her, studying her reaction.

"Thank you, but I don't need it," Rachael replied curtly.

He raised an eyebrow. "Mrs. Williams, must you always argue with me?"

He was enjoying this, amused by her discomfort. It was infuriating. Just like him.

Rachael clenched her fists, refusing to meet his gaze. He finally turned and walked away.

Moments later, Sara appeared, eyes wide.

"A-are you all rrright?" she asked.

"Yes, Sara, I'm fine. It's all just a silly fuss over nothing." Rachael softened her tone. "But I may need to lean on your shoulder to get to dinner."

"I c-c-can hel-help."

"Of course you can. I appreciate it." Rachael held out her hand. "Here, help me up, and let's get to supper before there's any more commotion over my ridiculous ankle."

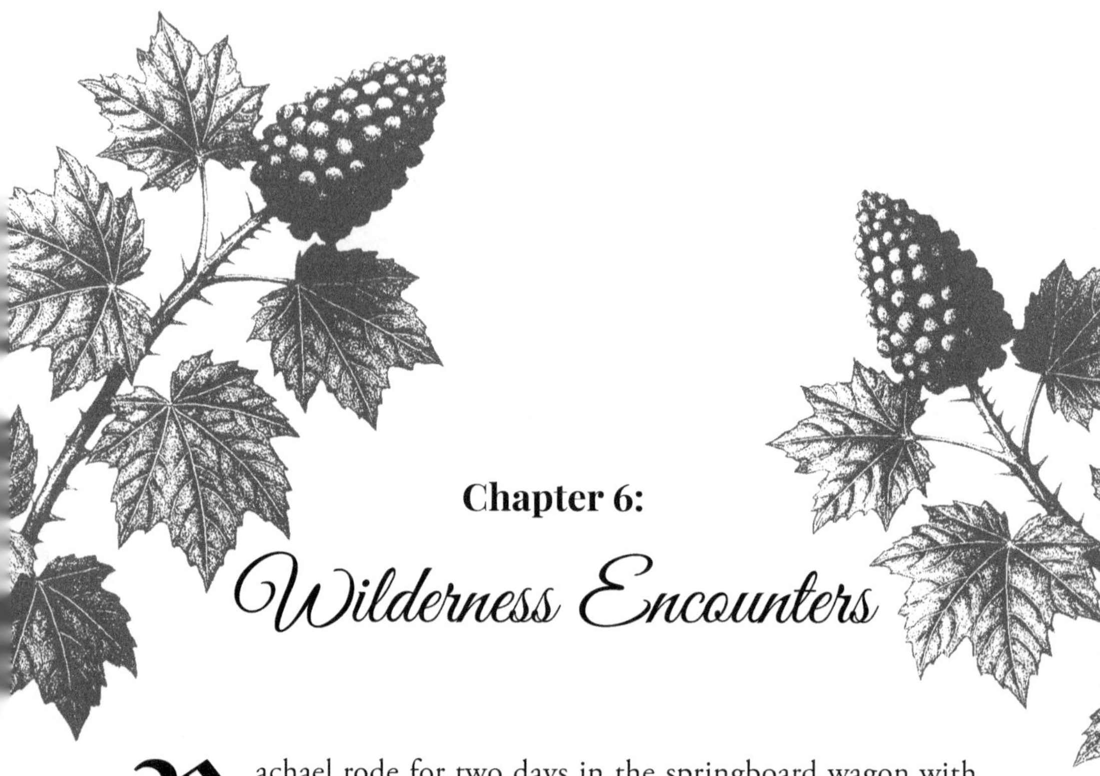

Chapter 6:
Wilderness Encounters

Rachael rode for two days in the springboard wagon with Cookie. She had to admit, he was a good driver. The mules responded quickly to his calls.

"Come, team. Big team. Get up, Billy. There, get Jake up."

The dirt track was deeply rutted from the wagons ahead. Other wheel paths paralleled the main trail. She assumed those were created to avoid the inevitable mud holes that bogged down the main route after rain. The road meandered through low sandy hills and gullies, and though it was flat, the dust and flies were relentless. She swatted at them constantly and began to wish she had brought a veil.

Cookie seemed to love his mules. On the first day, he told her:

"A male's called a John, and a female's a Molly. They're smart animals. They can smell a mile ahead. If there's a predator or buffalo herd nearby, they'll stop, put their ears up, and face the danger. Many buffalo hunters owe their lives to mules."

Rachael found them strange animals, unlike horses. She still preferred Little Red.

After that first day, Cookie's conversation dwindled. She suspected his earlier talkativeness had more to do with the little bottle he kept under his seat than anything else.

By the third day, the swelling in her ankle had gone down. She laced up her boots and longed to return to her horse. The wagon seat was unyielding, and her hips and back ached. Cookie also carried a particular odor that made sitting next to him increasingly unpleasant.

She woke early, excited to be free of Cookie's company. But to her disappointment, Mr. Grey ordered her to ride in the Dixes' wagon that day. He delivered the news with a firm expression that brooked no argument. Camille would ride the horse instead; it was a good day for it, with flat terrain and no river crossings. Mr. Miller would accompany her, and James would serve as head drover for the day. Mr. Grey wanted to test him.

Rachael wanted to object. She had managed to be polite to Cookie, but Mrs. Dix was another matter. Still, Camille was her friend and deserved the chance. And it was only fair to give James his opportunity, too. She resigned herself to the decision.

Maybe, she thought, *I've been too hard on Mrs. Dix. After all, she's Camille's aunt. This could be a chance to understand her better.*

Mrs. Dix placed a pillow on the wagon bench as far from Rachael as possible and heaved her stout frame onto it, spreading her skirt under her.

Rachael stepped onto the wagon wheel, spoke, and eased herself into the seat. She tried not to wince as her sore ankle touched the floor.

Mrs. Dix glanced at the foot, grunted, and then turned toward her husband.

Daniel raised his whip, and the wagon lurched forward.

"You'll find this wagon slow after gadding about on that horse," Mrs. Dix said. "I'm not surprised you hurt your ankle. It's not something a woman should do—riding. It's unseemly. Unladylike. So ungraceful, perched up on one of those great beasts. Why, my older sister even jumped fences on horseback. Mary always got away with everything. She did as she pleased and never cared what people thought.

I, on the other hand, did everything I was told. Our poor mother suffered terribly from Mary's antics, so much so that—"

Rachael cut her off. "Mrs. Dix, perhaps your sister simply had a different nature. People are all different."

"There are rules, Rachael, and they should be followed, especially by women. A woman's duty is to make a pleasant home for her husband and bear children. Women shouldn't be riding horses. It's simply coarse."

Rachael braced herself, hoping to stave off another lecture on femininity.

"You did notice that I ride side-saddle. Although," she added, "I've considered wearing pantaloons and riding astride. I was pleased to find a pair at Fort Hall. It seems many women are seeing the sense in them."

Mrs. Dix snorted. "Doesn't surprise me. You don't seem to understand the etiquette required of a married woman. Does your husband approve of all this gallivanting around on horseback?"

Rachael looked over the yoke of oxen, noting how their ears twitched as if they, too, were listening. "Why, Mrs. Dix, any husband worth having would want his wife to be comfortable. And considering I'm far more comfortable on a horse, I'm sure John wouldn't mind. I noticed Mr. Dix makes sure you're comfortable. He even handed you that pillow."

"Hmph," muttered Mrs. Dix. "Doesn't change the fact that it's not ladylike. Not in the least."

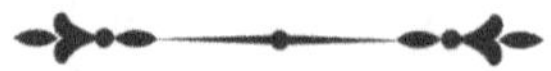

As time passed, the party fell into a routine. They rose at four each morning, packed the tents in the dim twilight, and ate only hardtack, maybe a cup of tea if the fire had held. All quickly learned not to drink water that hadn't been boiled. Mr. Grey insisted. Even so, many still suffered bouts of dysentery.

Mr. Grey's "cure" was extreme: eat nothing but dried fruit and drink only boiled water. Rachael wasn't sure it was wise. She stopped eating altogether and sipped water cautiously until the worst passed. As a result, her dresses now hung more loosely from her frame. She would consult Martha's mother's book; surely, there was a better remedy.

Because the sheep moved more slowly than the wagons, the drovers and Mr. Miller left first each morning, often without breakfast. The wagons followed, drawn by oxen, and then Cookie's springboard wagon came last, rolling out by four-thirty. Mr. Grey enforced this schedule rigidly. Anyone late faced a sharp tongue and sometimes worse.

Rachael had twice defended James, who often overslept, and Ann, who struggled with morning nausea. Reading about early pregnancy in her green book gave Rachael a better understanding of Ann's discomfort. She was increasingly grateful for Martha's gift and for her own visit to the mercantile store, where she'd purchased an herbal medicine list. These remedies were helping, especially for the women who had difficulty managing their cycles during the journey.

During midday stops, Rachael watched for familiar plants she'd studied with her father, ones that might help with digestion, fever, or other ailments. Mr. Grey frequently scolded her for wandering off. He warned of the dangers of getting lost or being taken by Indians.

His ultimatums infuriated her.

Her indifference infuriated him more.

But Rachael would do as she wished.

The site of this nooning was the most beautiful they had ever encountered. The party lazed beneath a grove of trees beside the clearest of burbling springs. Grabbing a biscuit, once again burned on the bottom by Camille but filled with the ever-present bacon, Rachael declined the beans. She headed up the glade with her gathering bag, chewing as she scoured the area for anything useful.

The day had turned warm. Rachael left her shawl behind and pulled the front of her sunbonnet farther over her face. Only this morning, she'd noticed her hands had turned a dark brown from the sun. She'd lost her gloves long ago. But if she had stayed home and married Richard, she might be embroidering a christening gown, something she would hate, and sitting on a sofa, heavily pregnant, sipping tea with friends all afternoon.

How much better it was to be here, living an adventure of her own making in pursuit of her plants.

That afternoon, it felt good to be alive and stretch her sore muscles after so much time riding. Soon, she left behind the camp sounds: the murmur of adult voices, children playing, the rhythmic snorting of oxen pulling up grass. Now, she heard only the calls of birds and the song of the small stream that meandered alongside her.

The cook fire's scent was replaced by that of sun-warmed grass and something sweet she couldn't quite name. A golden-crowned sparrow darted across her path, and she paused to watch it land on a large bush nearby.

It was covered in blue-black berries.

She wandered closer.

Later, she would admit she lost track of time. She began plucking the berries one by one, dropping them into her bag. She even spoke to the bees buzzing around the fruit, assuring them there was enough for all. Her hands soon stained purple, but she didn't care. Every so often, she popped a ripe berry into her mouth. Its rich sweetness was a welcome contrast to their dry hardtack.

She imagined their smiles when she returned with this bounty, an unexpected treat. With that thought, her hands worked faster.

Then, a shadow fell over her.

She froze.

A grunt sounded just behind her, low and deep. Her heart pounded. What could it be? What should she do? Instinct pinned her to the spot, and it may have saved her life. For if she'd bolted, the bear might have attacked.

The she-bear rose on its hind legs, sniffing the air. Rachael could smell her musky, animal stench. The bear was close.

"Don't move."

The voice came low and firm.

The bear dropped to all fours, turning toward the speaker.

"Git, bear. Git!" the voice commanded. "Git you!"

A rifle cracked. Rachael whipped around.

It was James; he must have followed her up the glen, perhaps hoping to shoot a rabbit for supper.

The bear reared up again, now focused on him.

"I said, git! Skedaddle!" James shouted, raising the rifle again. He fired a second shot into the air.

The bear hesitated, then turned and bounded off into the thick underbrush to their left.

For a long moment, they could only look at one another, breathless.

"Oh, James, are you all right?"

James swiped a hand across his forehead, pushing his blond hair back. His hands trembled slightly, though pride shone in his eyes, the proud, tremulous bravery of a young man who had done something right and dangerous and hadn't yet fully processed either.

"It's late, Mrs. Williams. We'd better get back. Mr. Grey was already packing up and complaining about you wandering off again. He had that look." James grinned.

"You mean the look of thunderclouds just before the deluge?" Rachael's heart was still pounding. Her knees shook so violently she doubted she could stand. Her mouth tasted metallic. A bear—a bear! She hadn't realized how large they could be. The teeth alone…

"Worse," James said. "Seems we two vex him more than most. Come on, or it'll be the whip for both of us."

"He wouldn't dare—"

"Wouldn't I?" came a low voice behind them.

Rachael flinched. That voice was ominously calm. She knew that tone. It carried the clap of thunder before the storm.

"I came looking for you, Mrs. Williams, and here I find you dilly-dallying with James."

"We—" Rachael began.

Mr. Grey turned to James. "I heard two gunshots. Where are the rabbits?"

"I'm afraid I missed, sir." James glanced quickly at Rachael and managed a small wink.

"But, Mr. Grey, look!" she said, lifting the berry-filled bag. "I managed to gather all these berries. Surely the company will be glad for a change in diet. We're all tired of—"

"You're complaining? You don't like the food?"

"I just thought—"

"It doesn't matter. Clearly, you haven't thought at all." His voice grew sharper. "You've both made us late again. This is intolerable, Mrs. Williams. From now on, I forbid you to leave camp during the nooning."

Rachael's chin rose. Her cheeks flushed.

"I'll do as I please, sir. You're not my master."

"Oh yes, I am, lady. Don't forget it." His voice now rumbled like thunder. "You agreed to follow my rules when you joined this company, and I won't be gainsaid."

His voice rose to a roar. Then he turned sharply and stomped back down the trail, shouting over his shoulder, "And hurry up, both of you!"

"Well," James said, eyeing the sky, "we'd best not test him. Let's go. We're already in enough trouble."

As they turned to follow, Rachael retrieved the bag she had dropped when the bear appeared.

"Let's just keep the bear between us," she said quietly. "No need for anyone else to know. Between Mr. Grey and your mother, we'd never be allowed to leave camp again. A bear! It still feels unbelievable."

"You know, Mrs., if you hadn't been standing behind her, I could've shot that bear." James' eyes gleamed with imagined triumph.

"Well, I'm glad you didn't. We invaded her space, and she was only defending what was hers."

"Still wish I'd gotten her. Think of all that meat! And I could've had me a bearskin blanket. Would've been something."

"Well, you didn't. Let's hurry." Rachael gathered her skirt and quickened her steps.

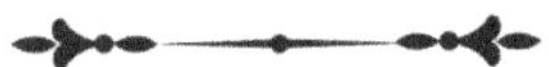

Rachael's legs trembled. She still couldn't believe how close she'd come to a bear attack. Just an hour ago, she'd been so happy, so confident, wandering the glen and gathering berries. Now, she had to admit she'd been foolish. It had never occurred to her that real danger might lurk in those peaceful woods.

If James hadn't come…

The thought chilled her. As much as she resented Mr. Grey's temper, perhaps he wasn't entirely wrong. This journey held dangers she hadn't anticipated. She would need to be more cautious.

Back at camp, the first thing she saw was Mrs. Dix.

The older woman stood with her hands on her hips, her mouth pinched tight with fury.

"James, get over here right now! Your father needs help yoking the oxen. As usual, he can't do it alone."

James left Rachael's side and trotted off to help his father.

"Mrs. Dix," Rachael said, approaching with her gathering bag. "Look what I've brought, big, fat berries. Won't it be a treat to have them baked into the biscuits? Such a—"

"I would ask that you stay away from my son, Mrs. Williams." Mrs. Dix's voice was sharp. "He has no use for the likes of you."

Rachael blinked. "Whatever do you mean? James and I are just friends. He's like a little brother to me."

"Well, if that's the case, then he doesn't need that kind of sister. Just leave him alone."

Rachael's heart kicked up as heat rose to her cheeks. Her temper flared fast and fierce. She remembered trying to save Mrs. Dix's rocking chair, offering her tea for her swollen feet, and being patient through every cold word and glare. And this, this, was her reward?

Something inside her snapped. "How dare you, Mrs. Dix? Why—" She stopped herself, pressing her lips closed before the fury could spill out. Her mouth was full of hot words.

As she turned away in anger, she collided squarely with Mr. Grey. He had clearly heard everything.

"Oh no, not *you,* too," she said. "Leave me alone. I've done nothing wrong."

Mr. Grey simply grinned. He said nothing, but the grin said plenty.

He'd heard the shouting. Had he misunderstood it, too? Did he think she liked James? That Mrs. Dix was right? That she, a married woman, was interested in a boy?

The humiliation burned deeper than her anger. Did Mr. Grey have no sense of who she was? It was embarrassing enough that he'd caught her losing her temper, but to think she fancied James? How utterly ridiculous.

She had never intended to marry again. Why would she want a man telling her what to do? She was a botanist, a scientist, destined for discovery. Once again, in her mind's eye, she saw herself lifting a Devil's Club root from the soil, penknife in hand. She had better things to do.

Without another word, she stomped off toward her tent.

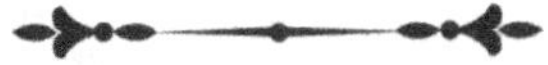

That night, the company assembled around the fire for supper. Rachael called it the 4Bs: *beans, bacon, and burned biscuits.* She'd once whispered the nickname to Sara, who had grinned, earning her a private victory. At least Cookie had drawn water from the spring they'd camped near at nooning. It tasted cleaner than usual.

She dutifully delivered her sack of berries to Cookie, who let out a joyful yelp that lifted her spirits. After the sting of Mrs. Dix's words, she needed it.

Looking around, Rachael spotted Sara perched on her usual barrel seat, plate already in hand. She joined her.

"Hi, Sar. Where's your mother?"

Sara pointed toward their wagon, where shadows moved inside. Rachael could just make out the silhouettes of Reverend Robert and Ann. Ann appeared to be lying down. Robert knelt beside her. Praying, Rachael guessed.

"Is she not feeling well again, Sara?"

Sara nodded and pointed to her own head, then her stomach.

"Oh dear. I'd hoped the nausea would be easing by now. I'll make something for her. Sara, do you remember when Christopher was born?"

Sara's eyes widened. She shook her head, no, her lips tightly pressed.

Rachael paused. Something in the child's face told her that Sara remembered more than she was letting on. But now wasn't the time to press.

"Never mind, child," she said gently, tucking a strand of hair behind Sara's ear and patting her hand. "We'll see her through this."

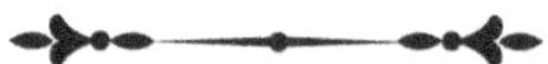

Later, after tucking Sara into bed, Rachael waited until Reverend Robert had joined the men at the fire. She took her chance and crept quietly toward the wagon.

There hadn't been time for another private conversation with Ann since that long-ago evening at Westport. And still, Ann refused the tea Rachael had offered. The tea Martha had recommended, steeped from Rubus idaeus leaves, is known to ease pregnancy symptoms. Ann insisted that only God's help was needed.

She would pray harder, she'd said.

But Rachael had made a promise. If she were to keep her word to Martha, she would have to find another way, either to be more insistent or more vigilant.

Yet, with every refusal from Ann, she grew more unsure of what to do next.

She called out softly before opening the canvas flap at the wagon's rear. "Ann, it's Rachael. May we speak for a moment?"

"Just give me a little time."

Rachael waited. From inside came the sound of something scraping along the wagon bed, an object being pushed aside. She stared at the ground, puzzled, then understood. The noise had been a pot. *She's been sick again*, Rachael thought.

"All right, come in," Ann said. Her voice was hoarse, barely audible.

Rachael climbed up into the wagon and stopped short. It was stifling inside. The heat wrapped around her like a wet woolen blanket, and the sour smell of vomit confirmed her suspicion.

Ann's face, pale and drawn, lay in shadow.

"Why, Ann, you're ill."

"I'm fine, Rachael. It's nothing."

"Can I open the back of the canvas? Let some air in? It's like an oven in here."

"I suppose if you must." Ann's tone was weary. She pulled a heavy quilt tighter around her shoulders.

"But aren't you hot, covered like that?" Rachael asked gently. "The night air is cool and pleasant. You always said you loved to see the stars. Wouldn't some air do you good?"

"I'm fine here. Thank you."

Rachael clenched her jaw. Her frustration was rising again. *How could she help this woman if she wouldn't even admit to being unwell?*

She decided to be direct.

"I made a promise to your Aunt Martha, and I intend to keep it. But to help you, I need to know more about Christopher's birth. And why the doctor warned you not to have any more children."

Ann's eyes remained fixed on the wagon roof.

"This birth will not be like that one," she said finally. "This baby is a gift from God. Not that Christopher wasn't, but Robert and I prayed so long for this child. Robert says the Lord has told him this birth will be different. He says the headaches, the nausea, all of it, it's a test. A witness to my faith."

Rachael stayed silent, listening, though each word unsettled her more.

"We prayed for strength tonight," Ann continued, her voice dreamy now. "This child is part of the plan. Our mission. To bring God's word to the savages. If I die giving birth, then that, too, is the Lord's will."

Rachael's heart sank.

Die? And so simply, so placidly, Ann said it.

Rachael's scientific mind reeled. *How could a woman believe that dying in childbirth, out here in the middle of nowhere, was part of a divine plan?* Did she believe every word Robert fed her? Couldn't she think for herself? *I need facts*, Rachael thought. She needed to understand the risks to help prevent them. That was what science was: preparation and prevention. Facts, not fatalism.

She tried a new angle.

"I am sure this birth *will* be different," she said carefully. "But I still need to understand what happened before, what happened with Christopher's birth."

She hesitated, then took a chance.

"Ann… couldn't it be that I am part of God's plan, too? Perhaps He sent me to help you. To look after the children, to help you through this birth. If you don't tell me what happened, if I don't know what to prepare for, maybe you're preventing me from fulfilling my purpose in His plan."

Ann's eyes glistened. Her hands released the quilt, bunched in her lap.

Rachael's gaze dropped. On the quilt, stitched in careful, looping letters, was a verse:

"Those who believe in Me shall not be punished but rewarded in the Kingdom of Heaven."

Ann looked down at the quilt in her lap. "I never thought… You could be part of His holy plan." She seemed to brighten, the pallor on her face easing slightly. "It's true. We are all part of the grand plan. Perhaps you're right, and you were sent to help me. I suppose I should tell you what you want to know. It would be wrong of me not to. I see that now." Her lips lifted in a faint smile. "Of course, I must speak with Robert, too. But first, could you get me a cup of that tea you mentioned? The one for the nausea? I suppose being sick into that pot isn't doing me, or the baby, any good."

Rachael nearly shouted a hallelujah. Instead, she said with quiet relief, "I'll be right back with it. Let me help you sit up, and I'll take that bucket."

Ann hesitated only a moment, then nodded. "And could you tie back the canvas? It's so hot in here."

"I'll gladly do both."

Rachael climbed down and quickly tucked the pot behind a bush near Cookie's wagon, hoping no one would notice. The fire still glowed, and Cookie was pouring water for the last of the evening tea. She caught his eye, offered a soft thank you, and returned with her steaming tin cup.

"It'll take a few minutes to steep," she said, settling beside Ann in the wagon and tucking the quilt gently over her again. With the flap tied open, a soft breeze drifted through the wagon, already cooling the stifling heat.

Setting the cup between them, she asked gently, "Now, Ann, what happened? What do you remember from Christopher's birth?"

Ann looked toward the shadows at the front of the wagon. "I don't remember much. Only that it hurt… and it seemed to go on for hours, days, even. The doctor wasn't there at first. He was busy with another birth."

She paused, then continued, voice soft. "He said Christopher was a big baby, especially for someone like me. He told me to stop pushing… then reached in with some instrument and started tugging. Finally, Christopher came out. The doctor grabbed him and slapped him hard. I remember being sick at the sight of him, white and slippery." She shuddered faintly. "Sara didn't look like that. The nurse took him away to clean him up. Then… all I remember is the blood. So much blood. The doctor's face went pale as he bunched up all the sheets to stop it. But they were soaked through. I must've passed out. I woke up a day later, sore… but alive. The doctor said it was a miracle I hadn't bled to death."

Rachael pressed her hand to her mouth, stunned. *Traumatic labor. Massive postpartum hemorrhage. Possibly a forceps delivery.* The images sprang into her mind, textbook terms made terrifyingly real.

And Robert… he was willing to put her through this again?

How had he allowed it? How was Ann? Rachael's mind raced, filled with dread. What if she couldn't manage it? Even with Martha's mother's book, how would she stop the bleeding of that scale again?

She couldn't do it alone.

Mrs. Dix. As much as Rachael disliked her, the woman *had* given birth twice. She'd have to help. Rachael couldn't manage without her. But asking for that help… that would be delicate. And risky.

They would almost certainly be on the trail when labor began. There'd be no doctor, no clean hospital, no instruments. Nothing.

She would have to re-read every section of the midwifery book, especially the chapter on a hemorrhage. She would need to plan, gather supplies, and prepare. And, difficult as it would be, she'd have to speak with Mr. Grey. They would need to stop at a fort or outpost, somewhere; there might be help. This birth wasn't just dangerous.

It could be fatal.

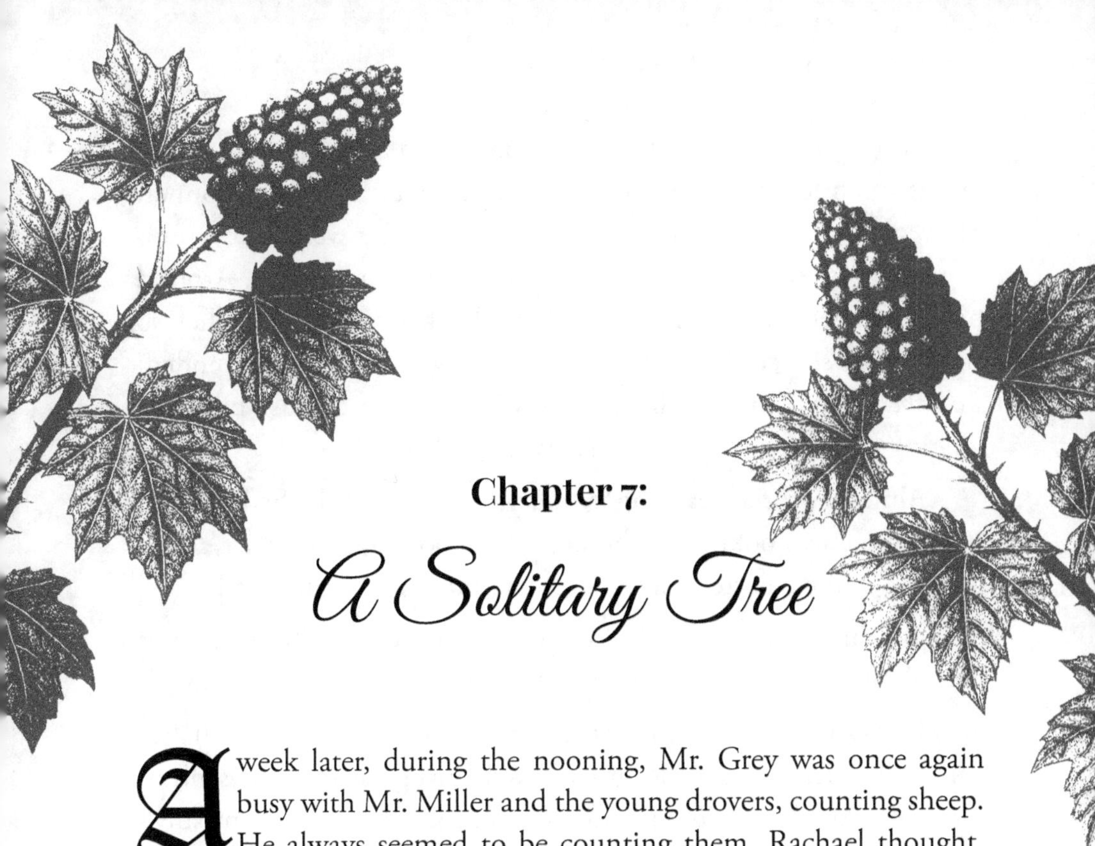

Chapter 7:

A Solitary Tree

A week later, during the nooning, Mr. Grey was once again busy with Mr. Miller and the young drovers, counting sheep. He always seemed to be counting them, Rachael thought. The other men were napping; the women were sewing. Rachael had no intention of sewing. She planned to use the time for something more practical, something that might actually help the company.

They were all still suffering bouts of dysentery despite Mr. Grey's rules about boiling water. Her book suggested white oak bark tea as a remedy, and to her relief, Rachael believed she had spotted a grove nearby. After the bear encounter, she was far more cautious. She wouldn't go far.

She found Cookie sitting in the shade of his wagon, a tin cup resting beside him. As she untied Little Red from the springboard wagon and fastened her collecting bag to the saddle, she said, "If anyone asks, tell them I've just gone up the trail a little. I'm hoping to find something to help with the, well... you know."

Cookie grunted but gave a faint nod.

Rachael pointed to a low rise in the distance. "Just to that next hill. You can still see it from camp." The route was flat and straight; she wouldn't get lost.

Feeling quietly triumphant, she mounted Little Red and rode out at a gentle walk. The breeze stirred her hair under her bonnet. How glad she was to be alone, away from the weight of group expectations, endless opinions, and whispered judgments. Around her, chokeberry and white gooseberry bushes tangled together so thoroughly she couldn't see where one began or the other ended. *Like the knots in my hair,* she thought with a grin, each bush probably longing to be free, to grow on its own. *Just like me.*

Almost without realizing it, she passed the hill she had pointed out to Cookie. Looking up the slope, she spotted the distinct, lobed leaves of white oak trees, shimmering faintly in the light wind.

Turning in her saddle, she looked back. She could still see the faint tendrils of smoke from the cookfire rising behind her. *Still close enough.*

In Martha's mother's notes, she had read that the white, flakey bark of this tree, when made into tea, could bring relief from dysentery. Urging Little Red up the incline, Rachael imagined the company's gratitude. Boiled water hadn't been enough. Dirt clung to everything, even the food. Maybe the cause didn't matter. *But now,* she thought, *I can offer something to help.*

At the grove, she dismounted and tied Little Red to a low branch. She pulled out her small knife and the leather pouch Hannah had stitched for her. Carefully, she began to scrape bark from the tree, just a bit, just enough. When the pouch was nearly full, she patted the tree's trunk.

"Thank you," she murmured, another ritual her father had taught her. Always thank the plant for what it gives.

Satisfied, Rachael tucked the pouch into her collecting bag and re-sheathed her knife. She swung up into the saddle, light with joy. The moment was golden.

A tune floated to her lips, one she hadn't sung in years. *Claire de Lune.* How had it come to her now? She smiled as she whistled the melody, her thoughts already on brewing the tea, offering it to the others, and making herself useful.

Then she heard her name.

"Mrs. Williams!"

She recognized Mr. Grey's voice. *Of course*, she thought. *He would be pleased. His dysentery was worse than anyone's.*

"I'm here!" she called back, beginning her descent down the slope, proud of her harvest, her horse, and her seat in the saddle.

She urged Little Red into a faster gait, trotting down the hill toward Mr. Grey. As she drew closer, she saw his face, red with fury, his jaw clenched, his hands gripping the reins so tightly that his big roan horse tossed its head and backed up in protest. He responded by kicking sharply into its flanks.

"Good God, woman! What do you think you're doing?" he bellowed. "You left the encampment without telling me. You know better than that by now. I—"

Rachael, stunned by the venom in his tone, straightened in the saddle. Her own frustration began to rise.

"I told Cookie exactly where I was going. You were counting sheep. I didn't want to interrupt—"

"Do you have any idea of the trouble you've caused? You could've gotten lost, hurt, or taken by Indians! Riding off during nooning? Alone? And with a horse? They'd love to have another horse! Have you no sense, woman? None at all?"

Rachael's temper flared. Her voice sharpened. "I knew exactly where I was. I never lost sight of camp. I stuck to the trail, saw a stand of white oaks, and went to collect bark for tea. A tea that helps with dysentery, something that could help everyone here!"

"I don't give a damn what it's good for!" he snapped. "I have a mind to never let you ride again. Certainly not for a while. Maybe that'll teach you something."

"But I was trying to help, don't you see—"

"No, I don't. Give me your horse's reins."

She dismounted stiffly, jaw tight, and handed them over without a word. What was he planning now?

"Now, get back on your horse," he ordered.

Seething, she rubbed her hands on her skirt and climbed back into the saddle.

He took hold of Little Red's reins and led her, like a child, back to camp.

Rachael rode in silence, her spine rigid. *He is deliberately humiliating me.* She refused to let him see how furious she was.

As they returned, the entire camp stared. Camille's eyes were cast down. Even Ann reached for Sara's arm to stop her from running to Rachael.

Enough.

She dismounted, untied her collecting bag, turned from the onlookers, and disappeared behind Cookie's wagon.

It was too much. She had done nothing wrong. She'd told someone where she was going, stayed close, found something useful, and this was the result? *Stupid.*

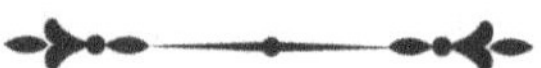

Later, alone in the tent, Rachael sat brushing her hair. The bristles snagged in the tangles, pulling painfully. Frustrated, she yanked the brush through the snarls, pointless. It only made things worse.

On impulse, she reached into her collecting bag, drew out her knife, and sawed at her hair. Long strands fell to the floor. She kept cutting until the ends reached just below her chin. When she stopped, breathless, she felt elated.

Her head was lighter. The burden of it all, the scolding, the scrutiny, the confinement, lifted. She shook her head. No heavy braid swung behind her, only curls brushing her cheek like a soft breeze.

She borrowed a small mirror from Camille's things. A different woman looked back at her. Her hair, now a golden halo, framed her face like a crown. She smiled at the reflection. She looked free.

Gathering the fallen strands, she wrapped them in an old scarf and tucked them into her satchel.

Then, head high, she left the tent and walked to supper.

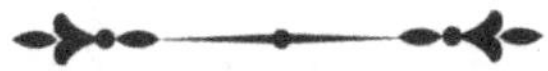

The camp fell silent as she approached. Eyes widened. Mouths hung open.

Rachael said nothing. She filled her plate with beans and bacon, skipped the biscuit, and took her usual place on the upturned barrel, as far from the others as possible.

A moment later, Sara broke free of Ann and ran to her, eyes enormous.

"Y-you ccc-ut yoor hhairr!" she whispered in awe, reaching toward the new curls.

Rachael smiled. "I did."

"CCaan I ccut mminne ttoo?"

Waiting for the sheep to cross yet another river, the company busied themselves unloading the wagons to let the contents dry. No matter how carefully they tarred the undersides, water always managed to seep in. Robert was off tending to the livestock. Cookie had started a fire, and Camille was baking, with her Aunt, as usual, hovering and correcting. Rachael spotted Mrs. Dix waving a finger and nodding her head in a furious rhythm. *What a tiresome woman.* She had never forgiven Mr. Grey for forcing her to leave behind her belongings; weeks had passed, and still, she brooded. *If I have to hear about that rocking chair one more time, I will howl.*

At the journey's outset, Rachael had hoped this small company might become like a family. But instead, the weeks had brought bickering, complaints, and a constant undercurrent of discontent, much of it aimed at Mr. Grey. To be fair, she often thought he deserved it. His treatment of her, especially, was so paternal, so condescending, never failed to enrage her. Still, she couldn't deny he knew the trail better than anyone. That alone had saved them more than once. Yet he spoiled it all with his short temper and uncompromising nature. They'd only been on the trail for a month. *What will three or four look like?* She sighed.

Glancing at the sky, she noticed a black cloud edging across the horizon. A storm was coming. Just moments ago, the camp had looked almost festive, clothes, sheets, and bedding flung across bushes and low branches to dry. Now, everything would have to be hurriedly gathered.

Lightning flashed. Then came the rain.

Rachael sprinted for her things, yanking damp garments from the brush and wrapping them hastily in a sheet of Indian rubber cloth. Around her, everyone did the same, throwing linens into wagons with frantic energy. The fire hissed out in a puff of steam. Bread was once again off the menu. She felt particularly sorry for Camille, who had changed into her cleanest clothes for the Sabbath, now soaked, her blue gingham dress and white stockings smeared with mud.

When the rain cleared and the sheep were once again rounded up after their crossing, Mr. Grey called a rest day. The group was weary. Rachael hoped the break would soften everyone's tempers, hers included.

She soon spotted Camille once again left to handle the family laundry. The children were busy drawing in the wet mud with sticks, so Rachael decided to help. Camille had been handed the entire family's wash again by Mrs. Dix, and Rachael bristled at how the girl was treated, like a servant rather than a niece. But Camille seemed unfazed, moving through her chores with practiced calm. *I could never be so patient,* Rachael thought.

Camille was always busy, always being told what to do. There was rarely time for conversation, and Rachael had been wondering for weeks about the mystery Camille had hinted at, her own reason for going to Oregon. Maybe now there would be a chance to learn more.

Grabbing her own laundry, her much-mended skirt, blouse, and undershirt, Rachael picked up her precious box of Armovr's laundry soap and walked toward her. *Surely Camille will be glad for the help.*

She found her kneeling at the edge of a shallow rivulet where it joined the main river. Camille had found a flat stone and was using it to pound the laundry clean. Small bushes, finally dry from the morning rain, stood nearby, perfect for hanging the wash. She was working on Mrs. Dix's blue linen skirt.

"Hi, Camille. I hope this will help." Rachael handed her the box of soap.

"Why, thank you. I'll just use a little, but it really does help. Sometimes, I feel like I'm pounding the dirt into the clothes rather than washing them out." Camille poured a modest amount onto the blue linen skirt and began scrubbing.

"If only we had a proper tub. We could keep the suds and get through this much faster. Now, they just wash downstream. It feels like such a waste."

"I know exactly what you mean. I hope to get something like that when we reach Fort Laramie."

"Perhaps. It does seem odd we don't already have one."

"Mr. Grey probably thinks it's too heavy," Rachael teased.

Camille tilted her head and smiled. "Indeed, he probably would."

As she laughed, her glasses slipped off her nose and into the water. Rachael lunged forward and caught them just in time.

"Better find a way to tie these on," she said, holding them up.

"Oh, dear, I certainly must. Seems I'm always losing my glasses."

"I bet Hannah has some string we can use. I'll ask her."

There was a pause, and Rachael shifted slightly, lowering her voice. "Camille, I don't mean to pry, but... why did you come on this trip?"

Camille glanced down, still scrubbing, then stopped. She sat back on her heels, eyes searching Rachael's face.

"Well, for one reason…to help my aunt. She took me in after my mother died. I was little then. I always felt I owed her something." Camille handed Rachael the damp blue skirt, and she hung it on a nearby bush. "But… there's another reason, too. I started to tell you before, but never finished."

"The other reason?" Rachael prompted gently.

Camille hesitated. "You won't share this, will you? I mean… not with anyone?"

"Of course not," Rachael said. "Especially if you ask me not to."

Camille looked out over the rivulet, her voice quiet. "I'm hoping to find my father. He left for California before my mother became ill and said he had 'gold fever.' Promised he'd come back rich as Croesus. But we never heard from him. Not until after she died. He doesn't even know she's gone."

"Oh, Camille…" Rachael whispered.

"He sent a letter from Sutter's Fort," she continued. "That's in California. I hope to find him there."

"Does your aunt know?"

"Certainly not. She disapproved of him, called him irresponsible, and said he broke my mother's heart. She blames her death on him."

"That's a heavy thing to believe."

"It's not true," Camille said quickly. "I know my mother loved him. She always told me she believed in him."

"Do you think he's still there?"

"I don't know," Camille said, picking up one of Henry's shirts and pounding it against the stone. "But I have to try. I've got a tintype of them on their wedding day. I'll show it to you later."

"I'd love that."

Rachael knelt beside her and began soaping her own garments. Mrs. Dix had gone on endlessly about how generous she'd been, taking in her "poor orphaned niece" after her "beloved sister's tragic death." But here, knee-deep in mud and wash water, Rachael saw something different: a bright, earnest young woman living quietly under the weight of someone else's story.

We could be true friends, Rachael thought, *if only she were free from all this drudgery.* There was something endearing in the way Camille tilted her head when she spoke, the way she was always losing her glasses.

I hope she has another pair, Rachael thought with a smirk. *Maybe that's why she keeps burning the biscuits.*

She reached out and touched Camille's shoulder gently. The impulse surprised her. She wanted to tell her the truth about everything. About the lie she was still carrying.

How can I have an honest friendship when there's this enormous secret between us? Can I risk telling her?

"Isn't it odd, Camille, that we both have private reasons for this trip?"

"What do you mean? You're going to meet your husband, are you not?"

Camille put down the stone and looked directly at her.

Rachael felt a flush rise in her cheeks. "Yes, of course."

"Is there more?" Camille asked, her wide eyes magnified by her glasses.

"No. I guess not, not really." Rachael looked out toward the river, watching a small log spinning helplessly in an eddy.

Camille continued to watch her.

Rachael dropped her gaze to the dress in her hands, gave it another swirl in the water, then stood and draped it over a nearby bush. She glanced again at Camille, kneeling at the river's edge, calm and focused. Rachael wondered if, in keeping silent, she'd just let something precious slip away, like the soap she'd offered and watched wash downstream.

The rolling hills glowed beneath a pearly dawn, their edges softened by mist and dewless grass. Rachael mounted Little Red, the bay horse, grateful it was her turn to ride again. Over their hard biscuits and tea, the company had muttered predictions about rain. No dew meant storm, they said, and it seemed they would be right.

Everyone had risen at four-thirty. The wagons, as usual, were the last to leave. Rachael had dressed in her best: a Lindsey-Woolsey skirt, a blouse, and two underskirts. Though ill-suited for the weather, she hadn't minded; if the rain came, Mr. Grey would surely take her into the wagon, as was the custom for women riders. That was one small concession he made.

Today, Mr. Grey was driving Cookie's springboard wagon himself as Cookie was off helping with the sheep. Ann rode beside him, seeking relief from her headaches in the smoother ride the springboard offered. Mr. Grey might have driven fast, but Rachael had learned to keep up. She could sit a canter as easily as rocking in a chair. She was proud of her firm, practiced seat.

Soon, a drizzle began. Instead of calling her into the wagon, Mr. Grey passed her an Indian rubber coat, oversized and meant for a man; it only half-covered her. She accepted it without complaint, oddly touched by the gesture. He hadn't coddled her but treated her like an equal. Ann leaned over and handed her an old sunbonnet, one without pasteboard stiffening, which would only wilt in the rain. Rachael tucked it under her chin, straightened her spine, and rode a little taller in the saddle.

Then the drizzle turned to rain. And then to a downpour.

Mud splashed up from Little Red's hooves, soaking her skirt. The coat clung to one side of her body while the other was entirely exposed. Still, she held her ground.

Mr. Grey looked over at her. "You'll be wet through by the time we get to camp. What a sight you'll be, covered in mud from head to toe!"

"And I will laugh, too," she shot back, smiling through clenched teeth. "Once we get to camp."

The storm broke in full fury. Thunder roared. Yellow bolts of lightning split the sky, and the air filled with the sharp, mineral scent of freshly struck flint. It was the worst storm they had faced so far.

Rachael became soaked to the skin. Water streamed down her neck, her bonnet collapsed under the weight of rain, and her blouse clung to her like a second skin. She shivered, chilled to the bone.

Mr. Grey yelled through the storm. "You'll need a fire when we stop!"

"Yes," she shouted back, her voice trembling. "A big fire!"

Although she had initially been pleased not to be treated like every other woman, now she wasn't so sure. Why hadn't he offered to take her into the wagon? Surely, he could see how miserable she was, soaked, shivering, and exhausted. Was he testing her mettle? Her determination? It would be just like him. Well, she wouldn't yield. She clutched Little Red's reins more tightly, fixing her eyes on the muddy, rutted road ahead.

She said nothing and rode on, a glowing coal of indignation burning in her throat. And what about Ann? Even if Mr. Grey *was* testing her, Rachael had expected some consideration from her. Why hadn't she spoken up? Rachael stole a glance at Ann, but her expression gave away nothing. Still, Mr. Grey drove on.

When they finally reached camp, Mr. Grey informed her that the grounds were too crowded with other wagons. They'd have to continue down the trail to rejoin the sheep and the rest of the company. Rachael said nothing despite the chill seeping into her bones. She had sworn back in Independence never to complain, no matter what. She gripped the reins and pressed on, guiding Little Red across a swollen creek where the water surged over her stirrups and soaked her skirts through.

They stopped at last where the others were waiting. Rachael dismounted, but when her feet hit the ground, a jolt of pain shot through them, numb, cold, unfeeling. Her wet wool clung to her skin. Groaning, she leaned against Little Red, burying her face in his damp, warm neck. He, too, looked miserable, his head low, ears drooping. He leaned gently back into her, and the gesture nearly undid her.

She admitted to herself then that she wanted help. She wanted someone, anyone, to notice. Her feet throbbed with cold. Her face burned with humiliation and fatigue. Her body ached with the wetness and weight of her sodden clothes.

Finally, Mr. Grey declared it too wet to pitch tents and suggested she climb into the wagon. She did, without protest. She couldn't tell him how desperately she needed dry clothes. Clambering up, she peeled off her wet skirt and petticoats, using them to towel herself as best she could. Her fingers were stiff, her teeth chattering uncontrollably. From her satchel, she pulled out another Lindsey-Woolsey skirt and blouse and pulled them on, still damp and shaking. She huddled in the wagon, waiting for warmth that wouldn't come.

No one offered help. No fire. No words. No gesture of care. She sat in the wagon alone. And maybe it was her own fault; had she been too proud? Too independent? Always refusing help? Was that why no one came now?

But beneath that independence, Rachael realized, was a quiet yearning, not for constant company or coddling, but for the simple comfort of being seen and cared for.

She lifted her hands and covered her eyes.

At that moment, abandoned, exhausted, and disheartened, Rachael questioned everything. Was this trip a mistake? The tears she had held back for days finally spilled down her cheeks. Yesterday had felt like a low point. Today, she had fallen further. Her body ached from the ride. She was sure she'd taken a chill. And deeper than the physical discomfort was the emotional sting: not one person had noticed her misery. Not Camille, not Hannah, not Ann.

And maybe they hadn't meant to ignore her. They all had families—husbands, children, siblings. They were consumed by their own needs.

And that was it, wasn't it?

They had their own people.

She had no one.

This wasn't just loneliness. It was something worse. It was *aloneness*. The deep, cavernous awareness that no one was tethered to her, that no one would come looking, no one would reach out.

And for the first time in her life, it frightened her.

Would she be able to live in Oregon alone? Could she carry on with her mission to find her precious plant, her purpose, if no one was there to share it with her?

She looked across the vast plain and saw a solitary tree, its branches bent in the wind.

Is that what I am? she wondered. A lone tree on a barren plain?

Later, when she rode in the springboard wagon beside Mr. Grey, she remained silent. Even when he tried to draw her into conversation, she refused. She had no desire to share herself. Not with him. Not with anyone.

On a steep descent, she asked to be let out and walked briskly behind the wagon, trying to lift her spirits by focusing on the world around her, the grandeur of God's creation, as her mother would have said. She noticed a small grove of trees arranged in what her father used to call a *fairy ring*.

But even that wonder failed to comfort her.

All she could see in her mind was that solitary tree. And the cold truth of being just like it.

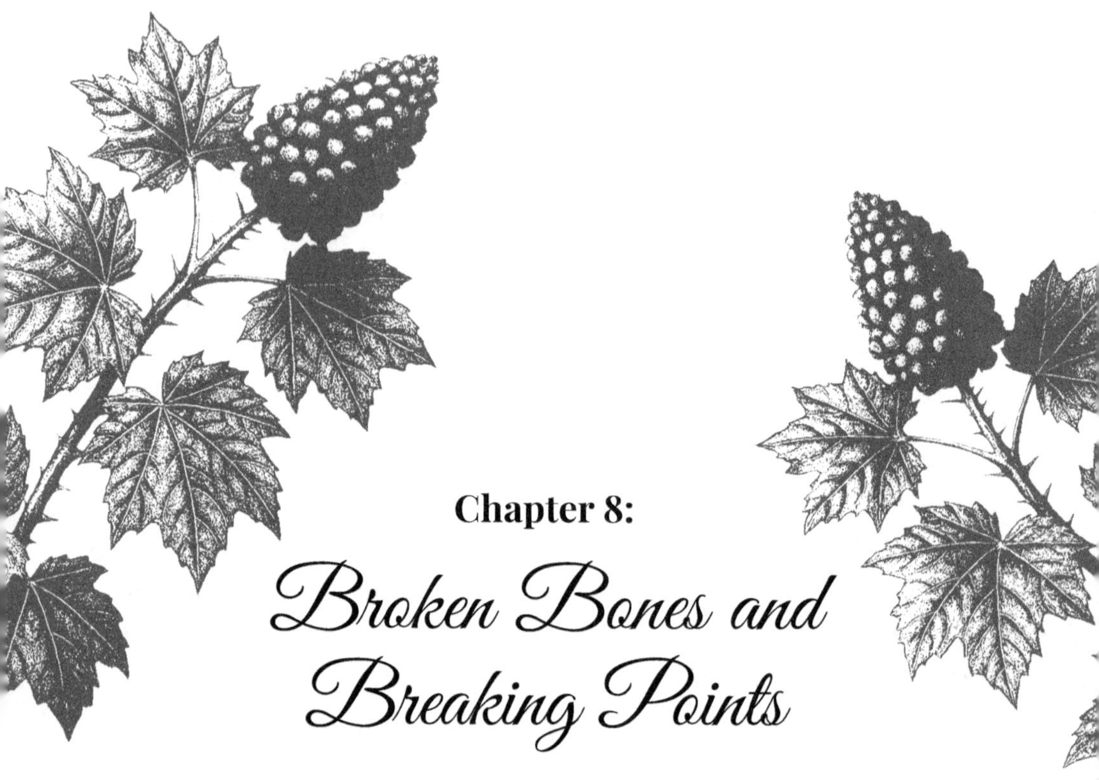

Chapter 8:

Broken Bones and Breaking Points

Four days later, Rachael climbed a small knoll during the noontime break. From the summit, she could just make out the winding course of the Little Blue River, its islands thick with trees. Closer to camp, the familiar outlines of the wagons and Cookie's buckboard punctuated the landscape. The sheep were barely visible in the distance, soft white dots against the prairie. She guessed they were between grazing spots near the river. The pasturage seemed good. *Much better than yesterday,* she noted.

Below, the men napped in the tall grass, hats pulled low over their faces, their forms slouched in exhaustion. Everyone was weary from the string of early starts that week. Mr. Grey had grown increasingly irritable, pushing them harder each day. They weren't meeting his mileage goals, and his agitation showed.

This afternoon, Camille, Mrs. Dix, and Mrs. Evans had draped their bedding across the wide, sun-warmed rocks near the river. Ann, meanwhile, lay curled in the wagon bed, claiming another of her headaches, now more frequent as her pregnancy progressed. Earlier,

Rachael had gently asked if she'd suffered the same during previous pregnancies. Ann had said she didn't recall. *Convenient,* Rachael thought. She made a mental note to check Martha's mother's book for remedies specifically tied to pregnancy. Another thought struck her. *Maybe it wasn't the pregnancy at all. Maybe it was exhaustion.* Rachael herself had battled headaches when too tired to sleep. She would ask Ann about her rest.

For now, it was blissful to be alone. On this journey, solitude was rare and precious. Most noontimes, Rachael was in charge of the children, inventing games or teaching them to build little boats of leaves and twigs to float down any nearby stream, things she had once loved doing herself. She had to admit she was good with children and usually enjoyed their company. But today, Robert had assigned Sara to look after the younger ones. Rachael took that as a small blessing and perhaps even a gesture of trust. Robert was usually cold and curt with his stepdaughter. She hoped Sara could manage the group: Roy, Christopher, and especially Henry were a rowdy bunch. She felt a twinge of concern but reminded herself she was owed this break.

She had seen the children disappear earlier into the stand of willow trees near the river. *Hopefully, there are no snakes,* she thought.

With a sigh, Rachael tilted her face to the sky. Puffy white clouds sailed overhead, bright in the afternoon sun. As a child, she and her parents had played a game, finding shapes in the clouds. A bear, a man in a hat, a fruit bowl. Her mother had once called it "God's greatest blessing to exercise the imagination." Rachael couldn't agree more. She smiled at the memory.

Then her gaze fell back to camp.

Her body went rigid.

She spotted Robert Godley gripping Sara by the shoulders, shaking her. He was shouting into her face.

Rachael dropped her journal and took off running down the hill, heart pounding. *What in God's name was he doing?*

As she got closer, his words rang out, sharp and cruel.

"What is it, Sara? You must tell us! No, no—I can't understand you! I swear your speech is the Devil's affliction!"

Rachael's stomach twisted. She saw the tears pouring down Sara's face. The child struggled to form words, her lips trembling, twisting, failing. Her mouth opened, but no sound came clearly. Only fragments. Her whole body shook with the effort.

"Stop it!" Rachael shouted, her voice fierce. "Reverend Godley, you're making it worse!"

She grabbed his arm and yanked him back, stepping between him and the terrified girl.

"Sara, breathe. Close your eyes. Just breathe." Rachael dropped to her knees, taking Sara's hands.

Sara's eyes were wild with panic. She clutched Rachael's hand tightly, tugging her toward the grove of trees.

"Crs—Crs—Crs—," she choked.

"Don't speak, child. Just take me."

Sara and Rachael ran, Robert thundering behind them, red-faced and shouting. Mr. Grey and Mr. Evans followed swiftly.

Beneath a stand of trees near the river, Rachael spotted a small figure lying still in the tall grass.

It was Christopher.

Roy knelt beside him, sobbing uncontrollably.

"Oh, my God. Please, God, do not take my son," Robert cried, shoving past Rachael to fall to his knees beside the boy.

As he did, a faint groan escaped Christopher's lips. He was alive.

Robert began to pray loudly, clutching at the boy's unmoving frame. Rachael held Sara, whose small body trembled against her.

Mr. Grey stepped up and placed a firm hand on Robert's shoulder, his voice calm but direct. Tom Evans stood quietly behind him.

"Prayers are important, Robert," Mr. Grey said, "but we must see what's wrong and where."

Robert went to scoop Christopher into his arms.

"No, don't move him," Grey ordered. "We need to look first. Moving him could make it worse."

Then, turning to Rachael, he said, "Come here. I'll need your help. Sara, take Roy and Henry back to the wagons. Tell your mother that your brother has been hurt, and we'll bring him to her. Can you manage?"

Sara nodded. Still shaken, she reached for Roy's hand and began leading the boys toward camp.

Rachael stepped forward, her chest tight. Guilt surged in her throat. *If only I had stayed with the children…*

Mr. Grey met her eyes. "Can I count on you?" he asked. His tone was not cruel, only commanding—unyielding. Rachael gave a single nod.

Together, they bent over Christopher.

"He's in shock," Grey murmured. "Look at his arm. It's bent unnaturally. Likely broken."

He gestured at the limb, twisted at an odd angle, swelling fast.

"Robert," Grey called, "Come steady his head while I examine the break. Rachael, you take hold of his feet."

"Christopher, can you hear me?" Robert whispered hoarsely. "Can you speak? Please, God, please…"

"Quiet, Robert," Grey said. "If the arm's broken, it's better he stays unconscious. What I'm about to do will hurt…badly."

"He's my son—"

"Hush," said both Mr. Grey and Rachael in unison. "Let us work."

Mr. Grey crouched low, easing his hands under the boy's body. As he gently tested the broken arm, Christopher whimpered and then gave a thin, piercing wail. Rachael felt bile rise in her throat.

The sight of the swollen, twisted limb made her knees wobble. She shut her eyes for a moment, willing herself not to faint. *Not now. You must stay upright. He needs you.*

She opened her eyes.

"I'm all right," she whispered, meeting Grey's gaze.

"Good." He turned back. "I need splints. Where's Robert? No matter, Tom, take my knife and cut four willow branches, the length of his arm, elbow to the wrist."

Mr. Grey stripped off his shirt in one practiced motion. "Rachael, I need your apron. We'll use it for padding and binding."

Without hesitation, Rachael untied her apron and handed it to him.

"I've done this before," Grey muttered, almost to himself. "And likely will again. Poor lad. I'm glad he's not fully conscious. This would be unbearable otherwise."

With clinical precision, Grey began to align the arm. His hands moved gently but firmly, feeling for the break, watching the boy's face for signs of pain. He also examined Christopher's hand, checking for circulation and nerve damage, though Rachael didn't dare interrupt with questions.

Christopher's eyes fluttered, and then he fainted.

It was a blessing.

Grey worked quickly. The willow branches arrived. He padded the arm with the soft fabric of Rachael's apron, then braced it with the straight sticks, wrapping it all tightly with more strips of the apron. When he was satisfied, he folded the injured limb across the child's chest and bound it securely in place with a piece of his own torn shirt sleeve.

Rachael watched Mr. Grey's actions with intense focus. Her mind buzzed with questions.

Why press the nails? What exactly was he checking for?

But she knew better than to interrupt. This was not the time.

Not far away, Robert stumbled into the brush and retched violently. Rachael turned away. She wished she felt more sympathy, but the memory of him shaking Sara, shouting that her speech was the Devil's work, stirred only anger.

With the arm secured, Mr. Grey carefully lifted Christopher and carried him toward the wagon. Reverend Robert followed silently behind. When they reached the Godley wagon, Ann came out to meet them.

Christopher's eyes, glossy with pain, locked onto his mother's.

"It hurts, Mama," he whimpered. "It hurts."

Ann knelt and smoothed his hair. Mr. Grey reassured her, "He's a good boy. Very brave. He'll be fine in a few weeks. I believe it's a clean break."

Ann nodded but said nothing more.

Rachael stood nearby with her arm around Sara, who trembled in her grasp. *Will Ann not even look at her daughter?* Rachael wondered, heart sinking. *Sara was frightened, too. Doesn't she see that?*

"Sara," Rachael said gently, "let's make some tea for your brother. And I'll need to prepare a comfrey compress; it will help ease the pain. I need your help. Could you go to Cookie and bring back some hot water while I get my bag?"

Sara said nothing, but her swollen eyes showed that she understood. She turned and walked off to find Cookie.

Rachael watched her go, proud of the child's quiet resilience. She was also struck anew by what she'd just witnessed. Grey had been calm, thorough, and, yes, kind. His hands, so often clenched in fury, had been steady and gentle. Even his tone with Ann had been reassuring. She had never imagined he could be that way.

Still processing it all, Rachael sighed. *Time to find Sara. That child needs comfort, too.*

The rolling hills were cast in pearly light at dawn, scattered with the silhouettes of lifeless trees. Rachael rode ahead on Little Red. After a breakfast of tea and a hard biscuit, the camp had quietly agreed that rain was likely; there had been no dew that morning.

They'd risen at four-thirty. The wagons were, as usual, the last to leave. She was glad today was her turn to ride. She had changed into her Lindsey-Woolsey skirt and blouse, adding two underskirts to brace against the chill. She had no oilcloth cloak, but if the rain worsened, she expected Mr. Grey would call her into the wagon; he usually offered that courtesy to women who rode.

Today, however, Mr. Grey was driving Cookie's springboard wagon himself. The cook was tending the sheep. Ann, suffering from another of her headaches, rode beside him, the springboard being less jarring than the Godleys' wagon.

Despite his usual speed, Rachael had no trouble keeping up. She was proud of her seat, confident now in her ability to hold a canter as easily as a rocking horse. A small satisfaction bloomed in her chest.

When the drizzle began, she waited for Mr. Grey to call her in.

Instead, he reached behind the wagon seat and tossed her an Indian rubber coat. It was clearly a man's, a long, heavy garment that covered only part of her, but she pulled it on and held her head high.

She was oddly touched. *He trusts me to ride on like one of the men.*

Ann, sitting beside him, removed Rachael's fine sunbonnet and handed her an older one, its pasteboard long since softened by storms. Rachael tied it under her chin, straightened her spine, and sat taller in the saddle.

The drizzle soon became a steady rain. Her skirt grew heavy and sodden. The cold crept in.

Mr. Grey glanced over at her.

"You'll be wet through by the time we get to camp," Mr. Grey shouted over the downpour. "What a sight you'll be, covered in mud from the horse's hooves splashing through puddles!"

"And I'll laugh, too," Rachael called back, her teeth clenched in a smile. "Once we get to camp."

The rain intensified. Thunder cracked overhead, and jagged lightning tore the sky, casting an eerie yellow glow. The smell of struck flint filled the air. It was the worst thundershower they had yet encountered. Rachael became utterly soaked. Blouse, skirt, bonnet, every inch of her clung to with cold, wet fabric. The rain trickled down the back of her neck, sending spasms of shivers through her body.

Mr. Grey shouted again, "You'll need a fire when we get in."

"Yes," she called back, chattering, "a big one."

At first, she had been proud not to be treated as delicate. Proud he hadn't offered her special consideration. But now, soaked through and freezing, she was unsure. *Why hadn't he offered to bring her into the wagon?* Was this another one of his tests, his way of measuring her endurance, her grit?

Just like him.

Well, she wouldn't bend. She gripped Little Red's reins tighter and focused on the muddy road ahead. Her mouth was set in a thin line. She said nothing, but a burning ember of indignation flared in her throat.

And what about Ann? Surely, he'd offer her comfort if she needed it. Why hadn't Rachael spoken up and challenged him? She glanced toward the springboard wagon, searching Ann's expression, but it was unreadable. Grey kept driving.

Finally, they reached the encampment, but the site was crowded. Mr. Grey announced they'd have to press farther down the trail to meet the rest of the company. Rachael swallowed her frustration. She remembered her vow made in Independence: *no complaints, no matter what.* She would keep that promise, even now.

They forded a swollen creek, the water rising past her stirrups, soaking her skirt. She gritted her teeth, legs numb, feet frozen, and pressed on. When they arrived, she dismounted and winced as her feet touched the cold, wet ground. Her wool skirt clung like a sodden rag. Leaning into Little Red's flank, she drew a bit of strength from his damp warmth. He seemed as miserable as she felt. He hung his head and leaned back into her.

Rachael longed for someone, anyone, to come to offer her a blanket, a word, a hand. She wanted warmth. Attention. Care. But no one came.

Mr. Grey, finally recognizing the downpour's persistence, announced that it was too wet to pitch the tents. Only then did he suggest she climb into the wagon.

She nodded stiffly, said nothing, and hoisted herself into the springboard. Inside, she peeled off her drenched skirt and two soaked underskirts. Using the dry edges of the fabric, she scrubbed at her clammy skin. Then, wrapping the wet layers into a bundle, she reached into her satchel and, with trembling fingers, pulled on a dry blouse and her other Lindsey-Woolsey skirt.

She sat inside the wagon, arms wrapped around herself, teeth still chattering. *Someone should build a fire for me,* she thought. *Someone should ask how I am.*

But no one did.

Maybe it's my fault, she thought. *Maybe I've turned them away with all this independence, so much that now no one dares offer help. And maybe that's not who I am after all. Or at least not all the time.*

She put her hands over her eyes. The tight control she had maintained since leaving Independence slipped away. The tears came, silent and hot. She wept not just from cold or exhaustion but from a deeper wound, the hollow ache of loneliness.

Had she made a mistake? Was this journey, the defiance, the hardship, worth it?

She didn't feel well. The cold had settled into her bones. But worse than the physical chill was the emotional one: no one had come. Not Camille. Not Hannah. Not even Sara.

Were they all so busy with their own needs that they hadn't noticed?

Or, she realized with a jolt, maybe it wasn't neglect at all.

They had families. That was the difference.

She had never felt truly alone before.

It was different from simply feeling lonely, missing conversation, or craving a companion. This was something deeper, something colder. The reality of being alone. And it frightened her.

Would she really be able to live alone in Oregon, find her precious plant, and carry on by herself?

She looked out over the vast plain and saw a solitary tree in the distance; its limbs stretched skyward in silence. *Was that what she was now?* A lone tree on an endless, empty prairie?

Today, riding in the springboard wagon with Mr. Grey, she had barely spoken. Even when he tried to make conversation, stiff, awkward though it was, she had turned away, uninterested in making the effort. She didn't want to engage. Not with him. Not with anyone.

Later, on a steep descent, she asked to get out of the wagon and walk. He granted it with a nod, and she moved briskly behind the rolling wheels, trying to clear her thoughts.

She told herself to focus on beauty, to take in the sweep of land, the grandeur of the sky. *Look up,* she reminded herself. *Notice the world God made.*

A tiny grove of trees nestled in a ring, what her father had once called a "fairy ring," caught her eye. Normally, such a thing would have delighted her. She would have run toward it with wonder, gathered leaves to press, and studied the bark and roots.

But today, it barely registered.

The lone tree remained etched in her mind.

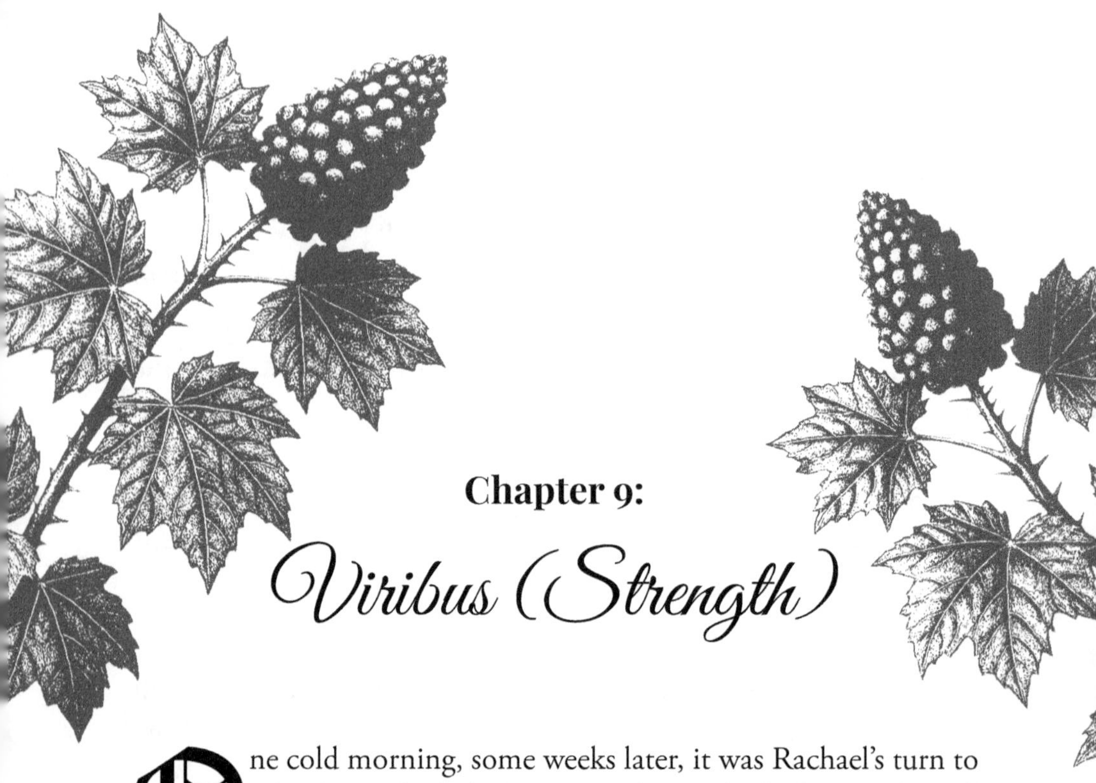

Chapter 9:
Viribus (Strength)

One cold morning, some weeks later, it was Rachael's turn to take down the ladies' tent. As she worked, she gave herself a stern internal lecture: *Enough feeling sorry for yourself.* It did no good. Still, she resolved that she would go on being independent and decisive. She would rely on her scientific powers of observation to guide her understanding of the people in this wagon party.

She thought again of that persistent feeling of being alone. It made things easier, she supposed. From now on, she will be friendly but not dependent.

Of course, she reminded herself that Hannah and Camille had to help their families first during the rainstorm. That was only natural. She tried to root out the image of the lone tree on the barren plain. But in the end, as the days passed, she simply shrugged her shoulders and went on. *After all,* she thought, *that tree is now part of me. Neither of us has a choice. We'll have to grow strong and stand alone.*

Lying the tent out on the ground, she placed the poles at one end and began to roll it tightly, using her knees to brace it in place as she turned it over and over until it was firm. Then she tied it securely with rope so it wouldn't unravel. Sitting on the bundle to catch her breath, she looked out over the camp.

The sheep, oxen, and horses grazed quietly around her, the wagons drawn up close together. Most of the others were now helping pack up the dishes. The sheep didn't seem to like the cold; they were bleating and milling nervously. *In my opinion,* Rachael thought, *Bo the sheepdog is worth three men.* Mr. Miller had told her that Bo was never allowed to eat raw meat, only cooked. "A dog that develops a taste for blood can't be trusted with the herd," he'd said. She found that both intelligent and fascinating. *There are so many things I don't know.*

That night, they camped beside a lovely, clear stream. The water burbled gently over smooth rocks, and there was a small gravel beach where Rachael had sat and soaked her aching feet after a long day's ride. The banks of the stream were lined with tall, graceful basswood and oak trees. Ivy wound around the trunks, cloaking the oaks from base to crown in green.

The men were now yoking the oxen in preparation for another day's travel.

When she mounted Little Red, her dress tore again. It had already been mended so many times it resembled a patchwork quilt. It was filthy, too, but there was no time to wash it, and only one other clean dress and skirt remained. Still, despite everything, no proper rest and scant food, she found herself enjoying this rugged life more than she ever thought possible.

What a magnificent, wild place this is.

The basswood trees towered above her, fifty feet high at least, offering sweet shade. Tom, Hannah's husband, had told her their tiny yellow flowers attracted bees. "Some people call 'em bee trees," he'd said. "You can even make honey from 'em if you know how." Rachael longed to see those blossoms and taste their honey.

This land and its plants...so different from anything I've known. She gazed up through the arching canopy and wondered if basswood bark had medicinal uses. She doubted Martha's mother had ever come this far west. *I'd have liked to linger here.* But she reminded herself of the journey's purpose: *The Devil's Club.*

With all she now knew about medicinal plants, her search for them felt more urgent than ever. And so, she reconciled herself once more: *Each day brings me one step closer.*

Rachael pulled open the heavy canvas and climbed into the back of the Godleys' wagon. Ann lay on a pallet on the floor, her long chestnut hair loosely plaited, her pregnancy evident beneath the blankets. She shifted into a sitting position, allowing Rachael to place a pillow behind her for support.

"Ann, you're looking better, not so pale. The tea helped. I'm glad I managed to find some of the herbs Martha's mother's book recommended at the mercantile store."

"I do feel better, Rachael. And I appreciate your kindness to Sara. She's grown quite fond of you."

"As I have of her."

Ann hesitated, her fingers plucking at the edge of the quilt. She looked up at Rachael.

"Is there anything to do about her stutter? It irritates Robert so much. Every time he looks at her, he's reminded of my first marriage. My first husband had a small stutter, too."

Ah, thought Rachael. *That explains why he calls it the 'Devil's affliction.'*

She nodded but said nothing. There was no point in contradicting Robert's views now, and she didn't want to embolden them either. Instead, she busied herself, helping Ann into the fresh nightgown she had brought. As she gently massaged a soothing almond oil salve into Ann's hands, Ann leaned back into the pillows and began to speak.

"Sara was eight when her father died. That was a hard time. I supported us by sewing for Charles' congregation. They even asked the cooks to give me their leftovers, though they never once invited us to supper." She shook her head. "They pitied us, but not in a kind way."

"I know something about public pity," Rachael said quietly. "The sideways glances. The shaking of heads."

"Yes, but I suppose it was wrong of me to resent it. They were trying to help. I see that now."

Rachael remembered the smug smiles she endured back in Geneva, the silent judgment from women her own age after her college rejection and broken engagement. The message was clear: *You got what you deserved.* Her ambitions had been too bold, too unladylike.

She turned her attention back to Ann.

"My brother Joseph brought Robert to Charles' church and introduced us. Robert was so passionate about his calling to bring religion to the heathens. He said I was part of God's plan and must go as his wife. I prayed on it. Finally, I agreed. It seemed like a God-given solution. A father for Sara. A fresh start. But I wish, oh, how I wish, he were kinder to her."

Ann's voice trailed off. Then she added with a sigh, "It's even harder now. Sara's been no help during this pregnancy. I thought she'd assist me, but she showed no interest. I've given up on her. And now she's drawing instead of reading her Bible. Robert is greatly displeased. So am I."

"She's quite good at drawing," Rachael offered. "And it helps her relax. Sometimes, when she talks with me, there's no stutter at all."

"Well, that's certainly not our experience. She stutters constantly. Sometimes, I think she does it on purpose to provoke Robert. And that doesn't excuse her from failing to read the Lord's word." Ann's eyes glowed with conviction.

Rachael remembered their lesson earlier that week, how Sara had carefully sketched the parts of the lily, identifying each one. She had drawn that first day in church, too. She was so proud of herself. Rachael wasn't sure which of them had beamed brighter with pride.

Why can't her mother see this in her? Why doesn't she try to understand her own child?

She unclenched her hands and gently smoothed the quilt over Ann. Looking around the cramped wagon, Rachael better understood why most families preferred to sleep in tents. Even in early fall, the heat trapped inside was stifling. There was barely room to reach Ann's pallet between the trunks Robert had lined up along both sides.

She wondered why they didn't have a family tent like the Evans. And why, exactly, did the parents sleep away from their children? It had always seemed odd. But now she began to understand. *Robert doesn't like Sara.* And so, Ann had turned away from her daughter, too.

Rachael's heart ached. *It must be so hard for Sara to make sense of all this. No wonder she stutters.*

Rachael tried to remain silent and keep her face neutral. She knew better than to argue with Ann. Was Sara's speech problem an embarrassment to her mother? Did Ann, too, believe it was the Devil's affliction? Her own sweet, bright child?

Rachael bit her tongue, her fingers trembling.

She reached for Ann's brush and offered to brush her hair, needing to calm herself. She remembered her own mother doing that, how soothing it had always felt. Rachael wondered if Ann had ever brushed Sara's hair. Surely, she must have when Sara was small.

"I'm glad that Sara has a friend in you," Ann said. "Perhaps you can talk to her about her stutter?"

As Rachael brushed, her hand began to move faster, drawing the brush through Ann's hair with increasing force.

"Ouch. That hurt," Ann said, turning her head.

"I'm sorry," Rachael replied quickly, slowing her strokes. Then, she stopped altogether and began to plait Ann's hair instead.

"Now," Ann continued, "tell me about your husband. I know nothing about him. How did you meet?"

Rachael's hands paused mid-braid. She had prepared herself for this question.

"Well," she began, tilting her head slightly, the brush still in her hand. "My best friend Elizabeth introduced us. John worked at the large animal vet clinic. He liked that I studied botany and didn't mind when I tramped through the woods in split skirts with my father, boots always muddy. He promised to build me a room for my studies. One day, he even gave me a flower press with a bouquet of wildflowers."

She smiled softly. "We wanted the same things. He understood me, he—"

"It's God's blessing to receive a man we can serve," Ann interrupted. "You must miss him very much. How terrible to be apart."

Her eyes shone with sympathy for a woman she believed was separated from a beloved husband.

"Yes, I…" Rachael's voice faltered. She set the brush down and turned away. A prick of tears burned in her eyes.

How foolish, she scolded herself. *Crying over someone who never existed.* She thought of Richard the last time she saw him. That disdainful look he gave her when she came to tea with his mother, boots muddy, completely unpresentable.

She shook the thought off.

"Oh, Rachael, you're crying," Ann said gently. "I've made you sad by asking questions. You're so lucky to have found someone you truly love."

Ann reached out, but Rachael turned away, brushing the tears from her cheeks.

"Yes," she said softly. "I suppose I am."

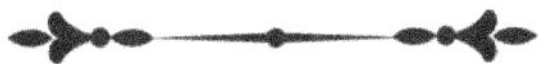

The party now stood on the banks of the Wakarusa River, staring at the wide, swirling torrent of mud-brown water. With its steep banks and powerful current, it was the most significant crossing they'd faced so far.

Rachael shivered.

"Mr. Grey, will it be safe to cross?" she asked, biting the knuckle of her hand.

Mr. Grey harrumphed. "Maybe in an hour or two. It's too swollen now. Too much debris. See there, like that log."

She followed his gaze to a massive oak limb spinning in the current, tumbling downstream with alarming speed. She could only imagine what would happen if such a log struck a wagon or a horse. Or a person.

Rachael shoved her trembling hands into her skirt pockets and turned her back on the river. *She would not let herself think about what might happen.* She had promised herself she would not show fear.

She was still ashamed about the scream she'd let out the day before when she almost stepped on a snake while plant gathering. She had seen what happened to the women who cried themselves to sleep, some even while holding their children. She had no intention of being one of them.

Two hours later, Mr. Grey finally decided it was safe enough to cross. The water was still high, but the debris had cleared. He would come after the wagons with the sheep.

He signaled for the first wagon, driven by James.

The boy had begged Mr. Grey to let him ferry his mother and stepbrother across, hoping to redeem himself after oversleeping that morning. After a long talk, Mr. Grey agreed on the condition that Tom Miller would ride beside them on his big bay horse.

"Hold on tight now, boy. Give the oxen their head when they hit the water. Don't be afraid to use the whip on them." Mr. Grey's eyes narrowed as he watched James, who nodded, gripping the reins tightly.

The wagon tilted and skidded down the bank behind the oxen. The animals surged forward, their weight keeping ahead of the wagon's bulk. As they entered the water, they snorted and pulled with power. James called out to them, "Hey, hey, move on there!"

The oxen held their heads high, swimming forward with steady resolve. His whip snapped in the air. Soon, their hooves found footing on the sloping far bank. James cracked the whip again, brandishing it over their heads to encourage the final pull.

Snorting and dripping, the oxen crested the top.

Mr. Miller's roan horse gave a full-body shake to rid himself of water, nearly unseating his rider.

The entire crossing had taken barely four minutes, but it felt much longer to those still waiting.

When the wagon finally pulled up the far bank, cheers erupted. Christopher and James whooped in triumph.

Now, it was Rachael's turn.

She fought the urge to close her eyes. If she stared between the ears of the steady mules, maybe she could pretend she was already across.

She sat on the buckboard bench between Hannah, who was holding her squirming five-year-old son, Roy, and Cookie, who would drive them across. Earlier, he had told her that mules were smart enough to sense danger and wouldn't enter the water they deemed unsafe. They'd often wait for another wagon to cross first.

She would have to trust the mules.

Silently, she unbuckled her boots and tucked them under the seat; no sense in letting them get soaked. She'd noticed earlier that Mr. Miller had done the same after crossing, his boots saturated to the thigh.

Old Bill called out, "Git up there, fellas. It's our turn now. Git!"

He raised the whip and urged the mules down the steep, muddy bank. His hand gripped the wooden brake lever, slowing the buckboard's descent.

The mules entered the water with a splash. The buckboard dipped, sending up spray. Rachael let out a small gasp.

From the opposite bank, Mr. Miller and James were waving wildly, shouting, and pointing upstream.

Old Bill raised the whip again, but it was too late.

A large branch, borne on the current, struck the buckboard on its upstream side with a heavy thud.

Rachael heard a scream.

She turned to see Hannah, but her arms were empty.

Roy was gone.

For a heartbeat, Rachael couldn't make sense of it. Then she saw him, small and flailing, bobbing downstream in the churning water.

Without a second thought, Rachael tore off her long skirt and dove.

Cold enveloped her. The river closed over her head. She kicked hard toward the surface, sputtering as she emerged.

She scanned the water. There, fifty yards ahead, Roy's small form bobbed in the current.

Rachael swam. Hard.

She'd grown up swimming in rivers. She knew the current would carry her faster than it would Roy, her weight pushing her along. If she didn't reach him soon, she'd be swept past.

She kicked with everything she had, arms slicing through muddy water. Her limbs began to numb.

Viribus… viribus, she heard her father say in her mind, Latin for strength.

She pushed harder.

Then, her fingers found the boy's suspenders. She yanked him close, tucking him against her chest, his head above the water.

Flipping onto her back, she let the current carry them, steering with her feet toward an eddy near the shore.

She saw only Mr. Grey and his big horse in the water. He was yelling at her to aim toward him. Moments later, her body slammed against the swimming bulk of that massive horse. The impact knocked Roy from her arms, but Mr. Grey caught him.

"Grab the stirrup!" he shouted. He had removed his foot from it.

She lunged and missed. The current began to swing her around the horse's flank, but her hand caught a length of leather tied to the saddle. With quivering arms, she hauled herself closer. Finally, her fingers found the stirrup. She clung to it, breathless.

She felt the horse's hooves touch the riverbed, and she let go as the roan lunged up the muddy embankment, Mr. Grey holding the child before him. On her knees at the bottom of the bank, Rachael tried to stand but slipped, nearly tumbling back into the water.

A rope struck her. Looking up, she saw James and a white-faced Mr. Grey above her. Her body shook uncontrollably from cold and something deeper…shock, perhaps. She vomited quietly into the mud and didn't care that she lay there in only her petticoat. Exhausted, she reached for the rope, looped it over her head, and cinched it around her waist. James hauled her up the slick bank.

"What the hell do you think you were doing?" Mr. Grey spat, his face rigid as his big hands gripped her shoulders.

"The child… I didn't think… the child," Rachael whispered. Her voice was hoarse. A metallic taste filled her mouth. Mud and water dripped from her; she was trembling all over.

"Don't ever, ever pull a stunt like that again!" Mr. Grey roared into her face. "You have no idea how dangerous that was. No idea!" He looked back at the river. His expression shifted, his face sagged with something more than anger. He let go of her.

"Don't do that again. It was reckless. I forbid it."

Even soaked and shaking, she was stunned. *Forbid it?* Why such fury? Yes, what she'd done was impulsive, but the child could have drowned. He must know that. She searched his face, expecting condemnation, but something deeper and unspoken shadowed his expression.

For once, she didn't argue. Didn't challenge. She was too tired. And somehow, she sensed this wasn't about orders or recklessness or wagons or rules. It was about something else.

She remained silent, letting his fury pass over her like another wave in the river.

Then he turned sharply and walked away without another word.

James stepped forward, draping a blanket over her shoulders. His eyes brimmed with concern.

Then, a gentle hand touched her arm. She turned.

It was Hannah, her eyes puffy from crying, Roy trembling in her arms.

"Thank you," she murmured, her voice thick with emotion. "Thank you."

She bent her head toward Rachael, then reached out and wrapped her in an embrace.

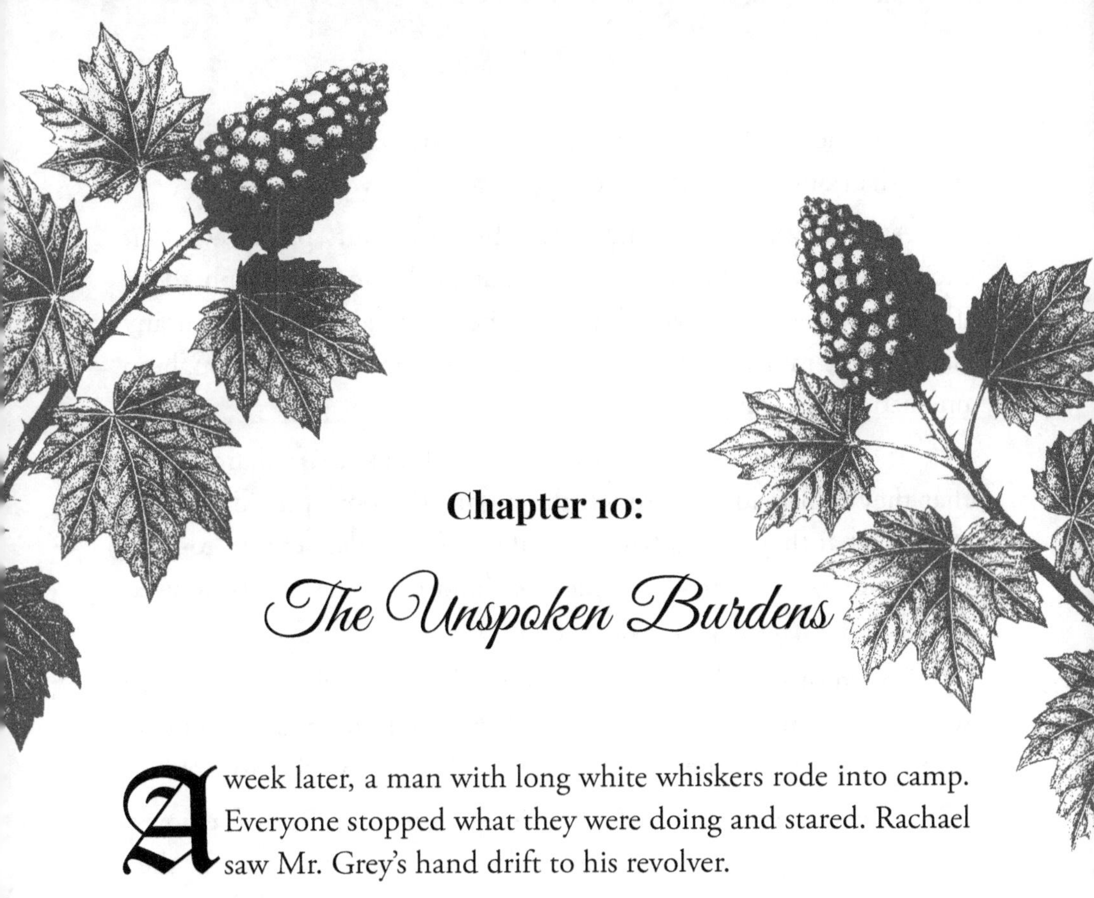

Chapter 10:

The Unspoken Burdens

A week later, a man with long white whiskers rode into camp. Everyone stopped what they were doing and stared. Rachael saw Mr. Grey's hand drift to his revolver.

The man dismounted, pulled a handkerchief from his pocket, and wiped his forehead. He spoke loudly enough for all to hear.

"Y'all best be alert. The Indians have been scattering emigrants' cattle and stealing our horses."

Mrs. Dix clutched James's arm. "You are not to go off with the sheep tonight. Absolutely not! I need you to stay here and protect us. Indians, why, those heathen—"

"Do you see any Indians at this moment, Mrs. Dix?" Mr. Grey asked flatly. "Please, calm down. James will be with the sheep, Tom, and the boys. There's no reason to worry. But I will set a watch anyway."

Then he turned to the men. "Gentlemen, may I speak with you in private?"

They gathered behind the cook wagon to organize the watch.

Rachael could feel her shoulders tensing. She fought the urge to keep glancing behind her. All those stories Mr. Grey had told her about women stolen or worse, came rushing back. He'd used them more than once to justify his disapproval of her wandering off.

A night watch was established, but the hours passed without incident. Still, Rachael's heart went out to the young sheepherders. Their eyes were wide with fear, and she doubted they'd gotten any sleep. In the morning, they swore they had heard Indians, though no one had seen a thing.

There was an air of camaraderie over breakfast, a shared relief that they'd all made it through the night. The boys puffed up with tales of what they would have done if they'd met danger face-to-face. The children listened with wide eyes, and even the adults allowed themselves a nervous chuckle or two.

That morning, the company did not leave as early as usual. They were only ten miles from the Kansas River, and rumor had it that many companies ahead of them were already backed up, waiting to cross.

When Mr. Grey signaled it was time to move out, Rachael enjoyed a pleasant canter across the prairie alongside James. But when they reached the ferry landing and waited for the wagons and the sheep, something was amiss: Cookie, driving the springboard wagon, was nowhere to be found.

Mr. Grey had specifically instructed him to stay with the ox-drawn wagons.

Tom confirmed he hadn't seen Cookie since he'd fallen behind earlier that morning.

There were two spots where the road forked. Mr. Grey guessed that Old Bill had taken the wrong path. He sent James after him with sharp instructions.

"You'd better find him," he said. "He has all the food, bedding, and tents."

Then Mr. Grey walked over to the ferryman and bent low to speak with him. Rachael noticed a small exchange. Something passed from Mr. Grey's hand to the ferryman's.

When he returned, Mr. Grey announced, "We're crossing immediately."

Rachael's stomach dropped. *What about James and Cookie?* she wondered. *Shouldn't we wait?*

But then she saw the line of wagons stretched along the bank and guessed Mr. Grey had made some kind of arrangement to move ahead. Judging by the scowl on his face, it hadn't come cheap. He was always muttering about the cost of the ferry.

Arriving before the rest, Rachael took the opportunity to study how the ferry worked. A thick rope spanned the river, fastened on both sides. Passengers rode in a scow, a flat-bottomed boat, pulled along the rope with the help of pulleys. It reminded her of the old canal boats.

One team of oxen was ferried first, followed by the two saddle horses, and then the women and children. The river was running swift and high, its banks steep and muddy, making the loading of livestock especially difficult.

All were frightened. Rachael held tightly to both Sara and Christopher. Hannah clutched Roy. The men would follow on the next scow with the other teams.

Mr. Grey had stayed back, still waiting for James and Cookie. Mrs. Dix was visibly agitated but calmed temporarily after Daniel and Camille reassured her.

Once across, the group moved away from the muck and dung of the riverbank to drier ground.

Dusk was fast approaching, and still, there was no sign of Mr. Grey, James, or Cookie.

Mrs. Dix fretted incessantly about James. Camille eventually gave her a spoonful of J. S. Merrell's FEM tonic, a nerve-calming concoction that Rachael knew from reading in Independence was mostly alcohol.

Only then did the group fully register the seriousness of their situation: Old Bill had all the food, the cookstove, utensils, dishes, and the tents, especially the ones used by the women and the Evans family. He also carried the Indian Rubber blankets and bedding.

They were, as Rachael put it, in *a fine pickle indeed.*

Tom had a stash of soda crackers and dried beef in his wagon, and they borrowed a tin pail from the ferryman's wife to collect water. It had to be returned promptly; she needed it for the evening milking, and it was the only one she had.

Soon, James crossed the river and approached the party. Mrs. Dix nearly fainted with relief.

He told them he hadn't found Old Bill. He'd assumed the cook would be back with the wagons, but all he'd seen on his return was Mr. Grey. James was surprised to find that the rest of the company had already crossed. Mr. Grey had stayed behind to find Cookie and promised he would bring him across himself.

As night fell and still no sign of Mr. Grey, an uneasiness crept through the group. The notion of Indians lurking near the ferry, however unlikely, given the number of people, clung to their thoughts like burrs. For Rachael, the absence of Mr. Grey made her feel oddly unmoored. Whatever she thought of the man, his presence usually meant some degree of order.

Sleeping arrangements were quickly decided. The men would do their best in the wagons. The women, lacking their usual tent, were to squeeze into the men's shelter stowed in the Evans' wagon. It was a long, miserable night—cold, cramped, and fitful. Most of them slept with one eye open.

Tension hung in the morning air like smoke. For breakfast, they managed a meal of smoked beef and pickles, courtesy of the Evans' supplies. There was nothing to drink but tin cups of river water that tasted faintly of iron, almost like blood.

Rachael tried to focus on the children, playing a game of tossing rocks into the river, but her eyes kept darting to the ferry landing.

Each approaching boat held the same hope: Mr. Grey, the springboard wagon, and their missing provisions.

Finally, much to everyone's relief, he arrived. He drove the springboard wagon himself. New mules were hitched to the rig, and his horse trailed behind. But Old Bill was not with him.

Rachael's shoulders, stiff from worry, released slightly.

Mr. Grey looked worn and furious.

"I looked for Old Bill until dark," he said through gritted teeth. "I couldn't track the wagon in the night, so I made camp. The ferry was closed anyway."

He looked as though he'd spent the night without much warmth—no fire, no food.

"This morning, I finally found him," he went on. "With another company. He'd been sitting there since noon yesterday, smoking his pipe like nothing had happened. I fired him on the spot. Told him he could keep his damn mules."

Gasps and murmurs stirred through the group.

"That company had some mules for sale, so I bought these. Cost me a fortune, but they'll have to do it. The springboard wagon is mine, after all."

He glanced around at them, his face hard.

"I worried about bringing an old man on a trip like this. Hired him out of pity. That's a mistake I won't make again."

Rachael noticed the glance exchanged between Reverend Robert and Mrs. Dix. Were they silently reconsidering her presence? But no, that was nonsense. She had cared for the children and made herself useful. Mr. Grey and she had even called a truce of sorts.

"From now on," he added, "I'll do all the cooking. Done it before. No complaints."

Rachael had her doubts that anyone would dare to complain.

He was already muttering that they were eating too much. With the food supplies now under his control and his temper fraying, she

expected rations would shrink even further. Still, despite her growling stomach, she was grateful. He had returned safely.

Two weeks later, Rachael was pulled from sleep by angry shouting.

Mr. Grey was berating James again. She crawled to the tent flap and peered out into the dim grayness. The sky behind the hills was barely touched with morning light. A quarter moon still lingered above the silhouette of the trees.

She sighed and wrapped her shawl tightly, tugging her boots over warm socks before stepping outside. Usually, she cherished the quiet hush of this hour, but not today.

"I told you, James. One more time falling asleep on watch, and I'd tan your hide. And now, two horses are gone!"

Mr. Grey yanked his belt from its loops and cracked it once beside James' legs.

The boy yelped.

Mr. Miller stormed over, boots half-pulled on and rifle in hand.

"What in the Sam Hill is going on here?" he barked.

"He fell asleep on watch again. Two horses were gone. Indians, most likely. You never hear them. They just creep in, untie the lines, and walk the horses away." Grey's eyes blazed. "Now we're delayed, and I'll have to go out and try to track them. I should give him another couple of lashes before I go—"

He paused, belt still in hand.

"But there's no time, not if I want to find those animals. Who knows how far they've gone."

Rachael immediately looked to the line where the horses had been tied. Little Red was gone. Only the two mules remained.

Her heart sank. Over the many weeks of travel, she had grown deeply fond of that small bay horse. Little Red had carried her across countless miles through cold, rain, fear, and fatigue. She had come to believe, in the silent companionship they shared, that the horse understood her. Now, the thought of him in the hands of strangers, or worse, was unbearable.

She thought of the dead horse she'd passed days ago along the trail. Though she had quickly looked away, the image of its bloated, rigid body was seared into her memory.

Mr. Grey threw his saddle on the one remaining horse, his own. It had been tethered to the springboard wagon beside his tent, within reach. He slept with his revolver tucked under the saddle, using it as his pillow.

At the start of the journey, Rachael had wondered why there were so few horses. Mr. Grey had explained that only horses of particular breeding and temperament could survive such a grueling expedition. It comforted her then, as she believed Little Red was one of those few.

"Damnation," Mr. Grey barked. "George, get the camp ready to move. Then you and the boys go on with the sheep. Ask Tom to have everyone wait for me here. Hopefully, I can catch them."

James was sitting up now, massaging his legs.

"And you, kid," Mr. Grey growled, glaring down at him, "I'll deal with you later."

Then, with a crack of the reins, he was gone, riding off at a gallop in pursuit of the stolen horses.

By now, the entire camp was awake.

Mr. Miller explained what had happened, then directed the group to eat breakfast, pack camp, and wait for Mr. Grey's return. He gave James a glare sharp enough to slice. James didn't look up. He just kept scuffing the dirt with the toe of his boot.

Mrs. Dix was livid.

"How dare he lay a hand on my son!" she cried. "Works him like a mule during the day and then puts him on watch at night? It's too much for a growing boy. He needs his sleep. I'll have words with Mr. Grey when he gets back."

Camille and Rachael exchanged a look. They both knew how ill-advised that plan was, but neither said anything. Camille simply shrugged. Rachael sighed and returned to rolling up her bedding.

After a meager breakfast of dried fruit, coffee, and hardtack, the wagons were readied, though the oxen remained unhitched. The mules were already harnessed to the springboard.

Rachael wondered idly why the Indians never took the mules. Perhaps they weren't considered valuable enough.

Her thoughts were interrupted by bickering between Henry and Roy. She looked around for Hannah, usually quick to rein in her son, but saw no sign of her.

"They would so!" Henry's voice rose with excitement.

"Would not!" Roy squeaked, his eyes wide with fear.

"Indians sneak up while you're asleep," Henry insisted. "You wouldn't even know they scalped you till morning. They hang the scalps from their belts."

"Do not! My pa would shoot 'em dead. Just like that!"

"Boys," Rachael said sharply, stepping between them. "That's enough. There are no Indians here now, and I highly doubt they'd take a child's scalp, especially not from boys who aren't even man enough to do their chores. Now scat. Go gather buffalo chips. Fill a bucket or go without supper. And take Christopher with you."

They bolted, still grumbling but grateful for an excuse to leave.

Rachael frowned. Still no sign of Hannah. Odd. She usually took her son's behavior seriously. Glancing toward the Evans' wagon, she saw Tom inspecting a wheel's iron rim. But Hannah was nowhere in sight.

She figured Hannah had likely gone to relieve herself. Privacy was a challenge out here. Early on, Rachael had been mortified by the communal system the women devised, standing in a circle, backs turned, holding their skirts to shield one another. But after weeks on the trail, modesty had given way to necessity. Now, it was just part of daily life.

At this camp, a proper latrine had been dug behind a patch of chokeberry bushes up the slope—a luxury, really.

With the extra time, Rachael decided to look for Echinacea to help ease Ann's persistent headaches. She believed she'd spotted some purple coneflowers when they had first arrived. Ever since diving deeper into *Martha's Mother's Book*, her interest in herbal medicine had grown. She took her penknife, a small sack, and set off.

As she climbed the slope, she heard a soft, pained groan.

Turning toward the sound, she found Hannah on her knees, arms wrapped tightly around her stomach. A moment later, she vomited into the grass.

Rachael rushed to her side. When Hannah was done, trembling, Rachael wiped her mouth with a clean handkerchief.

"You're sick. Did you eat something?" Rachael asked, crouching beside her.

Hannah's eyes widened in alarm. Then she doubled over and vomited again.

"No," she moaned. "It's not that. I'm…" Her body heaved once more, and she was sick again.

"Hannah, shall I get Tom?"

Hannah grabbed Rachael's arm in a tight grip. "No, please. There's nothing he can do, nothing anyone can do. I didn't want this. Not now. Not on this trip."

"Hannah, what is it?"

She eased into a sitting position, and Rachael helped her lean back against a large boulder. Her skin was pale, almost translucent, but her nausea had eased for now.

"I'm pregnant," she said flatly. "I thought I might be when I missed my courses these last two months, but I hoped it was just the strain of the journey. Now I know it's not. It's my greatest fear."

Rachael's mind raced. Mr. Grey had said he hoped they'd reach Oregon by early November. That meant Hannah's baby would likely arrive at least two weeks before that, if not sooner. And due dates, she knew, were only estimates. She remembered the line from Martha's mother's book:

"Baby will choose their own time, and usually at a most inconvenient time for the mother."

"You mustn't tell Tom," Hannah said urgently. "I've miscarried twice since Roy. It nearly broke his heart and mine. I'll wait until I'm four months along. Maybe then. You must promise me you won't tell."

"But won't he notice? Won't he see that you're ill?"

"He's a man, Rachael. Even as close as we are, he won't notice. And if he did, he wouldn't say anything. He doesn't want to hope again, not if it might end in disappointment."

"Oh, Hannah... What can I do? How can I help?"

"Just keep your promise. That's all for now. It's passed. We mustn't alert the others through our absence. Help me up. Am I presentable?"

Rachael nodded gently. "Here, let me brush off the back of your skirt. Smooth your hair, and we'll walk back together. Take my arm."

As they walked, Rachael's heart twisted with worry. She had already promised to care for Ann, but now Hannah needed her, too. She would search again in *Martha's Mother's Book* for anything on miscarriage prevention and pregnancy care. Her stomach churned with uncertainty. Could she truly cope with the responsibility of both women? She felt the weight of it settle between her shoulders.

She knew about miscarriage from her reading and knew that sometimes a not-fully-formed baby would simply fall from the body. She understood that when the waters broke, it was time. That labor could fool a woman into thinking it had begun when it hadn't. And then there were the worst cases: breech births, long labor, bleeding, and death.

No birth was ever the same. There were no guarantees. And Rachael, for all her reading, had never witnessed one.

She decided, then and there, that she would ask the other women for help. They knew she was to assist with Ann's delivery. But would they help her? Would they teach her? She hadn't asked yet, partly out of pride, partly from fear.

Ann's story of Christopher's birth still troubled her. Could she really cope if something went wrong? Hannah had given birth to Roy; surely she could help. And maybe, if she were brave, she could approach even Mrs. Dix. The idea made her stomach lurch, but Rachael knew it must be done. They were all women, and when it came to childbirth, they had to rely on one another. Liking one another was a luxury; helping was a necessity.

She thought of the women back in Geneva, chatting over christening gowns and baby blankets, never once discussing the realities of birth. There, it was considered unseemly to even mention such things. And yet, here on the trail, far from tea parlors and polite society, Rachael found herself immersed in the most unladylike subject and utterly fascinated.

As a scientist, she marveled at the body's design at nature's methods. No, she didn't share Ann's conviction that bearing children was a woman's divine purpose, but she respected the process. It was nature's plan. And now, it was hers, too.

As they descended the slope, Hannah leaned into her. Rachael placed a firm arm around her waist, steadying her. The warmth of that small gesture, that moment of vulnerability and trust, struck her deeply.

Hope bloomed in Rachael's chest.

Maybe Hannah would become the friend she longed for. That single moment of quiet intimacy decided it. Rachael would do everything in her power to help her. But first, she would have to be honest. Hannah needed to know just how little she still knew, how dangerous inexperience could be.

Still, Hannah had already given birth. Perhaps she would help with Ann. Perhaps they could help each other.

The tension in Rachael's shoulders eased slightly. She had a plan now. And though the prospect of approaching Mrs. Dix still made her uneasy, she reminded herself of what Ann had once said in Westport that she had offered to help her.

Perhaps it was time to follow through on that offer, for all their sakes.

When they returned to camp, Rachael gently released Hannah's arm. Hannah walked slowly back to her wagon, where Tom was waiting.

"Where were you? I was worried. You look ill. Are you all right?" Tom asked with a concern etched into his voice.

"I'm fine, Tom, don't fuss so. Rachael and I were just using what passes for a privy here."

Hannah cast Rachael a small wave across the camp.

Rachael tried to smile and wave back, but her mind churned. She would need to talk to Hannah again soon, and more pressingly, she would have to gather her courage and speak to Mrs. Dix. She glanced around the camp. No sign of her yet. A flicker of relief passed through her. Not today, then. Not yet.

She shifted her focus. It was time to check on Ann, who had taken the lull to lie down. Rachael had hoped to bring her some Echinacea, but she hadn't managed to collect it. Perhaps she would find more further down the trail. She would have to trust in that.

Then she heard hoofbeats.

Turning, she saw Mr. Grey riding into camp, dusty and exhausted, leading George Miller's big bay horse. But not Little Red. Her breath caught in her chest.

"Gee, thanks, Mr. Grey. I'm sure glad to have this feller back," George said, stroking the horse's thick neck. The bay tossed his head and nosed George's coat for a treat.

"Cost me a fortune, it did," Mr. Grey grunted. "Those Indians told me they'd found both horses, the big bay and the ladies' little red one. Said they were bringing them back to camp. Scalawags! I offered calico shirts with buttons like usual, but no, this bunch wanted gold. Five-dollar pieces. Per horse."

George raised his eyebrows.

"I said I'd give them one coin for the bay. Eventually, they took the deal. The other horse, your Little Red, Mrs. Williams, would've played out soon anyway."

Rachael stared at him, stunned. Her breath came quick, her heart pounding.

"You mean… you just left Little Red with them? You let them keep her? After everything she's done? She's come so far. Surely, she was worth five dollars! I—"

"Mrs. Williams," Mr. Grey cut in, his tone tired but firm, "I know you were fond of that horse. But you must understand, it's livestock. Not a pet."

Livestock.

She had thought he understood. Thought they'd been building some kind of understanding, some respect. She had believed he'd known what Little Red meant to her.

Apparently not.

Rachael clenched her hands at her sides. The sting behind her eyes grew unbearable. She turned away before the tears could fall, her shoulders rigid.

Behind her, another voice rose.

It was Mrs. Dix.

"Mr. Grey, I would like a word with you immediately. How dare you strike my son!"

Rachael didn't wait to hear the rest.

She couldn't bear it. Not now. Not with her heart breaking for a horse that had carried her so far and asked for nothing in return.

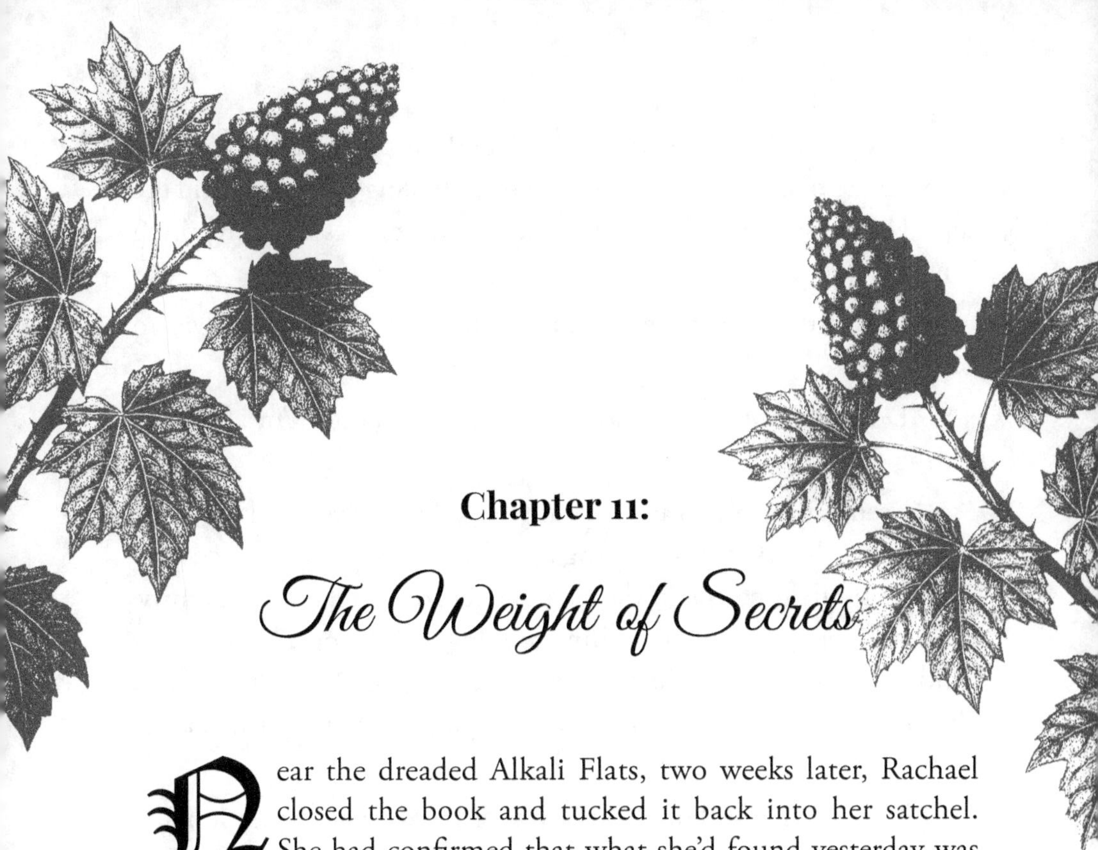

Chapter 11:

The Weight of Secrets

Near the dreaded Alkali Flats, two weeks later, Rachael closed the book and tucked it back into her satchel. She had confirmed that what she'd found yesterday was indeed Black Haw. Using her penknife, she scraped some of the red-brown bark, cutting two or three small branches from the shrub. She had read that the bark, or even the wood, could be brewed into tea to help prevent miscarriage.

Though Rachael had read the midwifery book many times, what she found most valuable was Martha's mother's cramped but legible notes and carefully drawn illustrations of each plant and its uses. She only wished the woman had also included precise recipes, how much bark to use, how much water, and how long to steep. She thought about it often. The difference between healing and harm could come down to the smallest amount. In the absence of exact guidance, she resolved to use the smallest possible dose and observe closely. It still left her uneasy.

Back at camp, the supper fire had already been lit. A large pot hung from the tripod, steam rising into the dusty air. Mr. Grey stood at the rear of the springboard wagon, slicing bacon with a large knife before dropping it into the iron skillet. Soon, he would add beans to the boiling water.

Rachael had already stripped the bark into smaller pieces. She dropped them into a tin cup, ladled in some boiling water, and held the cup to her nose. The aroma wasn't unpleasant, prunes and something like damp wood.

She left the cup to steep on a flat stone and wandered over to Mr. Grey.

"Do you think you could sharpen my penknife? I'm afraid it's getting dull."

"Been at your plants again, I suppose. What are you making now? Who's sick?" he asked, not looking up as he chopped. She noticed how confidently he used the knife, no stranger to a kitchen, apparently. For a moment, she imagined him cooking in Clatsop Plains for his children. How old were they? Odd, they'd never spoken of his family. She wanted to ask, but if she did, he might ask about her husband. Better not to.

"Mrs. Williams, didn't you hear me? I asked you a question."

"Sorry, I guess I was daydreaming."

"I asked who's ill."

Rachael hesitated. She couldn't tell him the tea was for Hannah. She had promised to keep that secret. "Um, actually, it's for me. I thought I'd try it out... see if it works."

He turned toward her. "Are you sick?"

"No, of course not."

"Mrs. Williams," he said, pausing with the knife raised, "you're not answering the question."

"If you must know, it's... for a woman's problem." She blushed. Hopefully convincingly. She hated lying, but she was getting better at it.

"Oh," he said, suddenly uncomfortable.

He turned away and grabbed an onion, chopping it quickly and adding it to the skillet. Rachael seized the moment to change the subject.

"Do you have time to sharpen my knife? I could leave it here and come back after supper."

He grunted a yes without looking up.

She walked back to the stone where her tea was steeping, picked up the cup, and turned to leave.

Behind her, his voice came again, eyebrows lifted. "Well, aren't you going to drink it?"

Did he know she was lying? Was that raised eyebrow a sign? Did he want her to drink it to prove something?

All right, then.

She lifted the cup, gave it a sniff, and raised it to her lips. She only pretended to sip, but even the steam burned her mouth.

"Ouch, it's too hot. I'll take it to the tent and let it cool." She turned quickly before he could say anything else, feeling his gaze on her back.

He was the most infuriating man. Watching her so closely, why couldn't he leave her be? She had *work* to do, important work.

As she passed behind the springboard toward Hannah's wagon, she spotted Mrs. Dix climbing down from the Godley wagon. From inside, Ann's voice floated out:

"Thank you, Mrs. Dix. Your advice and help are greatly appreciated. Why, I feel better already!"

Rachael felt her body tense. What was this about? She didn't have to wait long. Mrs. Dix strode directly toward her, something clutched in her hand.

"Well, hello, Mrs. Williams. I hope that the tea you're holding isn't for Ann. We've just had a conversation about her condition. I gave her a spoonful of my special tonic, and she already felt better. I told her I didn't think she should be drinking any more of your teas. I know you're always reading that book her aunt gave you, but that doesn't change the facts. It doesn't qualify you to act as, well, a midwife. You have no children. You've never even witnessed a birth.

The tonic I gave her was made by a real doctor. After all, you're just a... what do you call it, a plant finder?"

"I am not a plant finder, Mrs. Dix. I am a botanist." Rachael's neck flushed as her temper rose. "And Jane, at the mercantile store, said your tonic contains mostly liquor."

"Balderdash. I don't believe you. It's certainly been a help to me!" With a huff, Mrs. Dix turned and marched off toward her wagon.

Rachael walked briskly toward Hannah's wagon, her temper cooling as Mrs. Dix's words echoed in her mind. *She wasn't qualified as a midwife. She'd never given birth. She'd never witnessed one. Hadn't she herself worried that morning about getting the tea proportions right?*

Mrs. Dix wasn't entirely wrong.

But still, Rachael had made a promise to Martha.

She paused and looked up at the darkening sky, seeking the soft shimmer of the first evening star. She remembered Martha's instructions: *There will be other mothers along the way to help, but I want you to know the specifics of complications and what to do when things go wrong.*

That was why Martha had chosen her. That was why she made her promise.

Mrs. Dix didn't have that knowledge. She did. She had the education, the books, and the mind for this work. And she would use them.

She nodded, satisfied with her reasoning. Her spirit steadied; she reached Hannah's wagon and called out that she'd come by with some tea.

Hannah's face appeared from the back of the wagon. "Good," she said, "it's just what I needed, a good visit and some tea."

Rachael smiled. She couldn't have agreed more.

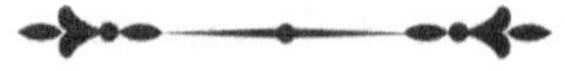

By the time they reached Chimney Rock, the land had changed completely. Yesterday, the sun had scorched them mercilessly as they traveled through what Rachael suspected was a desert, though she had never seen one before. There wasn't much dirt, just fine red sand and towering rock formations that blazed under the relentless sun.

Even now, in the early morning light, Rachael could make out a tall spire in the distance. The landmark every wagon train watched for was Chimney Rock. A stone pillar rising out of the earth like some relic of another world. After passing it, they would reach Fort Laramie, hopefully within two days. Everyone looked forward to the Fort, where they could restock food, supplies, and spirits.

Beyond that lay Independence Rock. Most wagon trains aimed to arrive there by the Fourth of July. Now, it was nearly mid-August. As Mr. Grey kept reminding them, they were late and dangerously so.

The sun baked them hour after hour. Heat waves shimmered across the sand, playing cruel tricks on the eyes, mirages of distant water that always disappeared.

They were rising by three o'clock and moving by four at the latest. Since losing Little Red, Rachael often rode in the springboard wagon with Mr. Grey. He said little. When she asked him questions, he only grunted in reply.

At first, Rachael thought he was angry again. But then she noticed the deep purple circles under his eyes. He looked utterly spent. Of course, he was taking the midnight-to-three watch shift. Then, with barely a breath, he woke the company and helped prepare the cold breakfast of dried fruit and hardtack.

Rachael realized he was as exhausted as everyone else. Maybe more.

More than once, he had fallen asleep while driving the mules. Rachael often wondered how he hadn't tumbled right out of the wagon, but somehow, he never did. His head would simply drop forward onto his chest, and the wheezing would begin, followed quickly by snoring. At first, Rachael had been alarmed and had shaken him awake, but by now, she simply took the reins from his limp hands and let him sleep. They never spoke of it. She imagined he was embarrassed by his inability to stay awake. She had become a confident driver and only woke him if they approached water. Despite following the Platte River, there were few running creeks to cross in this stretch.

As the light brightened, the sun backlit the cliffs along the trail. Rachael longed to stop and take in the spectacle, the towering walls, their colors shifting moment by moment, as though a vast, rose-tinted curtain was being drawn back across the sky. But the trail demanded her focus.

Then, without warning, the wagon jerked left.

The whole rig tilted as the left rear wheel slipped in the shifting sand. There was a sharp crack, and the wheel's spokes shattered where they entered the hub.

Mr. Grey jolted awake with a snort and reached for the reins, but he was too late.

The mules halted of their own accord, standing still and uncertain. Mr. Grey shoved the reins back into Rachael's hands and leaped down to inspect the damage.

It had happened so fast that Rachael hadn't even felt fear until now. Her hands began to tremble violently, and she could barely hold the leather lines. They could have died. If the wagon had tipped completely, they might have been crushed. And it was her fault. She should have been paying attention, watching the trail, not dreaming of the sky.

Climbing down, she saw just how badly damaged the wheel was. Her heart thudded.

Tom's wagon had been right behind them. He halted his oxen and came forward to examine the break.

"Truthfully, Mr. Grey, I worried this might happen," Tom said, crouching beside the broken wheel. "These wagon wheels are drying out from the sand. I've been driving wedges into the felloes to tighten the tires, but there's only so much you can do. Those spokes—" He shook his head.

Mr. Grey rubbed his chin, thoughtful but grim.

Rachael stood still, wanting to apologize but unable to speak. She held her breath.

"Do you think you can fix it, Tom?" Mr. Grey finally asked.

"I'm afraid what we need is a wheelwright," Tom replied. "Someone who really knows wheels could make it right. How far are we from Fort Laramie? Might be one there."

"About thirty miles, give or take. I reckon there's someone. The army's got to get their wagons fixed somehow."

Rachael stared at the shattered wheel. The spokes were splintered, fractured like bones. Would they have to leave the wagon behind and come back for it later?

By now, the other wagons had stopped. A crowd had formed, curious and concerned.

"Golly gee, that wheel done broke," Henry declared, inching toward it.

"Stay back, lad," Tom warned. "With the wagon tilted like this, it's dangerous. We need to right it first. That means we unload as much weight as possible."

"I'll get the pole," Tom added, heading to his wagon. He returned with a long, thick wooden pole, longer than the one they had once used to test for water in the sand.

Was there water under this trail? Rachael wondered. *Could that have caused the slip?* But she didn't have time to linger on questions.

Mr. Grey had already formed a human chain to unload the wagon.

"Start from the back, opposite the broken wheel," he directed. Rachael noticed how carefully he chose that side. It would keep the shifting weight from bearing down on the broken wheel and worsening the damage.

"For now, just stack the goods over there." He pointed to a level patch about eight feet ahead on the trail. "We'll divvy up what goes into the wagons afterward. Daniel, here, take this tarp. We'll pile the goods on top of it."

Rachael stood and joined the line, offloading the wagon. Tom, Daniel, and Reverend Robert handled the heavier goods, working together to carry large barrels or roll them across the sand. The routine was familiar; every time they needed to ford a river or lighten the load to climb a hill, they had to unpack the wagons. Everyone knew their role.

The children helped, too. Rachael smiled with quiet pride as Sara and Christopher struggled to carry the heavy bean pot between them. Ann, perched on the first barrel unloaded, began organizing the growing pile of goods. She didn't speak to the children or praise their efforts.

Why was it always so hard for her to give them a kind word?

Rachael's thoughts were interrupted when she spotted Hannah struggling with the heavy box of plates. She rushed to her side.

"Hannah, should you be lifting something like this?" she whispered urgently. "It's dangerous. You could strain yourself." Her glance dropped to the barely visible roundness under Hannah's skirt.

"I'm fine," Hannah murmured. "Don't fuss. It would look odd if I didn't help." She flicked her eyes toward Tom.

"He still doesn't know?"

"Hush," she hissed. "I promise I won't take anything this heavy again. I'll admit it makes my back ache."

"Hannah, I just don't—"

"Enough, here comes Tom."

"Hannah, maybe you shouldn't be doing that," Tom said gently as he approached. "You've been complaining about your back lately."

"I'll do my share. Don't blather. It's how I was raised."

Though Rachael admired her determination, she wished Hannah would be more cautious. She recalled reading something about back pain in early pregnancy, but couldn't remember the specifics. She'd consult the book again later.

She decided to change the subject. "Hannah, it was my fault the wheel broke. Mr. Grey fell asleep again, and I let myself get distracted. If I'd just kept my eyes on the trail…"

"For goodness' sake, Rachael, you're always taking everything on. You heard Tom, this would've happened even if Mr. Grey were driving. Now, let's put this box down before we drop it."

Rachael sighed. She still wished it had been Mr. Grey driving.

When most of the wagon had been unloaded, Mr. Grey called the men over and laid out the plan. It was clear he'd spoken with Tom and agreed on the next steps.

They ran a pole over the front axle and under the rear one, creating a lever that would lift the damaged wheel clear of the ground.

Christopher, Henry, and Roy eagerly volunteered to help, but Mr. Grey waved them off. "Too dangerous. Stand back."

Rachael pulled Sara close and watched, fascinated. Tom approached the broken wheel with his tools. He used a key to loosen it and then pounded it with a rubber mallet until it came free. The shattered wheel flopped sideways in the sand like a broken spider.

Then Tom lashed the long pole over the front axle and beneath the rear, creating a tilted brace. The far end of the pole dragged behind the wagon, trailing in the sand. It looked precarious but clever.

"That should work," Tom said, wiping his brow with a handkerchief.

"We'll need to go slow," he added. "If the axles stay balanced, we should make it to the Fort. Let's hope no other wheels go. This is my last pole. I'll check all the wagons before we move."

"Well done," Mr. Grey said. "I've heard of this trick but never done it myself. I reckon the length of the pole makes all the difference?"

"Yes, sir. Eight feet or so gives the right angle. I'm glad it'll help."

Mr. Grey grasped Tom's hand firmly. "It was money well spent, bringing you on."

Tom looked down modestly. "Just doing my job. Couldn't have come without the work discount anyway."

"One more thing," he added. "Best to walk the mules ahead a ways. Get them used to the way it feels, dragging that pole. It'll spook them otherwise."

"Sound advice," Mr. Grey agreed.

Rachael watched the exchange, heartened by the mutual respect. She'd never imagined something so simple could solve such a big problem. And though she still wasn't sure it would work, seeing Mr. Grey's satisfaction gave her hope. Her chest felt a little lighter.

Soon, the goods were redistributed among the other wagons. The Dixes couldn't carry much. Mrs. Dix made a great show of tucking the skillet under her wagon seat. The rest of the company did what they could, squeezing in boxes and bundles wherever space could be found.

Rachael noticed Tom making the rounds, tapping each wheel with his hammer. She was grateful to him. He had a quiet competence that was easy to overlook but essential. Mr. Grey had been right to hire him, and Rachael was finally willing to admit it.

She felt a little twinge of guilt when she thought about the small splash of water she reserved for Hannah's rosebush, still tucked into her satchel. She had considered leaving it behind once or twice, but keeping it alive had become a personal vow. It was no longer just a plant; it symbolized her hopes for Hannah and the fragile new life growing inside her.

Watching the others' work, Rachael was surprised that Mr. Grey hadn't said a word about her driving. Maybe, just maybe, it really wasn't her fault.

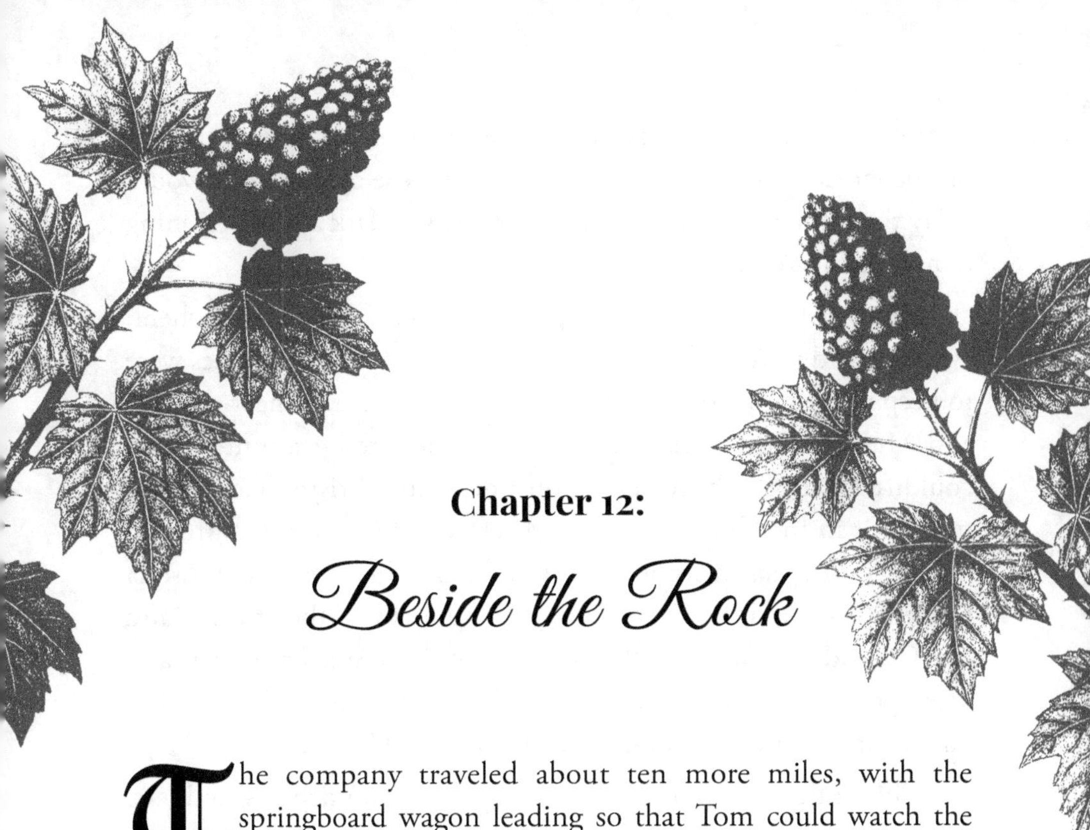

Chapter 12:

Beside the Rock

The company traveled about ten more miles, with the springboard wagon leading so that Tom could watch the drag on the pole. Mr. Grey guided the mules carefully across the rocky landscape. Rachael walked beside Sara, Christopher, and Roy, keeping the children occupied with rhyming games and teaching them to kick the smaller stones down the trail like marbles. When they were tired of that, she told them the fairy tales of Hans Christian Andersen, the same stories she had cherished as a girl. She could still remember the feel of the worn pages and the faint, musty scent of the book, rubbed smooth by her small hands.

As they moved along, she kept an eye on Hannah, who held her arms tightly around her waist. At least once, Rachael saw her bend forward slightly, a flicker of pain shadowing her face. She glanced toward Tom, but he was still focused on watching the wagon wheels and didn't seem to notice. Rachael hoped they would stop soon. It had already been a long, weary day.

At last, as dusk descended, they crossed a shallow stream. Tom followed behind the springboard wagon on foot to ensure it made the crossing safely. Everyone was bone-tired, but Mr. Grey insisted they press on across the creek. He always made a point to camp on the far side, explaining that if the waters rose overnight, it would delay them the next day. Tonight, with the sky dark and threatening rain, it seemed especially wise.

Tents were pitched quickly, and trenches dug around them; everyone had learned the hard way how essential those trenches were to keep water out. Cooking implements were gathered near the fire, and Mr. Grey had already started. For a few tense minutes, they couldn't locate the heavy cast-iron pot until Christopher recalled putting it in the Godleys' wagon. There was a fair bit of confusion as people rummaged through barrels for the flour and baking soda needed to make biscuits. Sara hauled water from the stream, and Mr. Grey added wild sage, the last of the onions, small potatoes, and dried penstemon to the stew. To Rachael, it smelled delicious. For one night, at least, they'd be spared the dreaded beans.

She pulled her mother's shawl tighter around her shoulders, warding off the evening chill. Around her, the other travelers sat wearily near the fire. Though clearly exhausted, there was a note of quiet pride among them, a subtle satisfaction at having endured yet another trial together. For the first time, Rachael sensed the early spark of camaraderie. Even Mrs. Dix, for once, seemed in good spirits, bending over the stew pot and offering Mr. Grey unsolicited advice. Rachael smiled into her shawl. She knew just how much he disliked being told how to cook.

The children played Cat's Cradle by the fire with a piece of yarn. Sara carefully arranged the string around her brother's fingers while Roy demonstrated how to form Jacob's Ladder. Sara looked up at Rachael with a triumphant grin. Not a single stutter in her instructions. Rachael beamed back, pride warming her chest, and turned to find Hannah so she could share the moment.

But Hannah was nowhere to be seen.

Rachael scanned the camp. Tom stood with Mr. Grey, deep in conversation. Perhaps Hannah had gone to rest in the family tent.

Rachael circled behind the Evans' wagon and lifted the canvas flap, but the tent was empty.

Her heartbeat quickened.

Listening carefully, she heard something—faint, rhythmic sounds like grunts. She turned towards a large rock a little way off. The noises were coming from behind it. Her first thought was of an animal. But then she thought of Hannah.

Rounding the rock, she stopped cold.

Hannah was crouched low over a shallow hole dug into the rocky soil. Her hair had fallen loose, sweat dampening the strands against her face. Her eyes were closed, and the sounds she made had shifted from grunts to short, trembling groans.

For a moment, Rachael could only stare.

"Hannah, what is happening?" Her eyes flew open as another groan escaped her lips.

Rachael dropped to her knees and gently pulled Hannah's hair back from her face. She looked down and froze.

The hole Hannah had dug was filled with blood, dark as rust, speckled with what looked like coffee grounds and torn flesh.

Now Rachael knew.

She had lost her baby.

"Oh, Hannah…"

Hannah's gaze met hers, her face contorted with pain and sorrow. Her eyes were red-rimmed, tears sliding silently down her cheeks, falling into the earth. With a final, guttural sigh, she tried to stand. Her knees buckled.

Rachael caught her.

She held Hannah against her chest, her arms wrapped around her trembling body, and began to rock her gently, just as her own mother had once done in times of grief.

Neither spoke. The world narrowed to the sound of their breathing and the weight of sorrow between them.

Finally, Hannah pushed back slightly. They still held hands, staring into each other's eyes, silent. The depth of this moment, its wordless intimacy, etched itself into Rachael's soul.

"We need to close the hole," Hannah whispered. "We need to bury it. I can't look again. Can you do it for me? Please... I can't."

Rachael nodded. She helped Hannah sit against a nearby tree, turned her away from the rock, and gently removed her mother's shawl, wrapping it around Hannah's shoulders.

Before covering the hole, Rachael looked again at what lay within. A wave of sorrow washed through her, mingled with a strange flicker of scientific curiosity. *So this is what a miscarriage looks like,* she thought, bits of tissue and blood, fragments of what might have been a child.

She knelt, her hands trembling, and quietly returned the soil over the small grave. Her heart ached for Hannah and the fragile life that would never be.

And Ann... she thought. *Ann's time is still to come.* And for the first time, she felt thankful that Mrs. Dix, difficult and quarrelsome though she was, would be there to help.

She closed her eyes, offered a silent, wordless prayer, then turned back.

Rachael helped Hannah into the tent and guided her gently onto the pallet. "Lie still. I'll bring some warm water and cotton. I'll make some excuses. They won't know. We'll get you cleaned up and changed."

Hannah didn't respond at first. Then, her voice rasping, she murmured, "Get Tom. I was wrong not to tell him. I just... hoped..."

She closed her eyes again, tears soaking into the quilt.

Rachael left the tent and found Tom still deep in conversation with Mr. Grey over the condition of the wagon felloes. She touched his shoulder and drew him aside. She could feel Mr. Grey watching, but she ignored it.

In hushed, steady words, she told Tom the truth.

He paled, broke away from her, and rushed to the family tent.

Rachael remained where she stood. A moment later, she felt a hand on her back. Turning, she found Mr. Grey looking at her.

"Mrs. Williams, what is it? What's happened?"

Her lips parted, but no words came. She simply shook her head and whispered, "I need a bucket of warm water… and some cotton."

He held her gaze for a beat, nodded, and turned to get what she needed.

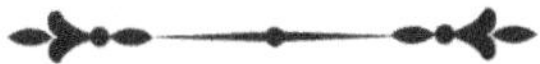

That night, after the camp had quieted and a fine rain began to fall, Rachael slipped out of her tent, the rose bush wrapped in burlap in her arms.

By the moonlight, she made her way back to the rock. She dug a shallow hole beside the small hidden grave, her hands steady despite the tremble in her heart.

With care, she planted the rose bush in the sandy soil, Hannah's rose, the one she'd carried all these miles.

Hannah would never know.

But that didn't matter.

It was Rachael's own way of expressing care, understanding, and grief for a friend's terrible loss.

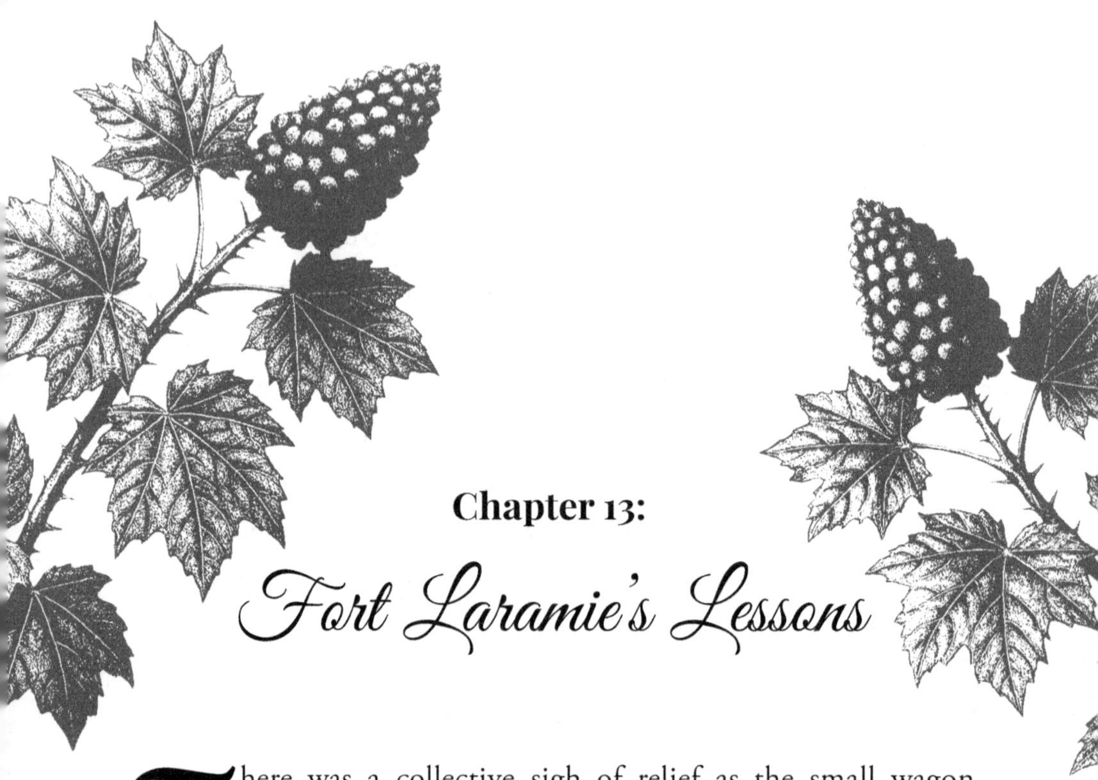

Chapter 13:
Fort Laramie's Lessons

There was a collective sigh of relief as the small wagon train limped into Fort Laramie. It was dusk, and the gates remained open. The sound of the poles scraping along the sandy stretch of road, leaving a deep rut marking their passage, was one Rachael suspected they would all remember for a long time. But they had made it. Tom and Mr. Grey's repair work on the springboard wagon had held.

Rachael's feet were swollen and sore, as she assumed, were everyone else's since nearly all had walked the final twenty-five miles following the wagon accident. As weary as she was, her heart quickened. She could see candlelight glowing in the windows of the fort and hear the low murmur of men's voices.

Across a narrow river flickered the campfires of more Indians than she had ever seen. She could just make out the tepees in silhouette against the lengthening shadows. She reminded herself they could not be dangerous, or surely the fort's gate would be shut.

Mr. Grey raised his hand, signaling the wagons to stop. He rode ahead and spoke briefly with the gate guard. Moments later, he waved the party forward, and they passed through the wide wooden gates.

Everyone looked around with interest. This was the largest fort they had yet encountered. A cluster of wooden buildings filled the compound—barracks, a mess hall, and other structures whose functions Rachael could only guess. It resembled a small town.

"We'll be allowed to camp within the fort walls tonight, in the southern section of the parade ground," Mr. Grey announced. "We're a small party and lucky to be the only company here. Three larger ones came through weeks ago. There's even room in the pens for the sheep and, if my money holds out, a bit of fodder."

A cheer rose from Mr. Miller, the drover boys, and James, who looked forward to sleeping with full stomachs for once, free from their usual dawn tending of the sheep.

Indeed, the respite was welcome for all.

Rachael found herself wishing the wheel repairs would take several days so she could explore. It had been a long time since she'd seen this many people. She was especially eager to visit the commissary. Would she find some of the herbs or dried roots mentioned in Martha's mother's book? She also hoped for a warmer coat and perhaps a new pair of boots. She mentally counted her money. It might just be enough. A flush of excitement ran through her at the thought of something new, something clean.

After they had set up camp, Mr. Grey called the party together.

"Tom and I just returned from the Wheelwright's forge. It will take two days to repair the wheel. I've asked Tom to inspect the other wheels as well since it'll be a long haul to the next fort. That means he'll have to remove some of them. I trust you'll all be cooperative."

He paused. "You've probably noticed all the Indians camped around the fort. They're here to trade, not trouble. You're in no danger. Just… stay out of the way."

He glanced directly at Rachael.

She returned his gaze, refusing to look away. The implication stung. *So he still didn't trust her to keep out of trouble?*

She would go where she pleased.

"Oh, and by the way," Mr. Grey added, "we've been invited to eat at the mess. I figured you'd enjoy a change from the usual. Don't expect much, but it probably won't be beans."

He was wrong.

The meal was, indeed, beans, though this time mixed with yellow mush. It was lumpy, but no one complained. At least it was different.

The women and children sat at a long wooden table at one end of the mess hall. The men joined the soldiers farther down.

James made a show of sitting with the men. He'd even washed his face and slicked back his hair.

Several Indian men sat at the men's table. Rachael scanned the room for Indian women but saw none.

As she ate, she watched the men's table. The Indians were silent, communicating through gestures. One soldier moved his hand sharply from left to right, and the Indian nodded in response.

It's a language, she realized. *Not one of sound but of movement.*

She couldn't understand what the signs meant, but clearly, the soldier did.

An enlisted man appeared with cups and a coffee pot. *Ah, coffee.* Rachael grasped the cup in both hands and inhaled the aroma as if she had missed it.

After tucking Sara in, perhaps she could come back here and read. She might even borrow a new book. She'd ask the cook after thanking him for supper.

What must it be like to live here in this fort?

After the meal, she'd try to find Mr. Grey and ask him, especially about the Indian language. There was so much to learn.

But when supper ended, Mr. Grey disappeared with the sergeant he had been talking to earlier. She suspected he had gone off to smoke and drink. He'd patted both his front and back pockets with enthusiastic anticipation.

As the other diners trickled out of the mess hall, Rachael noticed the young soldier who had been signing to the Indian was still seated with his companion, sipping coffee.

She stood, brushed off her skirt, and ran her fingers through her short hair, still aware that it was a novelty. Her own party had gawked at her when she'd first cut it.

For a fleeting moment, she wished she had worn something other than her usual wool skirt. But then again, it didn't matter.

She walked toward the men. The soldier saw her coming and stood up. He was tall and thin, with a pencil-thin mustache barely shading his upper lip. His red hair was cropped close to his head, but it was his hands that caught her attention—long, elegant fingers. *Artist's hands,* her mother would have called them.

Without thinking, Rachael glanced at his left hand. It was bare. She realized her own fingers were nervously turning her wedding ring round and round. Embarrassed, she forced herself to stop, resisting the impulse to tuck her hand behind her back.

"Good evening," she began. "I hope you don't mind my interrupting. I'm with the small party that just arrived. I noticed that—"

"Lieutenant Randall, at your service, ma'am."

Rachael found herself momentarily speechless. He had an accent, faint, unfamiliar, but more than that, he was... striking. She looked away toward the Indian, who was watching her openly, his eyes deep brown, almost black. His long black hair was tied back with rawhide. His large, powerful hands rested on the table.

"Oh…" she began again, recovering. "It's just that I noticed you were communicating using hand motions. I wondered, could you tell me about it? It's not something I've seen before."

Lieutenant Randall nodded toward his companion. "His name is Howahkan."

He made a motion with his hands. Howahkan laughed a deep, amused chuckle. His eyes gleamed with something Rachael couldn't quite read. He signed back.

Now, it was the lieutenant's turn to laugh.

Are they making fun of me? Heat flushed her neck. Her jaw tightened. Anger bubbled in her chest.

"I'm sorry, missus," the lieutenant said quickly, reading her expression. "No offense meant. It's just—no white woman's ever asked that before. Took us by surprise. You see… Howahkan's my brother."

Rachael blinked. She looked from one man to the other. *Brother?*

But they didn't look alike at all. The lieutenant was red-haired and pale; the Indian was dark, with black hair and brown skin.

"We grew up together," he said. "It's a long story."

He held her gaze for a moment.

"As for your question, yes, it's a language. There are many clans in the Lakota Nation, and not all speak the same language. So, they developed a hand-signal system, sign language, to communicate when they gather to trade. Everyone can use it. Tonight, since someone at our table spoke a different dialect, we used signs instead of speech. Using our language would've been rude."

Before she could stop herself, Rachael blurted, "Do you think I could learn it?"

The lieutenant's jaw dropped. "Why ever would you want to?"

"I do have a reason. I'm a botanist. I'm interested in what plants the tribes use for medicine. Mr. Grey has spoken highly of the woman healers, especially one named Mari, and the medicine men. I thought…"

She trailed off as Lieutenant Randall began signing to Howahkan.

Howahkan shook his head, then made a gesture: a crosswise motion over his chest, palm facing forward.

The lieutenant interpreted. "He asks if you have anything to trade."

Trade? Her mind went blank.

"A horse?" the lieutenant translated again, mimicking a sign Rachael guessed meant "horse."

She hesitated. "No. I did, but…" She stopped. *Better not to mention Little Red.*

Then she remembered her small hand lens. Could she part with it?

Before she could second-guess herself, she made a decision.

"I do have something that might be of interest. It's a small glass that, when you look through it, makes the thing you're looking at larger. It was a gift from my father…"

Rachael hesitated, but only for a moment. *He would have wanted me to find the Devil's Club,* she reminded herself. *Learning this language might help me.*

"Perhaps I could trade my hand lens?"

Lieutenant Randall stroked his mustache with one of his long fingers.

"You really do want to learn this, don't you?" he said at last. "You won't be able to learn a whole language in the few days you're here, but you could start. Forget the trade. I'd be glad to teach you. Tomorrow's the Sabbath. Why don't we start after morning services?"

"That would be fine indeed," Rachael said, holding out her hand. She expected a handshake, but he surprised her by lifting it and kissing it.

Still holding her hand, she felt her face flush again. She pulled it back gently. "By the way, my name is Mrs. Williams."

"Pleased to meet you, Mrs. Williams," he said with a slight bow.

She turned and headed for the door, her cheeks still warm. As she stepped out into the night, she heard the two men laughing behind her.

Let them laugh, she thought, lifting her chin.

She was pleased with the arrangement. Learning even a little of the language might be helpful, more than helpful, even.

Why hadn't Mr. Grey ever mentioned it? Surely, he must know some of it himself.

She smiled to herself. *Won't he be surprised when I sign to him for the first time?*

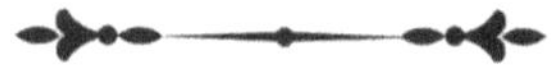

Rachael woke to the familiar sound of a rooster crowing. *A rooster? Then there must be hens and eggs!*

So excited she could barely contain herself, she leaned over Sara and gently shook her awake. With a finger to her lips, she motioned for quiet. The others were still sleeping. Together, they dressed quietly and crawled out of the tent into the pale morning light.

"Imagine, where there's a rooster, there are eggs. Do you think we could get some?"

The night before, it had been too dark to see much, but now Rachael could make out a dozen wooden buildings, fences, and animal pens. Two of the structures looked like small houses. As she watched, a woman emerged from one with a broom and began sweeping her porch. A small child followed behind her, dragging a ragdoll.

"There are women here!" Rachael whispered. "Look, Sara, families. That little girl might be just your age. You must be getting tired of your brother and the other boys."

Sara nodded and reached for Rachael's hand.

"Okay then," Rachael said with a smile, squeezing it. "Let's go exploring. Do you smell that? It's baking bread."

The aroma drew them across the yard and up the wooden stairs to a screen door. Rachael pushed it open and guided Sara inside. A large man stood behind a table dusted with flour, wrapped in a well-worn apron, a smudge of flour on his cheek.

"We're sorry to bother you," Rachael said, "but the smell of fresh bread was just too much to resist. It seems like years since we've had any. Would it be possible to buy some?"

"You wouldn't be the first," the baker said with a chuckle. "I'd be glad to sell you some. Looks like your young'un could use a little fattening up." He smiled at Sara.

"Oh, she's not my daughter. We're just friends. I—"

"You must be from that little wagon party that came in late yesterday," he interrupted. "Heard you broke a wheel. Bad luck. Lucky for you, the best wheelwright in the West is here. He'll set it right soon enough. Now, how about that bread?"

Rachael reached for her pocket and then froze. "Oh dear, I forgot my coin purse."

"No matter, missus. You can pay me later."

He looked directly at Sara. "Would you like some bread? What's your name, little lady?"

"M-my name is S-Sara. Yes, p-please, sir."

Rachael was surprised. Sara rarely spoke to strangers.

The baker glanced back at Rachael, then nodded and handed Sara a thick slice of bread across the kneading table.

"Well then, you shall have some."

Sara grinned, clutching the bread. "Th-thank you."

The baker rubbed his chin thoughtfully. "I could use your help later, young'un. I'm baking a batch of shortbread this afternoon. Need someone to taste it, make sure it's just right. Think you could help?"

Sara looked up at Rachael, who nodded her approval.

"Y-yes, sir!" she beamed.

"Well, then it's settled. I'll see you later. Look forward to it, little miss."

He handed Rachael a loaf of bread.

"And I'll be back with the payment. Thank you."

Rachael turned toward the door, Sara trailing behind her, happily chewing on the baker's bread. *What a kind man,* she thought. *He didn't even flinch at Sara's stutter.* How she wished everyone would treat the girl with such kindness. Rachael knew the stutter always worsened when Sara felt uncomfortable. *If only people always treated her with warmth, she might not stutter at all.* Oh, how she wished that were possible.

Later that morning, Rachael sat beside the Godleys in the mess hall, where Sunday services were being held. She looked around, noting the officers' wives and their children, and how she longed to talk with other women. She turned in her seat, glancing behind her for Mr. Grey, suspecting, as usual, that he was sitting in the back, but instead, her eyes met those of Lieutenant Randall. He smiled and inclined his head.

Rachael quickly turned away, but not before Mrs. Dix caught the exchange. The older woman fixed her with a disapproving glare, her head shaking in clear judgment.

Ann's head was bowed over her prayer book, her lips moving soundlessly. Rachael sighed and reached for Sara, gently tucking a loose lock of hair behind her ear. She glanced down the row. Christopher sat beside his father, who looked more puffed up than usual, likely thinking he should be leading the service himself.

As the sermon dragged on, Christopher began to swing his legs back and forth under the bench. His father shot him a look, but the boy kept swinging. Robert reached over and pinched him. Christopher squealed, then clamped his mouth shut at his father's stern glare, tears forming in his eyes.

Frankly, I don't blame him, Rachael thought. This minister had now held forth on the wages of sin and damnation for forty-five minutes. She, too, wished he would bring it to a close.

She remembered her own childhood services and the sweet relief of hearing, *"The service is over; go in peace."* The congregation's heartfelt reply, *"Thanks be to God,"* had never felt more true than at the end of one of these fire-and-brimstone tirades. A laugh threatened to rise in her throat at the memory. She suspected Christopher felt the same.

Finally, the service ended, and the congregation began filing out from the front. Rachael admired the starched dresses of the officers' wives and their families. She fingered her own skirt, patched and faded, feeling a twinge of embarrassment.

Just then, she saw the same woman she'd spotted earlier that morning, the one who'd been sweeping the porch, walking down the aisle. A small girl followed her, still dragging a rag doll, and behind them came another girl about Sara's age with fair hair in thick braids.

As they passed, the braided girl smiled at Sara. Rachael turned to look at the girl beside her; she was beaming.

Rachael squeezed Sara's hand. "Look, Sara, she seems to be about your age. Would you like to meet her? Let's ask your mother, shall we?"

Sara nodded eagerly, but her hopeful smile faded as Ann took notice of the girls' exchange. Her brow furrowed, and Rachael's hopes sank. That was not a good sign.

Still, she tried. "Look, Ann," she said gently, "there seems to be a young girl about Sara's age. Surely, Sara would benefit from the company. She's had only the boys to play with on this whole trip. Don't you think?"

"No, I don't," Ann replied flatly. "She still has that terrible stutter. We wouldn't want them to think her strange."

Rachael felt her indignation rise. *How can she say such a thing in front of her child?* She stole a glance at Sara, who now had her head bowed over her lap, pretending to examine her fingernails.

"But don't you think that Sara—"

"And besides," Ann cut in, "I'm not sure I want her exposed to a girl who lives among the heathens outside this fort. What could they possibly have in common?"

Clutching her prayer book to her chest, Ann looked away.

Rachael bit her lip hard. The temptation to snap was overwhelming. *Does Ann not see the irony? Does she not realize her children are going to live among those same so-called "heathens" when she and Robert set out to save their souls?*

"I was planning to teach Sara some new embroidery stitches this afternoon," Ann added, her tone final. "She's well behind in her lessons. You'd like that, wouldn't you, Sara, dear?"

Sara's head dropped even further. "Yes, Ma'am," she murmured.

Poor Sara. Rachael knew she would hate that. She loathed sewing almost as much as Rachael did. But what could she do? Ann was her mother. Their relationship was already strained, and it was best not to press further.

Rachael stood and gently placed her hand on Sara's shoulder, giving it a quick squeeze. "All right then, Sara, I'll see you later this afternoon. Don't forget we have an appointment with the baker to check on his shortbread. I'll come and find you."

As she made her way out of the mess hall, she nodded briefly to the Dixes. Her heart ached for Sara's embarrassment and her mother's lack of compassion. She could feel the child's eyes on her back, but didn't dare turn around. She would have dragged Sara to meet the fair-haired girl if she could have.

She wasn't due to meet Lieutenant Randall until after 11:30, so there was time to visit the commissary. The prospect lifted her spirits. She hoped to find paper or a small notebook to record the signs she would learn that day.

As she crossed the parade ground, an idea struck her. *What if Sara took lessons with her?* She was bright. They could learn the signs together. Rachael could see her now, gesturing to translate for her parents. *What confidence that would bring!* It would allow her to participate without speaking. A splendid idea. She nearly skipped the rest of the way to the commissary, already planning to buy a notebook for Sara as well.

She climbed the wooden stairs of the porch and pushed open the door. The room inside was dim, filled with tables stacked high with goods. No one was in sight.

She drifted toward a nearby table, brushing her hand across a pile of buffalo robes. They were astonishingly soft. On the trail, she had seen buffalo only in the distance, shaggy, torn-looking creatures. These robes were nothing like that.

"Well, hello, missus. Didn't hear you come in," came a voice from behind a stack of goods. "I see you're admiring the robes. They're good quality. What can I do for you? My name's Jacob."

Rachael turned toward the voice. The man approaching had wild grey whiskers, thick eyebrows, and a pronounced limp. He was stout, but something about him, the twinkle in his eye, perhaps, made her instantly like him. His glasses reminded her of Camille's.

"Well, to tell you the truth, I'd like one of everything," she said with a laugh. "It's been so long since I've seen anything for sale. It feels like a wonderland."

"Many feel that way after a month or so on the trail." He smiled, showing his teeth. "One of everything would suit me just fine."

"What I really need is paper, or a notebook or two, and some pencils. I've been teaching a young girl to draw, and we're nearly out of paper. The pencils are only nubs. She's made wonderful progress, and I'm proud of her."

"I suspect she has a good teacher," Jacob replied, ducking his head and blushing slightly.

Rachael smiled. "Why, thank you, sir. I do try. So, do you have any paper? Or better still, two small notebooks I could buy?"

"Yes, indeed. Let me get those supplies for you."

Their conversation was interrupted by a flood of light as the door opened. A tall silhouette stepped inside. It was Lieutenant Randall.

"Well, look who's here." His eyes swept the room, taking in both Rachael and Jacob. "You're not trying to sell her one of your flea-bitten buffalo robes, are you, Jacob? He charges outrageous prices, ma'am. He's a crafty one, he is. Steal you blind if you give him half a chance."

"You know there are no fleas in my robes," Jacob grumbled. "Why—"

But Randall ignored him, turning to Rachael instead. "Best to know the prices first and how to bargain."

His words rankled. *Always trying to embarrass someone,* she thought, remembering the kiss on her hand the night before. That lingering touch. It hadn't sat well with her then, either.

She drew herself up, her tone polite but edged.

"Why, I'll bet I could guess the price for these furs. In fact, I consider myself a good judge of quality."

What was she thinking? Still, she didn't like the way Randall had spoken to Jacob, and certainly not to her.

"All right, Mrs., let's see how you do, shall we? How much would you pay for this one?" Randall reached the bottom of the pile and pulled out a beautiful coat. Rachael fingered the robe thoughtfully.

To her surprise, she saw Jacob move behind Randall and hold up six fingers. She glanced at him briefly.

"I think I would pay about six dollars," she said, "because of the quality."

"And this one?" Randall held up a smaller robe. "How much?"

"Well," she said, looking over Randall's shoulder at Jacob, who now held up three fingers, "three dollars. Maybe less, I'd have to see it more closely."

Randall smiled. "Well, Mrs. Williams, I'm impressed. You do seem to understand prices."

Rachael laughed. "Well, I did have some help."

Jacob had already returned behind his counter and was busy gathering up the notebooks and pencils she had asked for. Randall turned and regarded him.

Jacob looked at Rachael with a blank expression. "Shall I wrap them for you?"

"Yes, please. I'd like to surprise Sara with hers."

"And what can I do for you, Randall?" he asked curtly.

"Has my tobacco come in yet?"

"Haven't had a chance to look through the last shipment," Jacob replied. "But if it's there, I'll bring it to you, even if you don't deserve it, after calling my robes inferior."

"Well, thanks then, Jacob." He turned to Rachael. "I'll see you later for your lessons, Mrs. Williams."

"Yes, indeed, and I may bring Sara with me. She's a young woman for whom I'm responsible."

Randall raised an eyebrow. "I suppose that would be all right… If it must be. I was looking forward to having you all to myself." He winked.

Rachael stiffened. *He has a lot of nerve.* She held her tongue. Though she no longer found him charming, learning this language mattered too much to let his behavior get in the way.

Without another word, he turned and walked out the door.

Jacob burst into laughter. "Well, I'll be. I haven't had so much fun in a long time. You bested him. Glad to get his goat now and then."

"Couldn't have done it without you, Jacob."

"Believe me, my pleasure. What lessons is Randall giving you and the young lady? He's a bold one, that one. If you don't mind an old man saying so, best be careful of his kind."

"Don't I know it? But it's important. Lieutenant Randall is teaching me the sign language the Indians use."

Jacob's brows rose. "Well, he should know it well enough. He was raised with the Indians. He was taken from his family as a small boy. Considers himself one of them, in fact. Still, I'd keep my eyes open, ma'am, even if it's not my business."

"Don't worry, Jacob. I'll have Sara with me. And we're meeting in the mess hall."

"So, that's the young lady's name, Sara. I like that. Bring her by to meet me. I think I can find some rock candy hereabouts."

"Why, thank you. I will." Rachael took the packages, now neatly wrapped with string.

"Nice to meet you, Jacob. See you later."

"The pleasure is mine."

With her packages tucked under her arm, Rachael went off to find Sara. She quickly spotted Christopher and Roy playing a game with rocks. The boys always found ways to amuse themselves. This game involved a circle drawn in the dirt. It reminded her of marbles, a game she used to play with Richard when they were children. *Funny,* she thought. *I haven't thought of him in such a long time.* Life on the trail had crowded out everything else. Then another thought struck her: *Maybe Jacob has some marbles.* She'd ask when she brought Sara by later. Christopher and Roy might enjoy that.

She rounded the Godleys' wagon and found Sara sitting on a log, embroidery hoop in her lap, head bowed. She stabbed the needle through the fabric, tied a knot, and examined her stitches.

"Nice French knot, Sara. Where's your mother? I thought she was teaching you."

"She's ssleeping," Sara said, pointing to her head.

"Oh. Well, I'll check on her later. Best to let her rest. Why don't you put down that hoop and come with me? I have a surprise for you."

Sara's eyes lit up. "SShortbread?"

"Not yet, sweetheart."

They crossed the parade ground together. When they reached the mess hall, Randall was already there, sitting at the same table as the night before. Howahkan sat beside him. Randall frowned when he saw Sara. Rachael decided to ignore it.

"Lieutenant Randall, Howahkan, this is Sara."

"HHello," she said softly.

Randall's frown deepened. Again, Rachael ignored it.

"We're ready for our lesson now. Sara, we're going to learn a language that the Indians use to communicate. It doesn't involve speaking. It's done through hand signs."

Sara's eyes widened.

They sat down on the bench across from Randall.

"Where shall we start? I have many things I want to learn, especially about medicine. I—"

"Our people do not just start asking questions," Randall interrupted. "It's considered rude. First, you must greet someone properly. Later, you may ask your questions."

"Oh." Rachael thought of Mr. Grey; he would like this language. He hated being pestered with questions. *Maybe I could learn to ask him things in sign instead.*

"You'll find that some of the signs just make sense," Randall went on. "It's pantomime. You should understand them naturally."

He made a quick gesture, waving his hand toward Rachael.

She paused, mentally sifting through possibilities.

Howahkan made the same gesture toward Sara, his palm open, waving toward his own chest, then repeated it.

Sara looked at him, forehead wrinkled in concentration, and a small smile appeared.

"C-come. C-come."

Howahkan nodded, smiling in return.

"Now you try," Randall said.

Sara repeated the gesture.

"And this one?" Howahkan placed his palm flat against his chest.

"S-stay?"

"And this?" He repeated the same hand motion but waved it quickly back and forth in front of his chest.

Sara tilted her head, puzzled. She leaned against the table. "G-go?"

Howahkan guffawed, then spoke to Randall in a language Rachael didn't recognize. It must be theirs.

Sara turned toward Rachael, her face full of questions.

Howahkan made more signs toward Randall.

Randall laughed. "It appears the teacher is becoming the pupil. Howahkan says she's brilliant, but her tongue is stuck."

Rachael's heart ached. She wished she could explain to Howahkan that Sara's stutter wasn't her fault, that it got worse when people mocked her or made her nervous.

But she was proud of her nonetheless. Watching Sara respond, stumbling at first but growing more confident, Rachael noticed that the stutter was lessening. And Howahkan seemed to enjoy the lesson, too. The signs did make sense. Most were simple gestures people made without thinking, often while speaking. For Sara, it was like a balm, a way to communicate without struggling.

Rachael sat up straighter, excitement rising.

Over the next two days, she and Sara met with Randall and Howahkan in the mess hall for two hours every afternoon. In between, they often stopped at the bakery. A quiet friendship bloomed between the baker and Sara. She stuttered less and less around him, her smile growing freer each day.

Ann, preoccupied with her pregnancy, scarcely noticed Sara's absences. Once, she complained to Rachael that she'd hoped Sara would be more helpful during this time. Rachael had simply nodded. Whenever possible, she brewed tea from the herbs Howahkan had shared during a lesson. He'd pointed to his stomach, made a rounding motion, pregnancy, and then gently patted his belly to signal a calming effect. She hoped he'd offer more insights, perhaps share other plants used by the healers.

There was still so much to learn.

She had also visited Jacob again, now a favorite among the children. He had given each of them rock candy and even produced a small sack of marbles for Christopher, who promptly stashed them in his pocket. Rachael suspected he even slept with them.

Jacob had arranged for her to trade herbs with an Indian woman, her first time using the signs on her own. Though her skills were still developing, she managed well with pantomime. It thrilled her to see communication unfold without words.

Mr. Grey, who had spent the past days out hunting with a friend, gathered the company that final evening to announce the springboard wagon was repaired. All the wheels had been checked. He praised the Wheelwright's skill and commended Tom for his efforts.

Rachael, distracted by lessons, the children, and helping Ann, had hardly seen Hannah. But tonight, she spotted her beaming at her husband. They looked so close, so united. *Would I ever feel that way about a man?*

Then she thought of Richard and the mistake she had nearly made in marrying him. *It doesn't matter now,* she told herself. *I'll find the Devil's Club. I'll learn about these plants. I have too much to do to worry about any of that.*

She stood a little taller, her heart steady. She was proud of her independence.

As they were yoking the oxen, a commotion broke out. Several soldiers galloped into camp, one with a young boy in front of him and another, a sergeant, his leg wrapped in a bloody shirt.

The soldier pulled up hard, and the boy slid into his mother's arms. She had already seen the sergeant ride in with her child and was rushing forward. Lieutenant Randall took the boy from her and immediately sent someone running for his brother and the medicine woman. Then, cradling the boy, he carried him into the mess hall.

Mr. Grey stopped harnessing the oxen and followed. Rachael watched him go with a flicker of pride. She had seen him in emergencies before; he'd apprenticed under a doctor, and he was always calm and capable. She knew he would be annoyed, but she followed anyway. *Perhaps I can be of some assistance,* she thought. The rest of the company moved toward the shade of the baker's porch.

Inside the mess hall, Randall gently laid the groaning boy onto a table. The door swung open, and Howahkan entered with the medicine woman. She carried her collecting bag, her movements purposeful. She stood still for a moment, taking in the room, then moved forward. It was clear to Rachael that this woman held authority. Both Randall and the boy's mother stepped back as she approached. She nodded to Howahkan and made the sign for *water* and *much*.

Rachael couldn't help herself. She stepped forward and made the sign for help.

The medicine woman looked surprised, then nodded. Mr. Grey frowned.

"No, Mrs. Williams," he said firmly. "This is not your place. Please go and join the others. You'll only be in the way."

But Wapun turned to Grey and signed rapidly toward Randall.

Randall translated. "It appears, Mr. Grey, that Wapun disagrees. She knows Mrs. Williams has been studying sign language and why. She says she wants her to stay."

Mr. Grey gave Rachael a dark, angry look, the kind she had seen before.

She didn't care.

She wanted to learn.

Wapun moved to the boy's leg and examined the wound. Howahkan returned with a bucket of water and cloth bandages. Wapun motioned for Rachael to come to the other side of the table and made the sign for the watch. Rachael nodded.

Wapun drew a knife from her belt and carefully slit what was left of the pant leg. There was little blood, but the cut was deep. Even Rachael could see that. Bits of cloth clung to the wound, and Wapun cut them free, then began to pour water directly over the fabric until the wound was fully exposed.

It was a deep ax slice into the boy's thigh. Though unconscious from blood loss, the boy was no longer bleeding. Rachael gasped as she saw the depth of the wound, white muscle visible beneath the torn skin. Oddly, instead of feeling sick, she found herself fascinated. The white strands looked like stretched rubber bands. *Tendons? Muscle fibers?* She itched to ask but knew better.

Two more buckets arrived. Wapun poured water steadily over the wound until the runoff ran clear. She gave a grunt and signed good.

Then she opened a wrapped bundle from her collecting bag. Rachael recognized the herbs, mallow and yarrow, crushed into a green paste. Wapun packed the mixture directly into the wound, layer by layer, then tied a large cloth tightly around the leg to keep everything in place. When it was done, she stepped back and exhaled heavily.

The boy's mother rushed forward.

"Will he be all right? Please, oh, please, tell me my son will be all right."

Wapun shrugged. She spoke softly to Randall in her native language.

Randall turned to the woman. "She says she hopes so. But you must watch closely for fever or redness. Keep the bandage tight and clean. She's done all she can. A birth is happening in her tribe; she must attend, but she says she will return if needed."

Rachael listened closely, watching each face—Wapun, Randall, the mother, the still boy. Her thoughts swirled, replaying what she'd just witnessed. She carefully reviewed Wapun's steps: cleansing the wound and using herbs instead of stitching. *Why hadn't she simply sewn it closed?* Rachael made a mental note to ask Mr. Grey later.

She turned to look for him, but he was gone. She heard the mess hall door slam. She hadn't noticed him leave; she'd been too absorbed in the moment.

Outside, she caught sight of the last of her party's wagons moving toward the fort gate. Panic surged. She ran to catch up, heading for Hannah and Roy at the back. Relief swept over her when she saw that her belongings had already been stowed in the Godleys' wagon. *But had he really intended to leave without me?* The thought ignited her anger. She had been asked to stay by Wapun. It wasn't as if she'd taken the liberty herself. The knowledge she gained might save someone's life one day.

She clenched her fists. *I'll speak with him tonight,* she vowed.

But as usual, Mr. Grey was the first to speak.

His tone was clipped and cold. "Once again, you've shown your determination to be where you shouldn't be. You held up our departure. And I'd like to know, from whom exactly did you learn that sign language, and why?"

Rachael crossed her arms. "From Lieutenant Randall. He was more than happy to teach me, in fact—"

"I don't like that man," Mr. Grey interrupted. "He's not to be trusted. And why didn't you tell me what you were doing?"

"You're hardly my husband or my father. I don't have to account to you for my actions. I saw an opportunity to learn something that might prove useful. So I took it."

His eyes darkened. "Happily, I am not your husband or your father. But while you are part of this company, you will do as I say, or you can walk back to that fort in the morning. I'm sure your precious Mr. Randall would be delighted to keep teaching you."

Rachael stood firm. "Oh, for goodness' sake, Mr. Grey. I'm not sorry I stayed to watch. I won't pretend I am. But I can see you're angry, and for that, I'll say I'm sorry."

"I am angry, Mrs. Williams. And I suggest you stay clear of me for a day or two."

He turned and stomped off down the trail.

Rachael watched him go, shaking her head. *Childish man.* She muttered to herself, "It'll be my pleasure, Mr. Grey."

Chapter 14:

Blooming Despite Thorns

A few weeks later, Rachael frowned as she spotted Sara trudging toward her. One of the girl's braids had come undone, her apron was smeared with dirt, and tear streaks cut through the dust on her cheeks.

Rachael patted the ground beside her. Sara nodded and flopped down, wrapping her arms around her knees and resting her chin atop them.

Rachael didn't speak at first. She understood the expression on the child's pinched face. It would take time for her to find the words.

Instead, she reached over and gently took Sara's hand, stroking it with her thumb while they gazed silently over the low hills.

Behind them, the doughy smell of baking biscuits drifted from the fire. Mr. Grey was at it again. To everyone's surprise, his biscuits were actually good. Camille had happily retired from her job of burning them and now stirred an iron pot Rachael knew held the eternal beans and bacon.

Hannah was down by the stream with a bucket. Tom crouched by their wagon, checking the wheels. Roy and Henry were nearby, playing a stick game in the dirt.

After a while, Rachael said gently, "Well, Sara, it looks like we're no longer in for the Four B's for supper. We'll need a new name. What do you think? Maybe Three B's—beans, bacon, and biscuits? Not as much fun, though."

Sara turned her head slightly, eyebrows raised, tilting her chin. Rachael had learned this was how she asked questions without speaking.

"How about 'Forever beans, bacon, and biscuits'? FBBB?" Rachael said with a smile.

Sara's face twitched, and a tiny high-pitched giggle slipped out.

"Well, at least you can smile and laugh. Are you ready to talk yet?"

Sara looked down, then back up.

"H-Harry," she whispered.

"Henry?" Sara nodded. "Take your time. Deep breaths. Tell me."

"Teased me… c-called me D-d-devil c-child."

Rachael stiffened. "Oh, Sara. That's so mean and so wrong."

Her voice sharpened despite her best effort. "Henry is cruel. He had no right. And you, you, are not a devil's child. You are a sweet, bright girl. Your stutter will pass. But cruelty like Henry's? I worry that won't."

She gently cupped Sara's chin and turned her face upward. "You don't believe what he said, do you?"

Sara gave a half-shrug.

Rachael's stomach clenched. Her temper stirred. She forced her eyes closed and tried to still her mind. But then Sara spoke again.

"A-and Chriss…t-turr."

"Christopher?"

Sara nodded.

"He was there too?"

A tear slipped down Sara's cheek as she nodded again.

"He didn't say anything?"

More tears.

Rachael drew a sharp breath, her fury rising.

She stood, pulling Sara up with her. "Come on. We're going to set this right."

Down the rise, they marched, hand in hand. At the edge of the camp, Rachael let go so Sara could slip away to her family's wagon. Her cheeks still burned with anger.

Only briefly did she consider cooling off, but then she tossed her head and kept going.

"Mrs. Dix, I want a word with you," she called. "Something important. I know you're behind your wagon. I can see your feet. Please come out so we may speak privately."

A moment later, Mrs. Dix emerged, scowling. She clutched a folded shirt in her hands. "And what do we have to discuss, Mrs. Williams?"

Rachael shut her eyes briefly. Focus. Be clear.

"It's your son. Henry teased Sara again, calling her the 'Devil's child.' She's very upset. I'm sure you've spoken to him about Sara's speech. That kind of cruelty is intolerable. It must stop. He needs to apologize, and there should be consequences."

Mrs. Dix stiffened. Her eyes narrowed, her shoulders squared.

She jabbed a finger in Rachael's direction.

"So you, Mrs. Williams," Mrs. Dix snapped, "are now an expert on child-rearing? To the best of my knowledge, you don't have any children. You and your high-minded ideas, you think you can tell me how to raise my son? Why, you—"

"Mrs. Dix," Rachael interrupted sharply, "if you don't talk to him, I will speak to Henry myself."

"If you do," Mrs. Dix hissed, "I'll bring it straight to Mr. Grey. We've all had enough of you handing out plants and calling it medicine. For all I know, you're trying to poison us! My sister's brother-in-law nearly died after eating mushrooms someone gave him. For all your talk of kindness and sweetness, I say you're just a plant fiend—"

At that moment, Hannah rounded the wagon, pulling Roy behind her. She had clearly heard the exchange. Roy shrank back, hiding behind her skirt, when he saw Mrs. Dix.

"Now, just a minute, Mrs. Dix," Hannah said firmly. "Mrs. Williams isn't the only one with concerns. I meant to speak with you, too. Roy told me that Henry dared Christopher to climb that tree, and when he fell, Henry ran off. He teases, and he's mean. Let's be honest; he needs to understand that what he's doing is wrong. I've punished Roy for not telling me the truth and for playing along. You should do the same."

Mrs. Dix sniffed, stiffened her spine, and lifted her chin. "Mrs. Evans, you're a mother, so I'll at least listen. But I've seen your child-rearing firsthand, and frankly, it's far too lenient. I've offered you advice, which you've ignored. And now you want to offer me advice? I'll talk to Henry, but I'm certain your boy was the instigator. My son told me Roy lies."

With that, she turned her back on them and marched away. The folded shirt she had been holding slipped from her hands and fell into the dust, forgotten.

Rachael clenched her jaw and fought the urge to stomp on it.

She turned to Hannah. "That woman's blind defense of her son is impossible. Maybe we should go to Mr. Grey."

Hannah nodded. "All right. We'll speak with him together. It's part of his job to ensure safety, and the children aren't safe around Henry. Mrs. Dix clearly won't do anything. I'm beginning to think the boy is a menace."

They huddled together, whispering a plan. They agreed the best time to approach Mr. Grey would be after supper, when he was most relaxed with his coffee.

Rachael asked Hannah to lead the conversation. Mr. Grey was already irritated with her for "wandering off" at noon to search for plants. True, she had proven herself with the white oak bark tea that helped everyone during the dysentery outbreak except Mrs. Dix, who continued sipping her dubious tonic. Mr. Grey had softened his stance some, but only so long as Rachael stayed close to camp. Still, his approval remained inconsistent.

That evening, they approached Mr. Grey while he leaned against a wheel hub, coffee in hand.

Hannah began. "Mr. Grey, I'm concerned about the children. Henry's behavior is escalating. He dared Christopher to climb that tree, and when Christopher fell, Henry ran. He continues to tease Sara about her speech. It's cruel. We've tried to speak with Mrs. Dix, but she won't discipline him. We're asking you to intervene for everyone's safety." She laid a hand gently on his arm. "Frankly, we need your help."

Rachael nodded, quietly reinforcing Hannah's words with steady eye contact.

Mr. Grey looked from one woman to the other. Then he shrugged. "I'm not the boy's father. I won't involve myself in trivial matters like children's squabbles. I've got a wagon train to lead. We're behind schedule, and you've seen how the pasturage is thinning. My sheep must reach Oregon before the snow sets in. That matters more than some child needing a firm hand."

Both women said "Oh" at once, exchanging a dismayed glance.

Rachael clenched her teeth to bite back the sharp words rising in her throat, but they burst out anyway. "But surely you see the danger, Henry's actions could seriously—"

Mr. Grey turned to face her, his jaw tight, his face flushed, running a hand roughly through his hair.

"I'll not be a nursemaid to children or women who can't sort out their problems with each other's children," Mr. Grey snapped. "Work it out yourselves. This matter is closed. Now leave me to the one time of day I usually can find some peace."

Rachael and Hannah exchanged a look and quickly withdrew.

"Well, Hannah," Rachael muttered, "that didn't go quite the way we'd hoped."

"Indeed not. I'm rather surprised by Mr. Grey's reaction."

"I'm not," Rachael said, exhaling hard. "But it still feels wrong. He always insists he's responsible for our safety and well-being. I guess I didn't really understand how limited he sees that responsibility. Still, maybe he's right. Maybe I was too angry to think clearly. What Henry did to Sara was cruel, but I suppose Grey's got bigger concerns. He's trying to get us across the mountains before the snow. I just wish he didn't have to be so gruff about it." She paused. "We'll have to find another way. Do you think we should talk to Camille?"

"That might help. But for now, I'm going to forbid Roy from playing with Henry anymore. Probably best we keep the other children away from him, too."

Rachael sighed and scanned the camp for Sara. The girl was nowhere in sight, but near the Godley wagon, Rachael spotted a small blue ribbon, the one tied to Sara's braid, lying forgotten in the dirt.

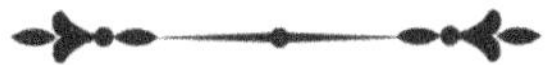

A week later, they were blessed with a rare, quiet hour before supper. Taking advantage, Rachael took Sara with her up the grassy hill that overlooked their camp. The air was warm, the scent of green grass thick in the breeze, and a gentle wind rustled the oak leaves.

Both were out of breath when they reached the top. They sat together on a large flat rock, Rachael handing Sara her pasteboard sketchbook and pencil.

"I'll let you choose today's subject," Rachael said, smiling. "Find something you'd like to draw."

While Sara wandered off to search, Rachael watched the camp below. Christopher and Roy played by the stream, tossing stones. His healing arm was still in a sling, but he was gaining strength. Rachael treasured this quiet time with Sara; it felt rare and precious. She had something important to say.

When Sara returned, her dress was muddied at the hem and her braid half-loose again; her mother would fuss about that, but her face lit up with excitement.

Hidden behind her back was a delicate flower. "Why, child," Rachael said, eyes widening, "an *Iris versicolor*! What a splendid choice."

She took the bloom gently in her hand. "See here?" she pointed. "This pattern on the sepal it's a kind of landing strip for bees. It guides them to the pollen hidden inside. The bee will then carry that pollen to another flower. It's how this lovely iris reproduces. The bees help make flower babies. Isn't that clever?"

Sara grinned shyly, eyes shining.

"Set it here between us," Rachael said, clearing a space on the rock. "Here's the hand lens. Look closely, and take your time."

Sara bent over her sketchbook, the flower in one hand, drawing with the other. Rachael worked beside her, carefully pulling the iris apart and sketching each anatomical feature—the spathes, petals, style branches, sepals, and ovaries. She intended to teach Sara the botanical names.

When she glanced up again, she saw that Sara had finished. The moment had come.

"Sara," she began gently, "I want to say something important. You only have to listen."

The girl nodded, her braid tumbling over her shoulder.

"I know you don't speak often. You're embarrassed. The others tease you. Even your stepfather calls it an affliction." Rachael's voice softened. "But it's not an affliction. It's a nuisance, yes. But it doesn't define who you are or what's in your heart."

Sara's eyes flicked downward, and her shoulders hunched.

"I've watched you. When you're calm and focused, like now, your words come more easily. It's when you're scared, or excited, or nervous that they stick, right?" She waited. "Just nod."

Sara nodded, eyes still on her lap.

"I don't care how you say things, child. What matters is what you say. You have things to say, important things. I'll always wait for you to finish. All right?"

A moment passed. Then softly, haltingly, Sara said, "Th-th-thank you, Rach…ael."

"You're welcome, dear heart," Rachael whispered.

She pulled Sara close and then nudged her gently.

"Now scoot in here," she said, "and let's look at our drawings together."

Ann should have been the one to have this conversation with her daughter, Rachael thought. But Ann was too preoccupied with her pregnancy and her unwavering belief that this child was God's unique gift to her and Robert.

Still, Rachael could sense that Sara understood her message that a person should be judged not by how they speak but by what they say. She remembered what it felt like at Sara's age, struggling to express her thoughts clearly. Her own words had often come out garbled as she tried to pronounce new and longer ones. Her classmates laughed at her, mocking her attempts at words like *profundity*, *profusion*, and *perspicacity*, not to mention the Latin names for plants.

But her father had always waited. Patient and attentive, he listened while they searched the woods for specimens. He'd never rushed her, never mocked her. He had gifted her patience, and she now vowed to pass that gift on to Sara. The girl was coming to mean more and more to her each day.

Rachael realized she was changing, softening in ways she had only just begun to understand.

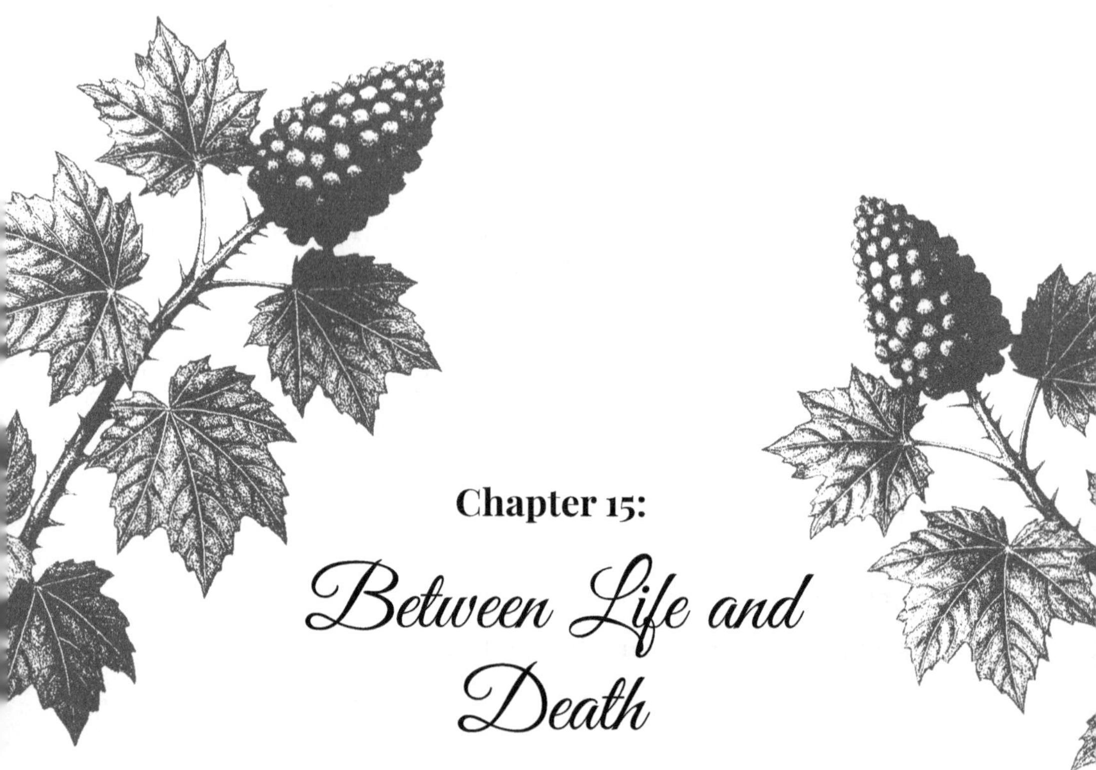

Chapter 15:

Between Life and Death

Most women and children walked during the day, but Camille's feet had become sore, so she took Rachael's place in the Godley wagon. That meant Rachael now rode in the springboard wagon with Mr. Grey.

"Mr. Grey, may I ask you a question?" she said hesitantly. "I know questions irritate you, but there's so much that's new to me out here. I'm curious. I want to understand what I'm seeing, names of places, birds, plants, the why of things."

The reins jingled in his hands as the wagon jolted over deep ruts left by those who had gone before. During their last ride, Mr. Grey had taught her how to read the tracks, to estimate how many wagons had passed and when. He'd mentioned learning that skill from the Indians he once traveled with. He'd also, she'd noticed, adopted their habit of answering in single, curt words or grunts when he was in a certain mood.

She hoped today wouldn't be one of those days.

"All your never-ending questions," he grumbled. "They get on my nerves. I'm neither your father nor your schoolteacher."

"Well, you're certainly not my father," Rachael muttered under her breath. Though looking at him, he might be old enough, she thought. She suppressed a smirk.

"But you are a sort of schoolmaster," she continued. "You've done this before. You know this trail. For me, everything is new—"

"Stop babbling," he cut in. "Just ask the question before I get too vexed to answer."

His voice was low and rough, like distant thunder. Rachael swallowed her frustration.

"All right," she said carefully. "What are those shallow depressions we keep passing on the trail? I must have seen at least ten yesterday. Are they... graves?"

Mr. Grey glanced at her, then back to the trail.

"Some are. Some are just old cookfires. The soil is alkaline. Fire leaves a mark. But yes, most likely, those are graves. Plenty of folks who were alive in the morning but dead by night. Especially when sickness went through, that's why I avoid other parties and insist on boiling all our water or going without."

Rachael turned to look out over the dry, pale soil and spotted another depression just off the trail. "I think... I'll choose to believe they were cookfires," she whispered.

"That's your choice," he said. "But don't let it fool you. This isn't a pleasure trip. It's hard living. For me, this is business. For you, it's a ride to your husband and that damn plant you're obsessed with. Hopefully, he's got the patience to answer all your endless questions."

Rachael blinked at him. She hadn't thought much about what came next, not really. Oregon still felt far away. She wondered suddenly if she would miss the trail, the rhythm of the days, the wild beauty, even the challenge.

"Yes," she said at last. "I suppose he can."

A small covey of birds crossed the trail ahead of them, their tiny crests bobbing as they ran in a tight line. Rachael bit her lip to keep from asking about them. After all, Mr. Grey wasn't her husband.

That night, Rachael awoke to the sound of someone softly calling her name.

Sitting up, she listened. There it was again. She reached for her shawl and felt around for her boots at the bottom of her blankets. She was glad, not for the first time, that she slept in her clothes. Nightgowns were long abandoned, too hard to wash, too easily torn. Her dress, though already in tatters, was easier.

Crawling to the tent flap, she tried not to wake the others.

Outside, Mr. Grey stood, shielding a lantern with one hand. He raised a finger to his lips and motioned for her to follow.

Without a word, she did.

Their destination became clear as they rounded the springboard wagon. Rachael could already hear the groans and cries of one of the young sheep tenders, Phillip.

"What is it?" she whispered.

"I'm not sure," Mr. Grey replied. "But if it is what I think it might be, we're all in trouble."

On the other side of the wagon, George Miller appeared with his arms full of blankets.

Mr. Grey knelt beside the boy and placed a hand on his forehead. "He's burning up with fever. Let's hope to God it's not cholera. Stand back."

Rachael stood frozen as Mr. Grey and George quickly spread the blankets on the ground near the boy's feet. Together, they dragged the boy, still groaning, from beneath the wagon and onto the clean bedding. A terrible smell filled the air: vomit, excrement, the sour stench of sickness. Phillip whimpered faintly, calling out for his mother in a voice like a kitten's mew.

Rachael clapped her hand over her mouth.

Wrapped now in blankets, the boy was being pulled farther from the wagons.

"What are you doing?" she asked. "Where are you taking him?"

"We need to move him away," Mr. Grey said. "If this is contagious, we can't risk exposure to the rest of the party. Don't touch anything. Go to the buckboard, get some sheeting, and tear it into strips. Here, take the lantern. Fill the bucket with water from the spring and soak the rags in it."

Rachael took the lantern and ran.

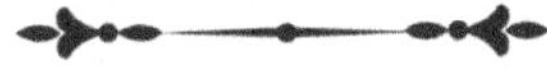

When she returned, she saw Mr. Grey kneeling over Phillip, his face lined with concern. George crouched beside him. The men whispered to each other in low voices she couldn't make out.

"I collected some feverfew the other day," Rachael said softly. "I could mix it with yarrow; he might be able to drink something. It might help."

Mr. Grey looked up at her.

"That's why I woke you," he said. "I was hoping you had something in your kit. That comfrey poultice you made for Christopher worked. Mari, one of the trappers' Indian wives, used comfrey to treat a man's broken wrist. I've seen plant potions work miracles. And if this is what I think it is, the boy will need one."

Rachael nodded and slipped away, lantern in hand.

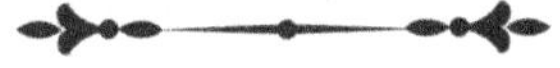

Back at camp, she stirred the fire under the cook wagon, added wood, and hung the kettle. Then she knelt beside the flames, unwrapped her medicine bundle, and laid out feverfew and yarrow on a flat rock. She crushed the leaves and flowers with another stone, her hands shaking slightly. Every second felt like an hour.

She watched the kettle. The water had to come to a full boil and stay there for five minutes. She held the lantern up, anxiously watching for bubbles. *Faster, faster,* she urged silently. She forced herself to count slowly to three hundred.

When it was ready, she ladled the boiling water into a tin cup for tea and poured the rest into her infusion bottle to steep.

Then, cradling the cup and lantern, she returned to where Phillip lay.

The boy's small form was still beneath the blankets. The soaked clothes she'd brought earlier lay scattered around him.

Mr. Grey and George Miller stood nearby, heads bowed.

Rachael approached and gently pulled back the blanket to see his face.

His skin had turned a dusky blue. His jaw was clenched, his eyes open but unseeing.

She covered her mouth.

She was too late.

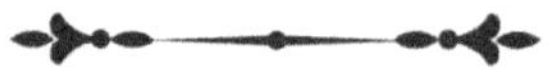

A second lantern came bobbing through the dark. Reverend Robert, still in his nightclothes, arrived breathless.

"Come quickly," he said. "Christopher and Sara are both burning with fever."

Rachael's heart dropped. Her stomach tightened, and Phillip's blue face flashed in her mind. She turned away, swallowing the urge to cry.

Clutching her medicine bag and the still-warm yarrow infusion, she followed Robert's swinging lantern toward the Godleys' wagon. She already knew: Ann must stay away. Exposure to this illness could put both her and the unborn child at risk.

At the wagon, Rachael ordered Robert to fetch Hannah. When he returned with Hannah and Tom, the three of them firmly insisted that Ann must leave.

Ann resisted at first but eventually agreed. As she climbed down from the wagon, she looked at Rachael with an expression so full of desperate trust that Rachael had to glance away.

Hannah and Rachael climbed into the wagon. The children lay curled on pallets near the front, their heads rolling weakly from side to side, low murmurs escaping dry lips. Their faces were pale, flushed only by fever. Neither was fully conscious.

Rachael crawled across the wagon bed toward Sara's pallet, Hannah close behind. She reached out, pressing her palm first to Sara's forehead, then Christopher's. She had never felt skin so dry, so burning hot.

She called for Tom, her voice firm despite the fear rising in her chest. "Bring clean clothes. Fetch cold water from the spring. And start boiling more. At the bottom of my bag is a packet of yarrow, which makes a strong infusion. We have to bring down their fevers."

Tom nodded and vanished into the darkness.

Rachael and Hannah exchanged a glance in the dim light of the lantern hanging on a hook in the wagon.

Hannah reached across to brush Christopher's forehead. "Oh, Rachael," she whispered. "He's burning up."

Rachael forced herself to take slow, measured breaths. "We can manage, Hannah. We have to."

"But—"

Tom returned with the bucket and the clean linens. "I've told Mr. Grey," he said. "He'll come when he's able. He's still dealing with Phillip."

"Bring two cups," Rachael instructed. "One for water. One for the tea. I don't know the exact dosage; we'll have to judge by feel."

From her medicine bag, Rachael pulled the small bottle of infusion she'd prepared earlier for Phillip. She poured a small measure into a cup and tried to get Sara to drink. Most of it dribbled out. Rachael gently pinched her nose, tilting her head back, trying to coax even a little down.

Sara gagged, but a few sips went down.

Hannah, watching closely, took the cup and mimicked the gesture with Christopher. Tom returned with a fresh bowl of the newly steeped infusion. It smelled earthy and pungent, like dirt and bitter flowers.

"Mr. Grey said he'd come by soon," Tom said. "He has to finish tending… to the boy."

Rachael nodded. She didn't need to hear Phillip's name. She turned back to the task at hand.

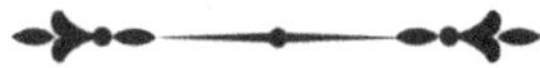

All through the night, the two women worked.

They bathed the children's faces and limbs in cold water, swapping out clothes as they warmed. They alternated water with the yarrow tea, counting minutes, gauging breathing, and watching for the smallest sign of change.

The hours stretched. The lantern dimmed.

And still, outside the wagon, they could hear Reverend Robert's loud, fervent prayers for his son's recovery. Not once did he mention Sara.

Rachael's mouth tightened. She wanted to throttle him. Instead, she caught Hannah's eye, and they shook their heads in silent understanding.

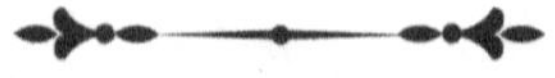

Finally, just before dawn, Hannah gave a cry: "He's sweating!"

Rachael rushed to Christopher's side. His forehead was damp. His breathing steadier.

Rachael nodded and motioned to Tom. "Tell Reverend Robert that Christopher is improving. He should tell Ann. She'll want to know."

They could hear Robert's booming voice soon after, his prayer of thanksgiving loud and clear.

But Sara was still limp. Her face had grown ghostly pale, almost translucent. Her sunken eyelids didn't flutter. Rachael placed a hand on her chest. Still breathing. But faint.

She turned for reassurance, only to find Hannah fast asleep, leaning against the side of the canvas.

Rachael wiped her eyes and turned back to Sara. She laid another cool cloth across the girl's forehead. Then, overcome by fatigue, she leaned back, just for a moment...

She awoke to a groan.

Sara.

She was soaked with sweat.

Rachael's throat closed. Tears spilled down her cheeks.

She leaned close and whispered into the girl's ear, "You're going to make it, sweetheart."

She kissed Sara's forehead, brushing back the wisps of hair sticking to her skin. Her nose still bore that soft scattering of freckles.

Rachael's body ached from hours hunched inside the wagon. She felt the needles of circulation returning to her legs. Gently, she smoothed Sara's hair again and crawled to the back of the wagon.

She needed air.

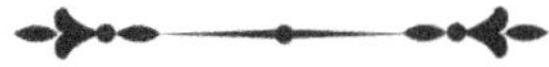

Dawn was breaking.

Mr. Grey appeared, his face gray and drawn. He came straight to the wagon and gestured silently for her to join him.

"How are they?" he asked.

"They're sleeping. No vomiting, no looseness of the bowels. Just a high fever. Christopher's sweating now. I think he's improving. Sara broke a sweat just minutes ago."

Mr. Grey rested his hand on his chin, rubbing it thoughtfully.

"I talked to the other boy, John, the one who tended sheep with Phillip," Mr. Grey said, his voice low. "I asked if he remembered Phillip drinking from the stream. He told me yes. Said he warned him not to, but Phillip replied he'd done it before and had come to no harm." He paused. "I had to ask if John drank it, too. He said no."

Rachael nodded slowly, feeling the heaviness in her limbs from the night spent tending to Sara and Christopher. She understood the weight of Mr. Grey's relief.

"Could the water have been the source of cholera?" she asked, her voice hushed. She remembered her own temptation at the last muddy stream when thirst had gnawed, and the sun had blistered her skin.

"I've spoken with the others," Mr. Grey replied. "No one besides the children has taken ill. I reminded everyone, again, not to drink anything that isn't boiled." He turned to her. "You're quite sure? The children didn't vomit? No looseness of the bowels?"

"Positive," Rachael confirmed. "Only fever. Hannah and I were with them all night."

He studied her for a long moment. His face was drawn with fatigue. She saw the exhaustion in the blue shadows beneath his eyes.

"Then perhaps we're spared," he said softly. "Thank God." He turned on his heel and walked away.

Rachael remained standing in the early morning light, watching his retreating figure. Then she tilted her face upward and sent a prayer skyward, one of deep gratitude. The children had likely suffered the grippe, not cholera. Still dangerous, still terrifying, but not the death sentence they'd feared.

Phillip's death haunted her. This journey was dangerous. But she also felt, grudgingly but undeniably, a growing admiration for Mr. Grey. His shoulders carried more than goods and livestock. She had seen something in his eyes last night, something painful. He was no stranger to loss.

She dropped to her knees beside the wagon and pressed her palms together. Sara had been so sick. Rachael had feared she wouldn't be able to save her. Perhaps, in the end, it had not been her hands but God's.

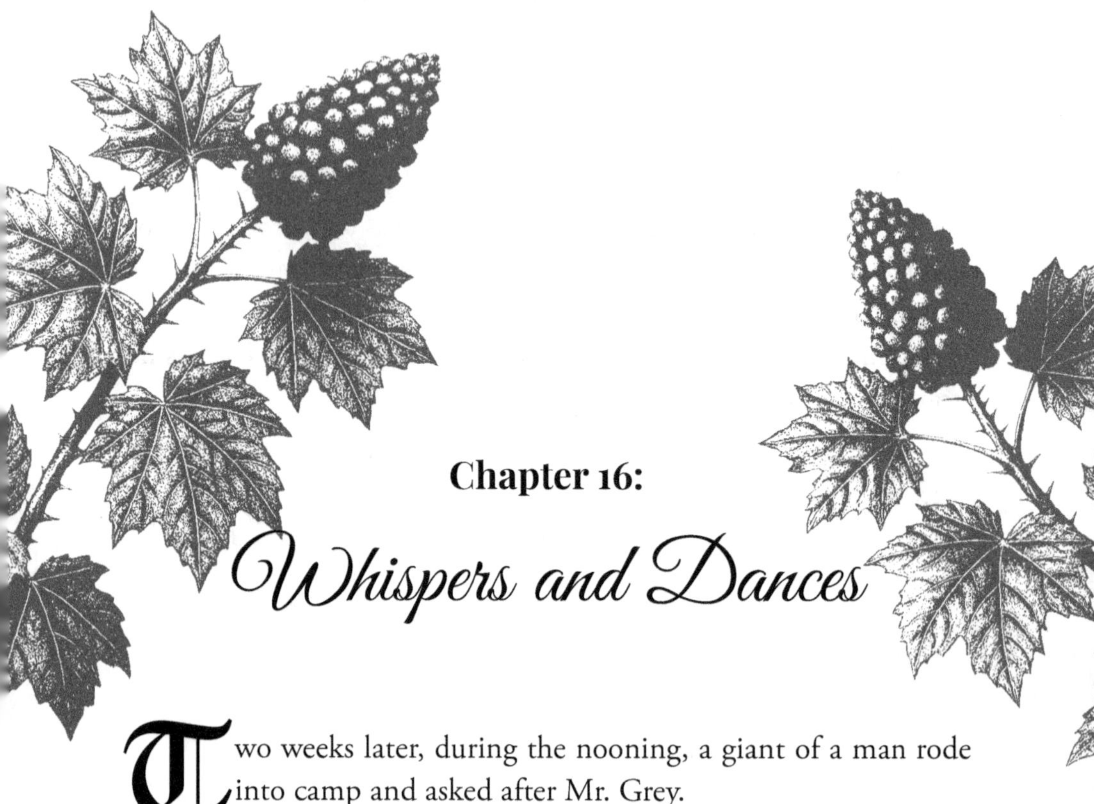

Chapter 16:
Whispers and Dances

Two weeks later, during the nooning, a giant of a man rode into camp and asked after Mr. Grey.

Rachael had just finished checking on Ann and was sitting near the cookfire when she heard the visitor ask Reverend Robert for the wagon master.

She turned to look.

Mr. Grey's face lit up with unmistakable pleasure. He strode across the clearing and gripped the man's hand in a powerful shake. Rachael watched, a little stunned. It was the first time she had seen him smile fully. The man beside him was enormous, bearded, with a mane of thick black hair and a booming laugh that echoed across the prairie.

They clapped each other on the shoulders and spoke in low tones. Rachael edged closer, curious, but couldn't catch the conversation. At last, the visitor mounted his horse and rode off in a cloud of dust.

Mr. Grey rang the triangle.

Everyone dropped what they were doing. Some men had rifles in hand, as the urgent clang had suggested danger.

"What is it?" Tom called out.

Mr. Grey looked down, drawing the toe of his boot across the dirt in slow arcs. The company held its breath.

"Charles, my friend, he and his party are just behind us," Mr. Grey began. "He came ahead to ask if we might share supper. Seems one of his men shot a couple of buffalo, and they've more than enough meat."

Murmurs of anticipation rippled through the group.

Mr. Grey paused dramatically.

"Of course, I told him no."

A loud groan rose from the crowd.

Then, his shoulders shaking, Mr. Grey looked up. A grin spread across his face.

"I'm kidding," he said. "We're going."

Laughter erupted. Someone whooped. Children began jumping up and down.

"I've kept us away from other wagon trains for a reason," he added more seriously. "Fear of contagion. But Sam tells me his group's been healthy for months. I trust him. We've traveled together before."

"Is his company large?" Rachael asked.

"Yes, Mrs. Williams. About twice our size. Women and children, too." He looked at her, the corner of his mouth twitching. "Though I suspect his women are more obedient than some in ours."

For once, Rachael didn't mind the jab. She smiled back, feeling, for a fleeting moment, like part of the company, not an outsider.

It was late July. The days had lengthened. The heat bore down with increasing force. They were still short of Independence Rock, a milestone most emigrants aimed to reach by the Fourth of July. That goal was long past.

The decision to walk a mile to the other camp for dinner was unanimous. The weather was clear. The moon would light their return. Someone had to stay and guard the wagons, and Mr. Miller volunteered immediately, his eye on the overtime pay. He cast a quick glance at Mr. Grey, who nodded silently.

Camille offered to bring him a plate of food, which he accepted with a shy smile.

Rachael, watching from the edge of the camp, noted the subtle exchange between them. There was something tender in the way Mr. Miller looked at Camille.

Camille was a sweet girl, hard-working, quiet, and possessed of a subtle mind, Rachael had come to appreciate in their brief exchanges. She often wondered how the girl kept her composure under Mrs. Dix's endless orders. Camille bore it with a quiet grace that, even after all these weeks, Rachael found remarkable. Had she been in Camille's place, she would have bitten her tongue clean through by now.

Rachael had intended to speak to Camille about her observations, about the way Mr. Miller watched her, the gentle, unmistakable glances, but she could never get Camille alone. Tonight would be her opportunity.

There was excitement in the air. The thought of fresh meat, new faces, and the exchange of trail gossip had the company nearly giddy. Hannah, Tom, and even Mrs. Dix immediately began rummaging through their baggage for small trade goods they might offer.

Before leaving, Hannah offered Rachael a hair clip to draw back her unruly curls and a delicate lace collar to adorn her faded lavender dress.

Rachael was touched. The collar gave the worn garment new life. She felt, if not beautiful, at least pleasantly presentable. Dignified. Transformed.

She slipped her medicine bag over her shoulder, hopeful that someone in the other company might know more about herbs, someone she could consult discreetly about Ann's delivery. The thought weighed on her. From all she had learned from Martha and her mother's book, it was not a matter of *if* there would be difficulty, but *when*.

Ann and Reverend Robert would stay behind. Ann was fatigued from the day's exertions and midway through her pregnancy. Rachael had agreed to accompany Christopher and Sara. Sara carried a large woven basket to bring food back for her parents.

As the group assembled, Rachael felt an odd flicker of pride. The women had tidied themselves, hair brushed, and clean aprons. The men wore their best shirts, faded but pressed. Mr. Grey, in his thin, oft-washed flannel, looked almost respectable. A worn leather bag hung from one shoulder. Tom, thanks to Hannah's attention, wore a clean blue shirt and a bright red handkerchief knotted neatly at his neck. Roy was dressed as always in his red cotton Henley, his pants held up with suspenders.

Then came Mrs. Dix.

Her robust figure was packed into a blue dress stretched tight across the back, and miraculously, she carried a parasol. Rachael blinked. *Where on earth had she hidden that?* Surely, Mr. Grey would have confiscated such a luxury during the wagon inspection. She must have smuggled it in. Rachael had to fight the urge to laugh aloud.

Camille emerged in a soft Delaine dress printed with tiny blue flowers. Daniel, her uncle, offered his arm and leaned in to whisper something that made her giggle.

Then came James, Mrs. Dix's prized rooster of a son. He strutted forth in black trousers and a too-tight lavender shirt, topped with a bolo tie. His belt buckle gleamed, and an oversized hat flopped over his forehead. Every few steps, he pushed it back. He had polished his boots to a military shine. Rachael bit the inside of her cheek to suppress her laughter and turned away.

Sara linked arms with Rachael, and Christopher took her hand. She glanced at his arm; it had healed well. After all the hardships they'd endured, tonight felt different. There was no dust in their mouths, no fire to tend, no crying child to soothe. Just the promise of meat and music.

She smiled, squeezed Christopher's hand, and gave Sara's arm a light squeeze. *Tonight, we are happy. Nothing can go wrong.*

In the distance, the squeal of a fiddle floated on the breeze. The basalt cliffs, dark chocolate against the pale dusk, cast long shadows across the prairie. The familiar scent of sage filled the air.

They reached the other wagon train and paused.

It was a chaos of camps, wagons in clusters, tents flapping gently, children running wildly between them in a game of tag. Laughter rose like birdsong. A wave of warmth passed through Rachael. This was what the community could feel like.

Christopher tugged at her hand. "Can we go play?"

"Soon," Rachael said. "Let's find where we'll meet first. I don't want to lose you in this crowd."

They found Hannah and gestured toward the boys.

"Think it's safe?" Rachael asked.

"With all these grown-ups? I doubt they'll find much mischief," Hannah replied. She pointed to a painted wagon with *California or Bust* scrawled in red letters. "We'll meet back here."

Roy and Christopher dashed off, their excitement palpable. Henry sprinted after them. Rachael and Hannah exchanged a hopeful glance. *Even Henry will behave,* Rachael thought. *Surely, the company of strangers will keep him in line.*

After everything, the death of young Phillip and the children's brush with fever, this gathering felt like a reprieve. A pause in the tension that had gripped them for weeks.

Mr. Grey led the procession, Mrs. Dix and Daniel trailing behind. Daniel still had Camille's arm and was murmuring something that made her blush.

Rachael raised an eyebrow. *Mr. Miller's not the only one watching her,* she thought.

James had already wandered off in search of boys his age, and the group agreed they would meet at the end of the evening and return to their own train together.

When they reached the fire, Rachael watched Mr. Samuel, Mr. Grey's friend, as the two men repeatedly slapped each other's backs in an exuberant greeting. Mr. Grey pulled a large bottle from his satchel. Sam gave a cheer and raised his tin cup. Mr. Grey poured a generous measure, then filled his own. The two men clinked their cups, metal ringing on metal, then raised them in a familiar salute.

"Here's to us," Sam declared. "Who would've thought we'd meet again on this damn old trail? Now, William, tell your company this fire is theirs for the night, and the food will be up soon. There's cold water to drink for your lot, but you and I, well, we'll enjoy something a bit warmer, eh?"

He turned and hollered, "Frank, drag up a few more barrels for the ladies!"

"Come, William," Sam added, gesturing toward the fire, "talk to me. Tell me how it goes with you and yours."

Rachael and Sara settled on barrels near the back, where they could watch without being too conspicuous. Sara was unlikely to speak among strangers, so Rachael chattered for both of them.

"Sara, what do you think? It's been months since we were in a crowd. Feels strange, doesn't it? But exciting, too."

She nodded toward the fire. "Look there, a woman's pulling a haunch of meat from the spit. And those... are those potatoes? Potatoes and meat!" Rachael gave an exaggerated sigh. "What a treat!"

Sara giggled at the accidental rhyme.

Soon, platters were passed, succulent slices of buffalo, golden potatoes, and biscuits stacked high. Tin plates and real utensils accompanied the feast. Rachael's heart nearly leaped from her chest. The comparison to their usual meal, beans, bacon, and biscuits eaten from battered cups, was almost comical. Even bacon didn't count as meat when you saw buffalo carved fresh from the bone.

The firelight flickered. A fiddler took up a tune, and laughter rose as couples twirled in a blur of calico and boots. The music was bright and infectious. Applause followed the dance, and the fiddler launched into another.

Out of nowhere, a boy of fifteen approached. He tipped his hat politely and asked where Sara's father was. He wished to ask permission to dance with her.

Rachael smiled. "Her father's not here," she said, "but I'm her chaperone. If she agrees, I give my consent."

Sara's eyes went wide. She shook her head frantically.

"Oh, go on, sweetie," Rachael said gently. "You don't have to know how to dance. Just let your feet follow the music."

The boy offered his hand, his green eyes sparkling. Sara hesitated only a second before placing her hand in his. He grinned and spun her into the crowd.

Rachael watched with delight, her foot tapping along with the beat. Sara grinned at her from the center of the dance. Rachael's heart swelled with joy and pride.

A shadow fell over her.

"Well, Mrs. Williams," came a familiar voice, "from the way your foot is thumping, I'd say you wouldn't mind a dance yourself."

She looked up.

Mr. Grey stood before her, hand outstretched. He had even shaved, she realized. His old flannel shirt had been scrubbed so thoroughly it looked nearly sheer. In spite of herself, she reached up and adjusted the tortoiseshell clip Hannah had lent her. She touched the lace collar.

"Oh, come now," he coaxed, "I don't bite. Not tonight, anyway. Let's just be friends, just for now."

He took her hand and led her toward the dancers. The fiddler struck up a reel. Mr. Grey's arm circled her waist, and they fell into step, joining the line.

He was light on his feet, surprisingly so, and she let herself relax. They swung around, slapped hands, and do-si-doed between clapping spectators. She risked a glance at him and found him grinning. *Why was he always like this?*

She caught herself smiling back.

The dance ended in laughter and applause. Breathing hard, flushed with warmth, Mr. Grey escorted her back to her barrel seat.

Sara returned, glowing with excitement.

"Wh-why, that was wwond-erful," she said breathlessly.

Rachael reached out and squeezed her hand.

"Yes, dear heart," she said softly. "It was wonderful indeed."

Rachael still felt a flush of excitement from the dancing. Her body tingled with the residual rhythm, her cheeks warm, her heart light. It had been so long since she had felt so free, so alive. And Mr. Grey, of all people, had seemed almost like a different man. He had grinned back at her, not with his usual irony, but with a softness, an ease.

She sensed a flicker of disappointment that the music had ended. For that brief time, they'd shared something she hadn't expected: comfort and a curious steadiness between them. Part of her wished the evening might stretch on endlessly. But no. She reminded herself not to be foolish. He was a married man. She had her purpose, her work, her plants, and her promise to Martha. A single dance, however pleasant, changed nothing.

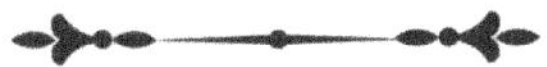

The moon shone silver on the trail as their company made the one-mile return to their own camp, spirits still high. Voices rang out into the night, off-key but enthusiastic:

"Camptown ladies sing this song… do-dah, do-dah!"

Laughter bounced between the wagon ruts. Rachael and Sara walked with their arms around each other's waists. From time to time, Rachael gave a skipping hop to keep their steps in rhythm, and Sara followed suit, giggling with glee.

Ahead, Mr. Grey, clearly a bit buoyed by the evening's whiskey, sang louder than anyone, his baritone voice rough but melodic.

Christopher, worn out from the evening's excitement, rode on his shoulders, his arms draped limply over Mr. Grey's forehead.

Rachael grinned. If only every evening could be like this—no illness, no arguments, no dangers, just community and lightness. For the first time, she thought, *perhaps we have become a real company after all.*

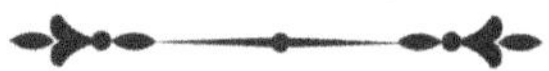

Back at camp, the routine settled in. Rachael helped Sara tuck Christopher into his bed, then placed the leftover food from the dinner into the Godleys' tucker box. She glanced once toward the fire and saw Camille sitting beside Mr. Miller. He was eating from a tin plate, and she leaned slightly toward him, speaking softly.

Rachael smiled. *Good,* she thought. *Very good.*

She turned to retire, but just as she was about to slip into her tent, a voice pierced the night.

"Excuse me, Mrs. Williams," came a sharp whisper.

Rachael turned. Mrs. Dix stood behind her, arms crossed, her face stiff with meaning.

"I want to speak with you. In private. There's something you ought to know."

Rachael's breath caught.

"A Mrs. Wolfberry from Geneva recognized you at the dance. She told me things. Things I'm sure you already know quite well."

Rachael blinked. *Mrs. Wolfberry?* That name stirred no immediate memory. Geneva was large enough, but gossip traveled fast.

"I don't recall a woman by that name," Rachael said slowly. "I can't imagine what she might have said."

Mrs. Dix narrowed her eyes, her tone clipped. She lifted her left hand and pointed deliberately to her wedding ring.

"She knew all about you. And I think you know what I'm referring to."

Rachael's face warmed. Her pulse thundered in her ears.

"For now," Mrs. Dix continued, "I will keep what I heard to myself. But I trust you understand me."

She turned on her heel and disappeared behind her wagon.

Rachael stood motionless for a moment, the air suddenly colder. Then she crawled into her tent, her heart hammering in her chest.

Her mind reeled. *Who was this woman? What had she said? What did Mrs. Dix now think she knew?* And, perhaps most disturbingly, *what would she do with it?*

It was so like Mrs. Dix to have sniffed out trouble in a place of joy. And so bitterly ironic that someone from Geneva, of all places, would appear now, just when Rachael had begun to feel she belonged here.

She lay down and pulled the blanket over her chest, but she knew it would be a long, sleepless night.

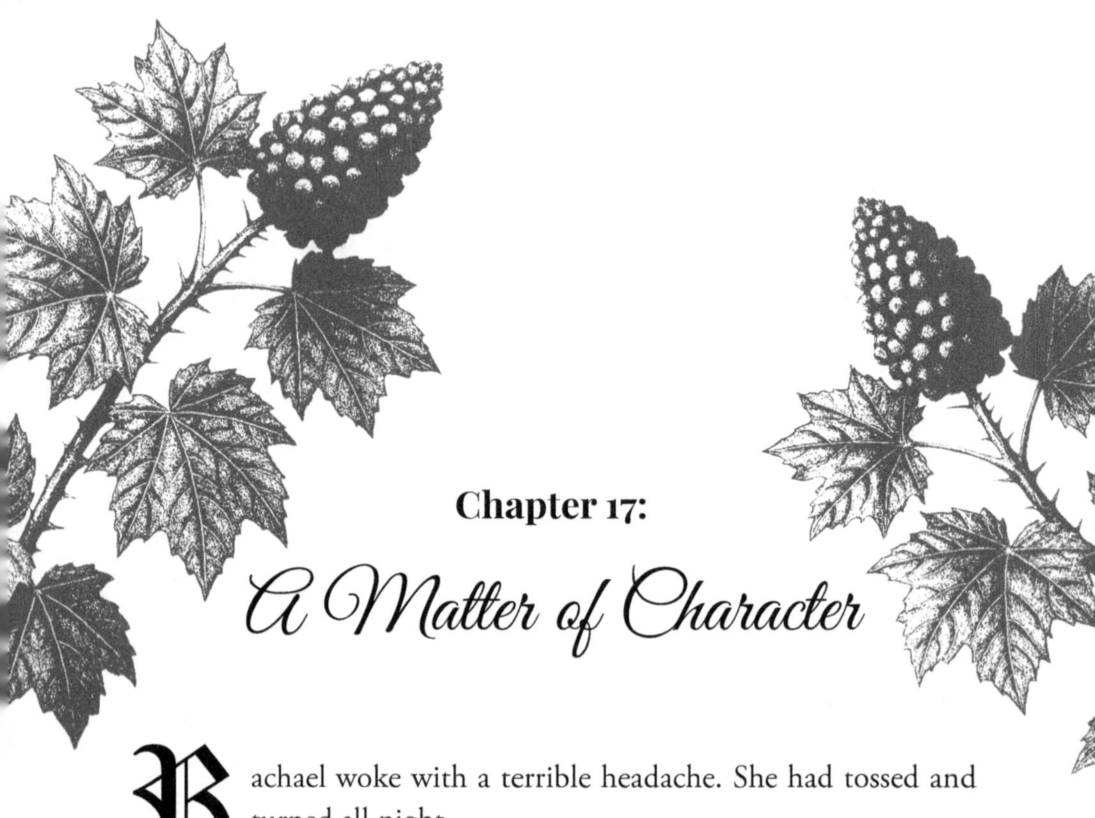

Chapter 17:

A Matter of Character

Rachael woke with a terrible headache. She had tossed and turned all night.

There was little doubt now that what Mrs. Dix had said was a threat. And she wasn't sure what to do about it. Surely, Mrs. Dix would tell Reverend Robert. And worse, Mr. Grey.

After all this time, Rachael still couldn't predict how either man might respond. She'd seen Mr. Grey dismiss Cookie without hesitation.

Would he be compelled to do the same to me?

She had, after all, lied.

Yes, she had kept her bargain with Ann and the Reverend. She had managed the children, tended to Ann as lovingly as Ann would allow, and used her knowledge of herbs to help the company on more than one occasion. But would that be enough to justify her presence?

Could she really expect them to let me stay, knowing I was a single woman who had lied about being married? The next outpost was still weeks away.

Would Mr. Grey wait until then? Or would he simply turn me over to another company? And would any of them take me, an unwed woman, traveling alone?

Her thoughts tangled.

Should I confess before Mrs. Dix did?

But it was already time for breakfast. The camp was stirring. Mr. Grey was bent over the fire. The sharp scent of coffee drifted in the morning air.

Last night, she had felt content. Today, despair gripped her. She wanted to run and hide. But no, she would wait. She would see what Mrs. Dix did next.

Could she even claim that Mrs. Wolfberry was mistaken? Of course not.

Over the following days, Rachael could barely concentrate. She tried not to watch Mrs. Dix but failed. Her shoulders were constantly set in a rigid tension, bracing for what might come. She knew Mrs. Dix could feel her eyes on her. More than once, the woman turned, raised her eyebrows, and smiled in a way that made Rachael blush.

Mrs. Dix held the power now, and she knew it.

A week after the feast, Rachael decided she couldn't stand it any longer. She would tell Mr. Grey herself. Better he hear it from her than from that woman.

But as if she'd read Rachael's mind, Mrs. Dix acted first.

Rachael looked up from washing her face in the stream and saw Mrs. Dix crossing camp toward Mr. Grey.

Rachael froze, face cloth falling from her hands into the creek.

Mrs. Dix touched Mr. Grey's arm, drawing him away from the others. She bent her head toward him, speaking in a low voice.

Once, she turned and glanced at Rachael.

Rachael's stomach dropped. She felt the blood drain from her face.

The two turned slightly, and now she could see Mrs. Dix's finger-wagging, her voice animated. Mr. Grey's eyes flicked in her direction briefly. Then he looked away.

He said something to Mrs. Dix, then returned to the fire.

Mrs. Dix, clearly satisfied, caught Rachael's gaze and pointed smugly at the fourth finger of her own left hand. Then she disappeared behind her wagon.

So that was it.

Rachael's fate was sealed.

He knew now. He knew she was a liar. And worse, she cared that he knew. Why did his opinion matter so much to her?

But it did.

A slow dread filled her chest. Still, she straightened her shoulders. She would speak to him. Maybe, just maybe, if he heard the truth from her, he would understand.

She spotted him by the wagons, just finishing his coffee. He was looking at her with an unreadable expression.

Her heart pounded. Her feet carried her forward.

"Mr. Grey, may I speak with you for a moment? Perhaps… alone?"

"Why certainly, Mrs. Williams. I'd like to speak with you as well."

There it was, Mrs. Williams. Was there sarcasm in the way he said it? She couldn't tell.

They moved away from the others, who were still sipping their coffee, blissfully unaware of the storm inside her. Her stomach churned. She had no appetite.

"Mr. Grey, I…" she began. Then stopped. She couldn't meet his eyes.

"Mrs. Williams," he said calmly, "Mrs. Dix and I just had a fascinating conversation. She told me—"

"Mr. Grey, I—"

"She said she met a woman at the feast last week. A Mrs. Wolfberry. Someone from your hometown. According to her, this woman informed Mrs. Dix that you had lied. That you are not married."

Rachael's eyes dropped to the dust. She couldn't look up. She couldn't bear to see the judgment in his face.

"I told her," he continued, "that I didn't believe her."

Her head snapped up.

"I've come to know you over these past months," he said. "You're headstrong. Opinionated. Frequently difficult. But I've never found any reason to believe you would lie. It's simply not in your character."

He shrugged slightly.

"And truth be told, I've already noticed that Mrs. Dix doesn't like you. I don't quite understand it. It seems to be a woman's thing. So I dismissed the whole idea."

Rachael stared at him. Wide-eyed. Breath caught.

She *wanted* to tell him the truth. She needed to.

"Mr. Grey, I—"

He placed a hand gently on her shoulder and leaned in.

"You've become a valuable member of this company. I appreciate most of what you've done for us, especially your interest in plant medicine. So, I consider the matter closed."

He looked her squarely in the eye.

"We'll speak no more of it."

She was frozen. Unable to breathe.

"Now," he said more briskly, straightening, "do you think you could, for once, be ready to leave on time and not go gallivanting after one of your precious plant specimens?"

"Yes, Mr. Grey," she replied, lifting her chin. Then, with emotion catching in her throat, she added,

"But, sir… I must say, I'm rarely late."

She turned quickly, back straight, and walked away, resisting the urge to run.

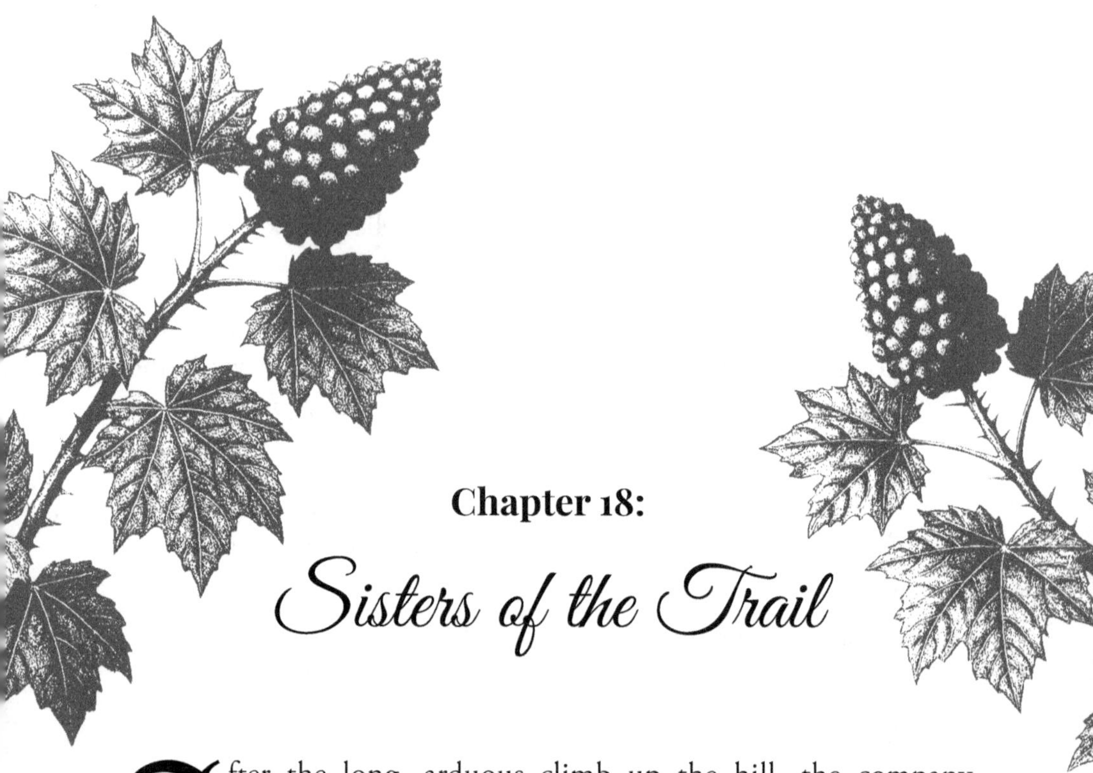

Chapter 18:
Sisters of the Trail

After the long, arduous climb up the hill, the company members were visibly relieved when Mr. Grey announced they would soon be able to see the Blue Mountains, the first major mountain range to cross. The Cascades would follow.

Rachael shaded her eyes with her hand, scanning the horizon. There, faint in the distance, rose the blue-tinged peaks veiled in shifting clouds. Despite the mild reassurance that many had crossed these mountains before her, a shiver ran through her. The peaks, massive and distant, seemed almost alive, like an army advancing steadily, muttering warnings only she could hear.

She drew her shawl tighter around her shoulders.

As it was the Sabbath, Mr. Grey declared a day of rest once the wagons had crested the infamous hill. At the summit was a small settlement that earned its keep by supplying worn-out travelers. A corral held mules and oxen; many of the party's animals were nearly spent. Mr. Grey had warned from the outset that some stock wouldn't survive the entire journey. Most travelers had saved money to replace what they could.

Mr. Grey seemed pleased to reunite with an old acquaintance: a French trapper with whom he'd briefly traveled on his first trip west. The man ran the small trading post with his Native wife. Their children were playing in the dirt with Christopher, Roy, and Henry, hitting rocks with sticks in a makeshift game. Henry, predictably, was cheating, moving his stone when the others weren't watching. That boy vexed Rachael to no end.

Ann, now heavily pregnant, rested on the trading post's porch in a creaky rocking chair, her hands cradling her belly. Her time was close.

Rachael imagined Mr. Miller and the drover boys must be grateful for the sheep pen, a rare break from herding. Everyone looked forward to a proper meal. Mr. Grey had promised coffee with sugar and perhaps some game if the trapper could spare any. Rachael's mouth watered at the thought of something sweet, even a single piece of fruit.

With Sara attending to her mother and Christopher absorbed in play, Rachael wandered behind the post. She discovered a building where bunches of herbs hung from the rafters. Some she recognized, but others were unfamiliar. She longed to speak with the trapper's wife. Perhaps sign language would help; she recalled the basics she and Sara had practiced at Fort Laramie. That playful memory returned: the joke they had played on Lieutenant Randall. It felt like a lifetime ago.

Rounding the shed, she saw the Native woman, stooped, weathered, and graceful, approach Ann's chair. The woman made a simple hand sign: one for "baby," another for "soon."

Then, out of nowhere, Mrs. Dix came barreling toward them, hands flailing.

"Get away from her, you heathen! Leave her alone. She doesn't need your kind of filth around, especially not now. Shoo! Get away from her!"

To Rachael's horror, Mrs. Dix shoved the woman aside. Ann started to speak, but pain flickered across her face, deepening into a grimace.

Rachael rushed forward. The Native woman slipped silently inside the trading post.

"Ann, what is it?"

Ann's complexion had gone pale, her features tight. A contraction rolled visibly through her belly.

"Come, Ann, let's find a place for you to lie down. Mrs. Dix, for heaven's sake, help me get her back to her wagon."

"It's that filthy woman's doing," Mrs. Dix spat. "She tried to give her something. I knew she was in trouble. Filthy savage!"

"Shush, Mrs. Dix. Just help me."

Rachael seethed. *Why was she so focused on the woman when Ann was clearly in pain? Couldn't she see the contraction? Would this be the kind of help Mrs. Dix offered during a birth?* Her shoulders tensed with doubt.

Later, with Ann resting and sipping chamomile tea under Camille's watch and no more contractions for the moment, Rachael returned to the trading post.

She needed to find the trapper's wife.

The interior was dusty and dim, stacked with hides, furs, tin pots, and dry goods. Toward the back, the trapper was unstringing a line of rabbits. Rachael asked where his wife was. He gave her a long, assessing look.

"You mean Mari?" he asked, then nodded toward a rear building with a tilt of his chin.

Rachael blinked. *Mari. Could this be the same woman Mr. Grey had once described? The healer?* She had no idea whether that was a typical name, but she knew, with certainty, she needed to speak with her now.

She had brought her medicine bag, hoping to trade knowledge or supplies.

Inside the drying shed, the smell of herbs wrapped around her like an embrace—pungent, sharp, earthy. She spotted plants she knew: boneset, comfrey, feverfew, yarrow, grouped in unfamiliar ways. Others she had never seen before.

The small black-haired woman at the back of the room was working, stripping leaves from a plant. Rachael coughed softly to announce her presence. The woman turned, and Rachael made the greeting sign. She smiled and returned the gesture.

Rachael motioned around the room, pointing to the neatly arranged herbs, then raised both fists at her sides, bringing them down and up again in front of her eyes, the sign for *many*. The woman nodded.

Rachael opened her bag to show her own bundles. Mari made the sign over her stomach for *pregnancy*, followed by a friend, and then *soon*.

Rachael nodded. *How I wish I knew more of the language,* she thought. But this, at least, was something. Mr. Grey had mentioned a woman with a talent for healing more than once. Surely, this was her. All around were herbs, roots, and jars filled with unfamiliar contents. Finding her here at this moment felt almost miraculous.

Rachael tried to remember the sign for *blood* but couldn't. Frustrated, she pointed to a small scratch on her forearm and rubbed it against the wooden table until it bled again.

The woman tilted her head with a curious expression as Rachael held up the trickling wound. Rachael made the *pregnancy* sign again, pointed to the blood, and then signed *much*.

The woman nodded and crossed the room, selecting a root from the drying rack and gathering other plants, including yarrow. As she returned to the table, Rachael leaned in to examine the root. She recognized it. *Shepherd's Purse,* she thought. It was listed in Martha's mother's book.

Through signs and pantomime, Mari explained she was giving Rachael two bundles: one for stopping bleeding and one for after childbirth. She wrapped them in cloth and tied each with rawhide strips in distinct knots so they could be told apart. Then, she indicated that both needed to be steeped in hot water as infusions.

Rachael opened her satchel again and placed her own modest collection on the table, offering something in trade. But to her surprise, Mari shook her head and gently pressed the bundles into Rachael's hands. Then she signed: *Help a pregnant friend.* She drew a circle with her finger, pointed to Rachael, then back to herself.

Rachael nodded deeply. "All women sisters," she said aloud, inclining her head in thanks. Mari returned to her work, and Rachael stepped away, quietly thanking the French trapper before heading out into the fading light.

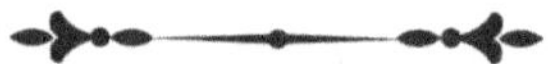

As evening descended, it was evident that the birth was imminent.

Mrs. Dix had arrived with her bottle of Elixir, insisting it would help Ann feel better. But after one spoonful, Ann vomited violently, her eyes bulging in distress. Rachael wanted to smash the bottle. The idea of giving Ann anything alcohol-laced in her condition was maddening.

Ann was growing more and more uncomfortable. She moaned and clutched at the quilt; her face was slick with sweat and drawn in pain. The contractions were speeding up.

It was time to inform Mr. Grey. *Could I send Mrs. Dix instead and hide her 'medicine' while I'm at it?* It was unlikely she could convince him to delay the trip, but Rachael would have to try. She had promised Martha that she would care for Ann, and she meant to keep that promise.

Leaving Mrs. Dix rubbing Ann's back and murmuring reassurances about God's hand, Rachael cast a glance at the wagon floor. There it was. The bottle. She told Mrs. Dix she would be gone just a moment, slipped the bottle into her skirt folds, climbed down, and hurled it into the thick coyote bushes.

We have to stop for a few days, she thought. *Ann needs time to recover; this isn't just another inconvenience on the trail.*

In most cases, wagon parties didn't delay births, but Ann's history demanded an exception. Surely, Mr. Grey, who had a wife and children waiting in Oregon, would understand.

She breathed a sigh of relief, thinking of the Indian healer nearby. If complications arose, help was at hand.

Outside the Godley wagon, Reverend Robert paced. The children had already been sent to stay with Hannah and Tom. Rachael would go now, firmly, and insist that the company remain until Ann had safely delivered and recovered.

They could make up the time later. It was worth it.

It had to be.

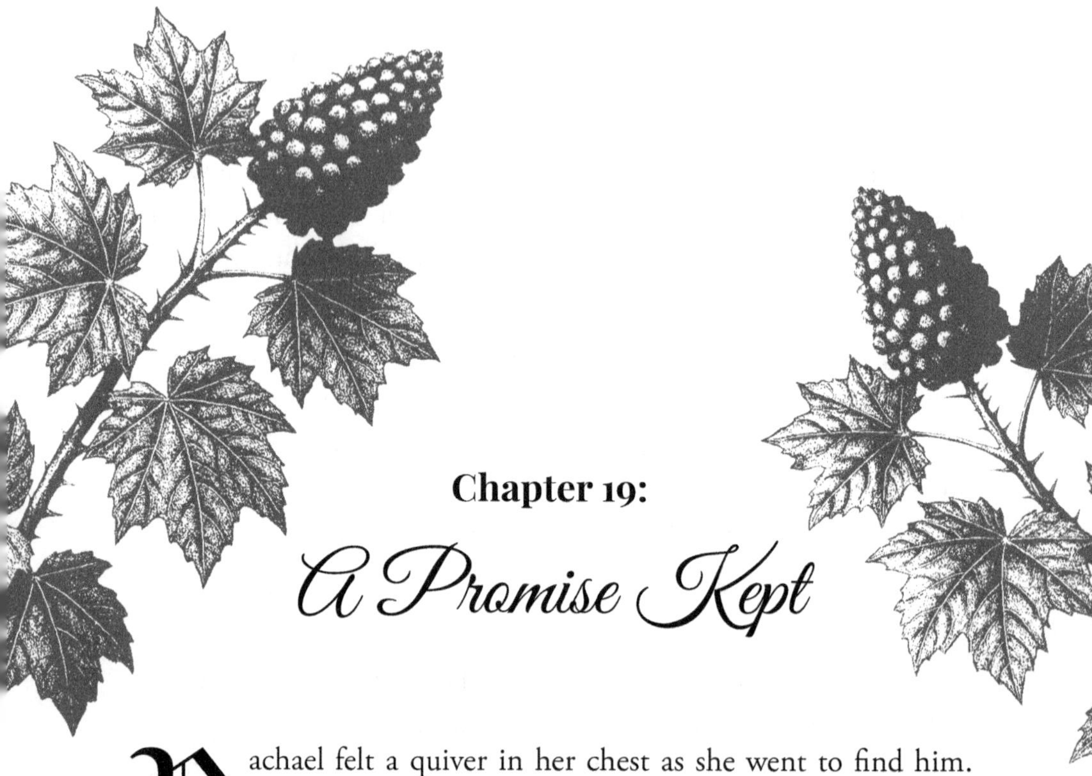

Chapter 19:

A Promise Kept

Rachael felt a quiver in her chest as she went to find him. She knew Mr. Grey hated being challenged, and decisions for the company were not hers to make, but none of that mattered now. Not with the baby coming.

As she suspected, he was in conversation with the French trapper at the post. She approached and stood beside him.

"So, you suspect there's snow coming to the pass soon?" Grey asked.

"Mr. Grey," Rachael began—

He ignored her.

"Yes, I do," said the trapper. "All signs indicate a coming storm."

"Then we'll leave at first light. Can't risk my sheep. We're already behind. It's a matter of business."

Rachael placed a hand on his arm. "That's not possible."

Grey turned, stone-faced. "This does not concern you, Mrs. Williams." He turned back to the trapper.

"Indeed, it does," she said firmly. "Ann's baby is coming. She's already in labor." She touched his arm again. "She can't continue in the morning, not so soon after giving birth. There's a real danger of hemorrhage. Even if the delivery goes well, the wagon jolting could trigger bleeding. Mari is here. She can help me if there's a problem."

"I disagree," he said flatly. "Every birth is different. You forget I've seen three babies born safely." He pulled his arm away.

"But you must understand," Rachael said, her voice rising, "Ann is weak. Even Mrs. Dix agrees. Surely—"

"You're interfering again, Mrs. Williams. Do not dictate to me. You've no idea how dangerous snow in the mountains can be. We could be trapped for days in freezing temperatures. I'm responsible for the lives of this company."

Rachael took a breath. His argument wasn't wrong. Staying might endanger everyone. But she knew he was also overly cautious, and this time, it might cost Ann her life. She tried a new approach.

"But surely, when your wife had her children—"

"You do not know anything about my wife," he snapped.

"But, Mr. Grey—"

His whole frame tightened, neck flushed, eyes narrowed. "I'm beginning to pity this so-called husband of yours, having to live with a shrew who thinks she knows best. He must not be much of a man."

Heat rushed to her face. Her arms dropped stiffly to her sides, fists clenched. She exploded.

"At least he would care more about people than sheep. I pity your poor wife. It seems you care more about your precious animals than any woman in your care. She—"

She stopped. Her hand covered her mouth. She'd gone too far.

He turned away from her, but not before she caught the flicker of pain in his eyes. She didn't care. Not now.

She steadied her voice. "I—"

He faced her again, eyes hard. "Mrs. Williams, I'll give Ann tonight and one day. No more. I'll send the sheep ahead this morning with Miller, the drovers, and James. If we're caught in the snow, it will be on your head."

"And you don't understand how dangerous this birth could be."

"I understand more than you know. Much more."

For some reason, she couldn't meet his eyes.

"Then it's settled. I'll send word when the baby is born."

"Do that."

She turned and walked away, legs shaking, but she had won. And she was right. She would keep the promise she made to Martha. She hurried to the wagon where Mrs. Dix sat beside Ann, overseeing her confinement.

Ann's belly was taut, rippling with the strain of her body trying to bring forth the child. It quickly became clear she was exhausted. According to Martha's mother's book, she should be pushing now, but Ann lay pale and wordless, spent.

Mrs. Dix's eyes darted wildly. She began praying aloud, her voice thick and urgent, her words tumbling over each other.

Ann's body still contracted, her stomach rock hard, but she was fading. The wagon flap opened, and Camille's face appeared, cast in the flickering glow of a lantern.

"How is she?" Camille asked, her eyes wide and luminous.

Rachael felt a wave of relief. Maybe Camille could help calm her aunt, who was growing increasingly unhelpful.

Rachael didn't know what else to do. She'd followed everything suggested in the book, but the baby had not progressed. Ann was weakening by the minute. Mrs. Dix, despite her claimed experience, offered no assistance, only frantic prayers, her wrinkled hands clutched tightly together.

It was maddening. Prayer wasn't enough.

Rachael leaned close to Camille. "Go. Go to the post. Bring Mari."

Camille hesitated, uncertain. But then she took another look at Ann and nodded, slipping out through the wagon flap.

At once, Mrs. Dix erupted. "You cannot, will not, let that heathen woman touch this poor girl! It's unnatural! I simply won't allow it.

Where is my elixir? Perhaps that will help. I forbid it, I tell you, I forbid it!"

She leaned protectively over the near-unconscious Ann as if to shield her from Rachael's decision.

Rachael's eyes turned steely as she steadied herself and glared directly at Mrs. Dix.

"You will permit it. Something is wrong. Can you help Ann? It seems not. I believe Mari can. She's a known healer. If you can't stand to see her help Ann, then you can, and should, leave Mrs. Dix. In fact, I insist on it."

She pulled Mrs. Dix's arms away from Ann.

"Please leave. Now."

Mrs. Dix sputtered, her face blotched crimson with rage.

"Do you even know that savage's name? I'm not surprised. If anything happens to Ann, I'll see you gone from this wagon train. I'll go to Robert and Mr. Grey this instant and tell them that you plan to allow… allow—"

"You must do what you believe is right, Mrs. Dix," Rachael said quietly. "And so must I. Now, please, leave."

When Mrs. Dix finally stormed out, Rachael was alone with Ann. She pressed a cool cloth to her friend's forehead, praying silently for help. Ann's stomach was taut and convulsing, but she wasn't pushing.

Rachael had never attended a birth. Her only guide was the book's advice: *bear down and force the baby out.* But how could she encourage that?

"Ann," she said gently, wiping the perspiration from her brow, "I've sent for help. Everything is going to be all right."

Relief flooded her when the canvas parted, and she heard the click of the beads on Mari's tunic as she stepped inside.

Mari didn't hesitate. She reached into her sack, removed a small vial, and held it to Ann's lips. Then she placed her hands on Ann's distended belly and began to massage it, gently at first, then more firmly.

Ann's eyes flew open in surprise. Mari held her gaze, breathing with her in and out, in and out. She exaggerated the motion, holding her breath, lifting her body, and pushing. Ann began to imitate her.

Still, the baby didn't move.

To Rachael's horror, Mari reached into Ann's womb. She felt for the baby's head with steady hands.

"Ah," she said, nodding.

Then, with firm yet careful pressure, Mari said something in her native tongue. She gestured for Rachael to help.

"It will hurt," she warned. "Help the child. Breathe this."

Mari began panting like a dog.

The next contraction came. Ann screamed.

Mari withdrew her fingers and nodded. She made that face again, eyes wide, lips taut, head lifted.

"Push, Ann!" Rachael cried. "Push! I see it. I see the head!"

Tears streamed down her cheeks as the baby was crowned.

With a great grunt and a final push, the baby slid into Mari's waiting hands. Covered in white, waxy fluid, its face was still obscured. Rachael watched anxiously as Mari wiped it with soft rawhide, then gently swirled her finger inside the baby's mouth.

A tiny cry rose.

Mari took her knife, cut the cord, and tied it off with rawhide. Then she looked at Rachael and made the sign for *male.*

In all the flurry, Rachael hadn't even thought to check. She watched as Mari swaddled the child and placed him gently onto Ann's chest.

"Joseph," Ann whispered. "Joseph."

A gush of blood followed, along with the placenta.

Rachael gasped, startled by the thick, red flood. The sight shocked her, but also sparked a flicker of scientific curiosity. *So this is the afterbirth... this nourished the baby...*

She wanted to look closer, but Mari swiftly bundled the placenta in a leather bag and tied it shut.

Then Rachael noticed the bleeding hadn't stopped.

A red river still flowed. Ann, too focused on the baby, didn't seem to notice.

Mari moved with precision. She sopped up the blood with the bedclothes and reached again into her bag. This time, she pulled out a bone needle and thread. She signed for Rachael to hold Ann's legs apart.

Without hesitation, Rachael complied.

Mari leaned forward and began to stitch. Rachael, captivated, watched the needlework. *Why, it's a blanket stitch,* she thought. *One of the few I know.*

It made sense. It was strong.

At last, Mari tied off the thread and signed: *Stop the blood.*

She took a small root, chewed it, and then placed the softened pulp into Ann's mouth. Still massaging her abdomen, she watched Ann closely.

Rachael, hands on her chest, remained motionless, transfixed.

She hadn't noticed Camille until she heard her retch at the tent flap.

Rachael turned. Camille had reappeared, pale and shaken.

Rachael gave her a small, understanding smile.

"Tell Robert he has another son. Get hot water and clean rags. Please inform Mr. Grey that Ann's baby has been born."

Camille nodded, her voice steady despite her pallor. Then she turned to carry out her task.

Later, when the bleeding finally subsided, Rachael crawled across the wagon bed to Mari, signed *thank you,* and reached for her.

Mari pulled her close, holding her while Rachael sobbed.

"I couldn't have managed without you. You saved her. Thank you… Thank you."

When her tears ended, Mari stroked her cheek with a gentle hand.

Rachael looked at the baby, now dozing on Ann's chest. Wrinkled and strange-looking, yet Ann was transformed.

Mari made the sign for *return*, nodded once at Rachael, and left the wagon with the placenta bundle and soiled linens, stepping into the new morning light.

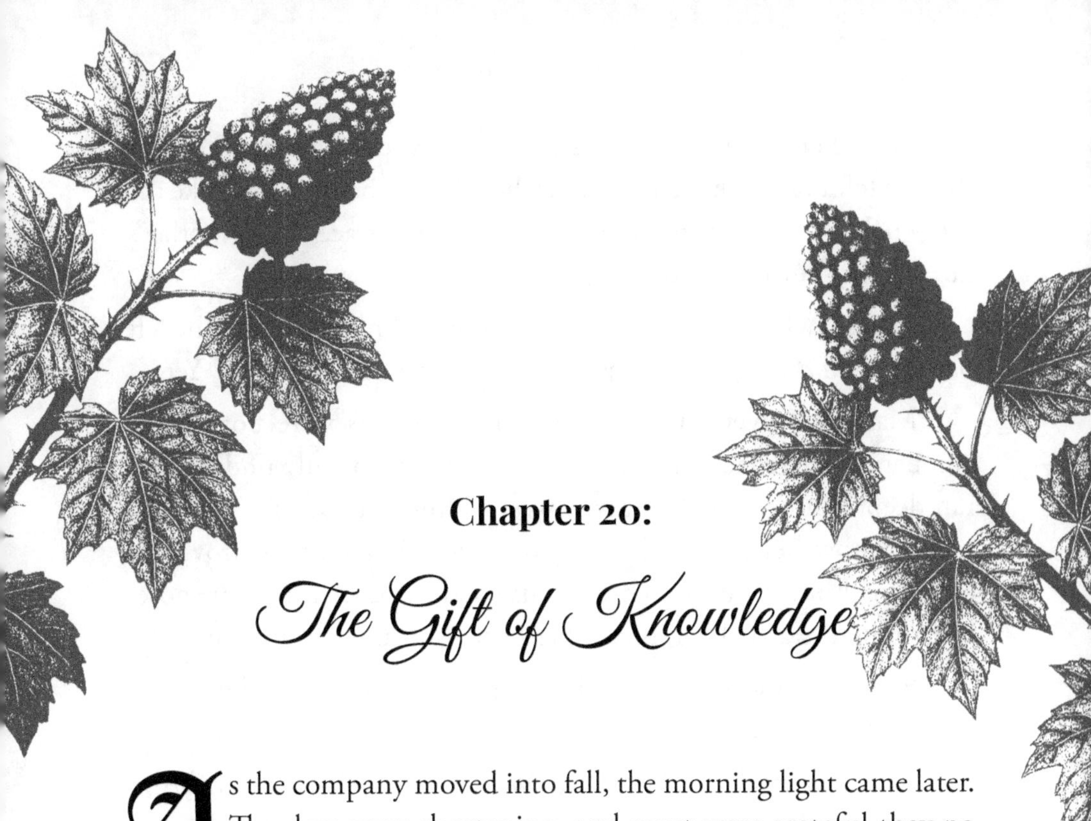

Chapter 20:
The Gift of Knowledge

As the company moved into fall, the morning light came later. The days were shortening, and most were grateful they no longer had to rise and depart at three or four in the morning. Even at five-thirty or six, the early air held a chill.

Mother and son grew stronger the day after Joseph's birth. The potion the trapper's wife had given Ann was taking effect. Her milk had come in, and the baby suckled. Both rested quietly. For the first time since the onset of labor, Rachael felt her shoulders relax. *Maybe,* she thought, *everything will turn out all right after all.* She resolved to write Martha that evening to share the birth of the small boy named Joseph after his father.

Rachael wanted to give the Indian healer woman a gift for her help. There had to be something of value in her belongings. She rummaged through her kit, surprised by what she had once considered important: a silver teaspoon of her mother's, a box of unused hairpins. Then she found five small embroidered handkerchiefs—lovely, but not quite enough. These, plus the hairpins, would be good for trade but not worthy of Mari's gift of knowledge.

Then, her fingers brushed tissue paper. She drew out her mother's shawl. Holding it to her cheek, she sighed, letting her fingers stroke the soft wool. She raised it to her nose, hoping for a trace of her mother's floral scent, but it was gone.

This shawl had always been her strongest link to the life she left behind. *Could she give it away?* It was her most personal item. Yet…

Mari had given much. Those handkerchiefs were nothing in comparison. Rachael's desire to learn from her, to truly understand, ran deep. Though she had come west to find the Devil's Club, she realized now her goal had changed. It wasn't fame that drove her anymore, but the desire to heal, to use plants for their true purpose. The thought startled her, but in her heart, she knew it was true.

She heard footsteps behind her, recognizable by the slight drag of the left foot. Mr. Grey.

After a brief silence, he asked, "Well, Mrs. Williams. How is Ann and her child? Stronger?"

Rachael's hand tightened on the shawl. Their last meeting had ended in anger. She blushed at the memory of her outburst but then lifted her chin. Her actions had been justified, and in the end, he had agreed with her.

"Yes," she answered briskly. "Thanks to God and Mari's skill."

Her voice warmed as she went on. "I find myself more and more fascinated by the power of plants to assist healing, to lessen pain, to restore health. I'm still learning. Perhaps in Oregon, I'll meet others I can study with. Will you teach me more of the sign language you know?"

She studied his face. Was he still angry? Did he still resent her for delaying the company?

Mr. Grey cleared his throat and met her gaze. "I'm glad Mari was there. Mrs. Dix came to complain, of course, but I silenced her."

Rachael wanted to ask how that would be useful knowledge, but his expression warned her not to press the subject.

"Mrs. Williams," he continued, "we both spoke out of turn last time. I won't apologize for everything I said; some of it needed to be said, but I do regret the remarks I made about your husband. I—"

Rachael interrupted. "And I am sorry for what I said about your wife and children. I…" But the sentence withered between them.

He looked away, then sighed. "It's over. Let's move forward. We leave tomorrow at first light. The sheep and drovers are three days ahead. It's late in the year. We must get over the pass."

"But Mr. Grey," Rachael said hesitantly, "couldn't we wait another day? For Ann and the baby?"

"Enough," he snapped. "We had an agreement. I've spoken with Reverend Robert, and he's agreed. So have the others. The only ones who objected were Hannah and Camille, but even they saw the reason. I told the company that anyone who doesn't leave tomorrow can stay behind and try to join another group. But their chances are slim. It's very late in the year."

"Well then," Rachael said, steadying herself, "I will stand by your decision as leader of this expedition."

"A wise choice, Mrs. Williams," he said crisply, turning on his heel and walking away.

She watched his broad back disappear into the dusk, feeling a strange mixture of relief and worry. *Had he made the right choice? If the wagon jostled Ann too much, might the bleeding start again? Would there be time to brew the tisanes she needed? They required hot water, and hot water meant fire. If she made them in the evening, would they still be effective by morning? How would she even store them?*

Mari came to say goodbye, carrying a large skin bag. Rachael wondered how much she understood. Clearly, she had witnessed the earlier conversation with Mr. Grey.

Mari signed a greeting. Rachael smiled and signed back.

As she did, she glanced down at her mother's shawl still folded in her hands. A decision took shape in her heart. She stepped forward and signed I give, flattening her right hand, moving it to the right, then up and down in front of Mari. Then she held out the shawl.

Rachael curved her fingers inward and tapped three times on her chest: *Mother.* She pointed to herself and repeated the sign.

Mari smiled gently, understanding. She took the shawl in both hands and examined it with care, her fingers moving lightly across the delicate woolen weave.

Then Mari handed her the skin bag, signing *for you.*

Rachael opened it. Inside, tied in neat bundles, were medicinal roots and herbs, some familiar, many not. She recognized a small packet prepared specifically for a new mother and baby. Boneset for high fevers. Yarrow for wounds or bleeding. Her fingers trembled as she held the bundles. It was a healer's kit.

Mari took out another pouch and gestured for her attention. She pointed to a knot, then to her stomach.

Together, they unpacked the bag. For each knot, Mari pointed to a part of the body that might help. One pouch, tied with a coral cord, was different. Mari signed *big* and then *all.*

Rachael signed *name?* and Mari said something Rachael couldn't understand. Then she signed *strong,* which also meant *brave.*

Rachael nodded slowly. She would be cautious with that one.

She studied each knot with care. Everyone was tied in a unique way. *Could she retie them?* She wasn't sure, but she would try. She had to try.

How she longed to stay and learn more from this wise woman. Perhaps, someday, she would return.

Unable to express the depth of her gratitude, Rachael signed *thank you* over and over again until Mari caught her hands and laughed, a deep, lovely, gurgling sound that made Rachael smile.

Then, Mari's demeanor changed.

She began signing quickly, her hands held close to her chest as if shielding the signs from view. The motions were quick and deliberate. Urgent.

Rachael recognized only a few: *water, children,* and *wife…*

She shook her head, confused.

Mari signed it all again, her face more intent this time. Rachael still didn't understand.

Mari's eyes darted past her, and suddenly, she dropped her hands. Over Rachael's shoulder, her husband was approaching.

In one last, swift motion, Mari signed a final word, a complicated one, but one Rachael remembered: *Think.*

Rachael nodded. Then, without another word, Mari turned and disappeared into the shadows of the post.

Rachael stood alone, clutching the bundle of knots and herbs, her mother's shawl now in Mari's keeping.

That was a message, she realized. A private one. Mari had hidden her hands when her husband neared and ended the signs abruptly.

What had she been trying to say?

That night, Rachael promised herself she would review every sign she knew, every motion and gesture. She would think about Mari's message until she understood.

Because she had to understand.

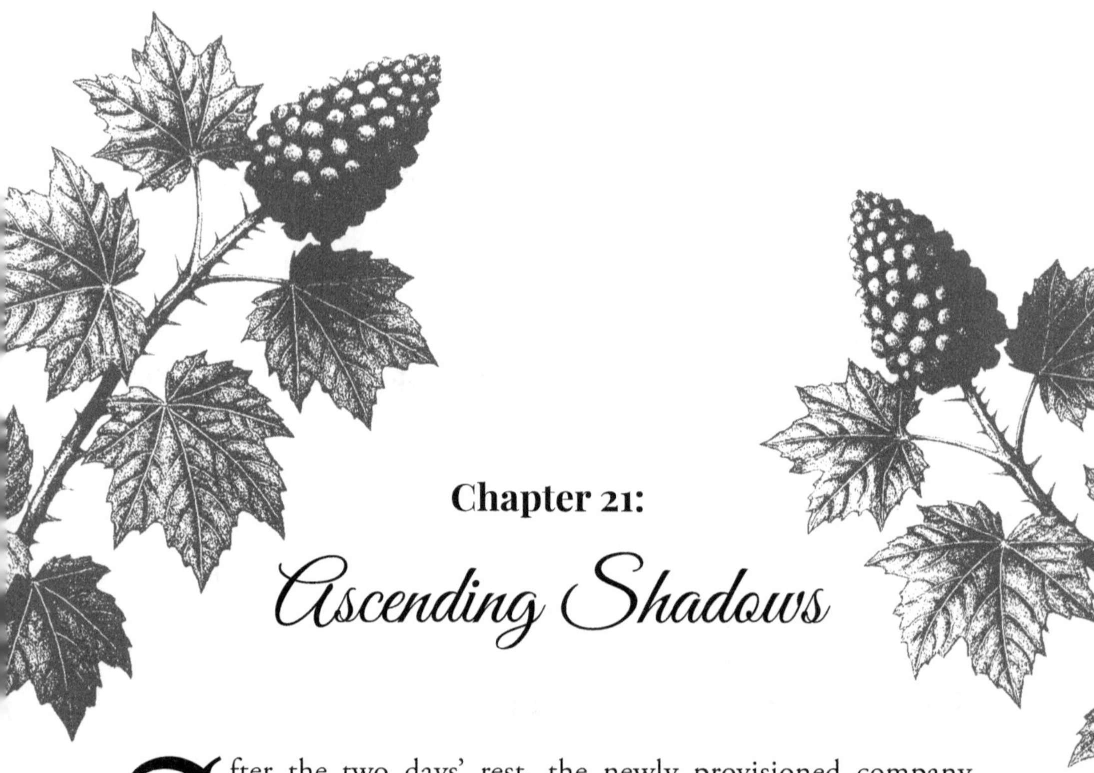

Chapter 21:

Ascending Shadows

After the two days' rest, the newly provisioned company was ready to leave the trading post, though later than Mr. Grey would have wished. The new oxen were difficult to yoke. Daniel's stepson James, who usually helped with yoking, had already left with the drovers. It took both Tom and Daniel to get the animals ready.

The springboard wagon had two new mules; the others had been traded, their feet raw from traveling across the basalt plains.

Rachael sat beside Mr. Grey on the wagon seat. He was his usual taciturn self. The wagon creaked and rattled as he slapped the reins, and the mules moved forward.

Ann and her infant son rode on a pallet in the back of their wagon while Reverend Robert walked beside his oxen. Hannah accompanied Sara and Christopher, who walked alongside their family's wagon as Tom guided the oxen. Sara was enthralled with her baby brother, whispering sweet words into his ear and stroking his back. Christopher, on the other hand, was less impressed. He preferred the company of his friend Roy.

With Daniel guiding their own oxen and Henry riding in the back, Mrs. Dix and Camille followed in their wagon.

Rachael had hoped for another saddle horse. She missed the freedom she'd once had on Little Red. But she hadn't yet found the will, or the right moment, to bring it up with Mr. Grey. That freedom, that independence, tugged at her spirit. She longed to learn more sign language from Mr. Grey, but again, she hesitated. He hadn't mentioned his intervention when Mrs. Dix had gone running to Robert, screeching about the "filthy savage" woman, Mari, who had helped during Ann's delivery.

Camille had quietly told Rachael what she'd seen: Mrs. Dix confronting Robert with that slur just after Camille had delivered the news of his son's birth. It was probably wise to stay silent for now, but Rachael's mind burned with questions nonetheless.

They made slow progress up a steep slope. Rachael feared they might have to unload the wagons and carry goods up by hand, something they'd done too many times before. The mere thought made her arms and back ache.

"I might as well walk," she muttered to Mr. Grey. "The mules have enough to carry."

He halted the wagon with a grunt, and she climbed down without another word.

Looking back, Rachael joined the children walking with Hannah and Camille. Of course, Mrs. Dix had remained in the wagon; she rarely walked if she could help it.

Sara and Christopher were content and cheerful. Rachael soon had them playing a rhyming game to pass the time as they trudged upward.

As she walked, she noticed how the scent of dust had vanished, replaced by the sweetness of pine. The tall trees stood upright and regal, their limbs high and narrow. She paused by one, examining a spot where golden sap oozed down the bark. She touched it and found it sticky, almost impossible to remove.

Pitch, she thought. In her Botany class back in Geneva, she might have learned the Latin name, but certainly not its medicinal use.

She was beginning to believe she could learn more here, on the trail, than in any classroom.

At the base of the pines, she spotted soft green moss. It looked thick and fibrous, and something about it struck her as useful. Perhaps it could help staunch blood? So many possibilities.

Martha's mother's book had been her faithful guide, but even she had never traveled this far. Rachael's heartbeat quickened. This, this discovery, this knowledge of the land, this was what she truly wanted.

Yes, she would still find Devil's Club. But no longer for the sake of fame. No longer to prove something to the Dean, who denied her.

She would find it out of pure, fervent curiosity.

Further along the trail, she noticed a few yellow mountain lupines blooming, even this late in the season. She knew its leaves made a helpful tea for nausea and bleeding. She'd already collected some along earlier slopes but couldn't resist picking a few more, tucking them into her apron pocket.

Sniffing the air, she wondered about the pine needles. *Did they have a use?* It seemed every plant around her had a purpose, a place in nature's pharmacy.

At noon, they stopped in a small, fragrant meadow ringed by pines and other trees she didn't yet recognize. How wonderful it would be to cook over wood again after weeks of buffalo chips. No matter how careful they were, the filth always got into the food. Here, the air was clean. The stench of the alkali flats felt a lifetime away.

She took a long, slow breath.

Dark clouds gathered overhead, and Rachael could tell that Mr. Grey had noticed them, too. He was determined to get them over the pass before nightfall. At the brief noon stop, the travelers were told simply to eat jerky and hardtack.

During that pause, Rachael and Camille checked on Ann. She lay listlessly on her pallet, her skin pale. Five-day-old baby Joseph slept peacefully on her chest. Ann gave them both a wan smile.

Rachael's concern flared. Ann had looked better yesterday. She and Camille exchanged a glance. There had been no fire built, so Rachael couldn't prepare the usual warm herbal infusion. But maybe she had a little left in the bottle she'd mixed with Mr. Grey's liquor.

She hurried to the back of the wagon for her medicine bag, pulled the stopper from the bottle, and poured three tablespoons of the mixture into a tin cup from the mess kit. Cold or not, it would have to do. She climbed into the wagon and gently lifted Ann's head so she could drink.

"Are you in pain, Ann?"

"No," she murmured, "just weak and tired."

"This should help you sleep, though I know riding in a wagon up this rocky, rutted road is hardly restful."

Ann gave a faint smile of thanks.

From Martha's mother's book, Rachael recalled that blood loss could slow the heart. Maybe that explained the pallor and exhaustion. But after the recent fight with Mr. Grey, she hesitated to bring it to him. She'd promised to support his decisions, and they were already ten hard miles from the trading post. This, she told herself, was Robert's concern. It was his wife.

She glanced across the encampment. Robert stood near Tom and Mr. Grey. They were clapping him on the back, congratulating him on the birth of his son. She studied his face, trying to read his mood. Then, as if by instinct, he broke from the group and strode toward the wagon.

"Sara and Christopher will go along with Tom's wagon. They've been enjoying playing with Roy. I'll drive ours with Ann and the lad. Well, Rachael," he said with a broad smile, "we'll soon be on our way. God's blessing has been great indeed."

"Robert, I'm concerned about Ann," Rachael said quickly. "She seems pale and weak. Should she really be traveling today? Perhaps a bit more rest?"

"Nonsense, Rachael. Of course, she's weak; she just gave birth, but she's strong. Look at the fine young man she's produced. Sometimes, you women who haven't given birth make too much of these things. It's the Lord's way, and He'll care for her. I have faith in that."

"But I—"

"Rachael, she'll be fine. Don't you trust in our good Lord? Say some prayers for her if it eases your mind, but she's well. I prayed for both of them two nights ago, and those prayers were heard, just as they were when she delivered a son."

"Robert, I really must—"

"The matter is finished, Rachael." He nodded toward the wagons. "Everyone's ready to move on. Now, please, step aside so I can climb up. Mr. Grey is in a hurry to reach the pass. He says we've still seven or eight miles to go. And look at the sky; we don't want to be caught in a mountain storm. They can be fierce up here. If it will ease your worry, I'll look in on her before we go."

He hoisted himself into the wagon and parted the curtain. "See?" he said. "Ann's fine. Sleeping just like the little one wrapped up in her shawl."

But Rachael's stomach remained tight. That feeling, low and cold and heavy, had been her warning signal since childhood. A deep, unshakable sense of dread gripped her.

Was this listlessness truly normal after a hard delivery?

She looked toward Mr. Grey, considering whether to try him again, but he was waving his arms at her, urging her to hurry.

She had no choice but to obey.

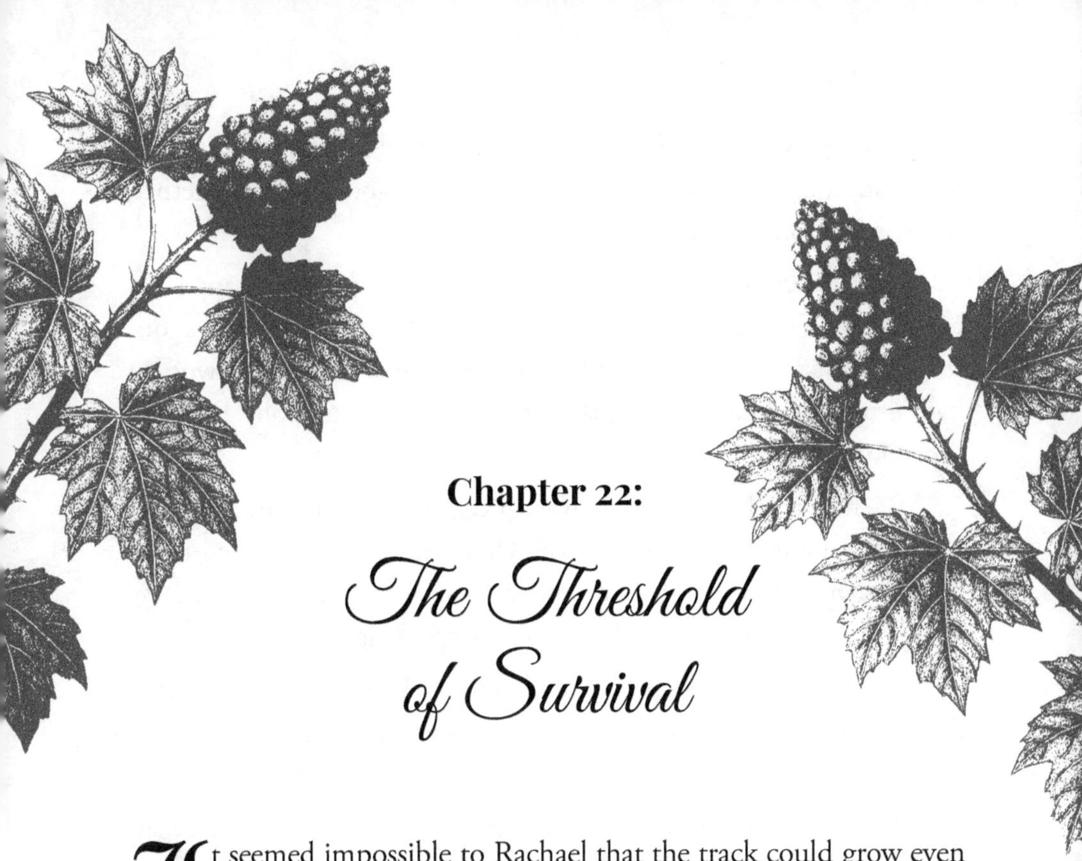

Chapter 22:

The Threshold of Survival

It seemed impossible to Rachael that the track could grow even steeper and rockier than the one they had traveled that morning. She began to wonder if, somehow, they had missed the trail.

Everyone was walking now, trailing behind the oxen and mules as they navigated around the obstacles: large rocks and trees spaced too narrowly for the wagons to pass. Even Mrs. Dix had left her wagon, supported by the ever-kind Camille. After all these miles, her stout frame was unaccustomed to walking. Her feet were terribly swollen. Rachael had offered her a remedy for the swelling, or at least a foot soak, but as always, Mrs. Dix refused anything she called "those Devil's medicines."

When the small group finally crested what they assumed must be the top of the mountain, they saw, to their dismay, the trail continuing up.

Mr. Grey urged them on, assuring them the summit was only a few miles farther. But everyone was exhausted. They had spent hours hauling logs and debris off the trail. Even the children, who had once seen it as a game, now drooped with fatigue.

Rachael moved to Sara's side and wrapped her arm around the girl's shoulders. She took Christopher's small hand in hers. Together, they pressed on.

As the incline steepened, the sky darkened. The sun disappeared behind thick clouds, and the temperature plummeted. The wagons stopped briefly so people could grab their heavier coats. The women had already stuffed rags into their bonnets for insulation. The men tugged their hats low over their ears.

Rachael reached beneath a wagon and pulled out coats and wool hats for Sara and Christopher. The children gratefully pulled them on, though Rachael noticed they were now too small. *They're growing,* she thought, a flicker of pride and worry sparking in her chest.

She took the opportunity to check on Ann, still tucked under the blankets. Rachael couldn't hear her breathing, but the blankets were drawn up over her head and the child's. She felt no alarm yet.

The company continued its slow, grueling climb. The trees began to thin, the slope grew sharper, and the dusk deepened.

Then came a sound in the distance, a rhythmic thump echoing through the hush of the coming night.

Rachael paused, listening. *A grouse? Was it drumming?*

She glanced back at Mr. Grey, who was frowning, forehead furrowed in concern.

There's something about a grouse drumming at dusk, she thought, struggling to remember. Her father had once mentioned it…

The sky continued to darken. Rachael and the other women stuffed their hands beneath their skirts to keep warm. The top still wasn't in sight. Mr. Grey and the springboard wagon had moved into the lead. He was hunched forward, scanning the trail, alert for something. *Wild animals? Bears? Mountain lions?*

A shiver ran through Rachael. She remembered the she-bear vividly.

Suddenly, a sharp yip pierced the air. Mr. Grey's voice.

They had reached the summit.

At that very moment, the first snowflakes began to fall, tiny slivers of white spinning through the twilight like bits of starlight.

How beautiful, thought Rachael. *How beautiful.*

"Hurry, everyone! Hurry!" Mr. Grey shouted. "We must reach a campsite before the snowfall thickens. There's a spot down the hill a bit. Brake the wagons on the descent. We'll hold off on using the chains for now. But we can't go farther tonight. The ravines on either side get dangerously steep. It's too risky in the dark and with snow."

The animals, just as weary as the people, stumbled and slipped down the slope. They followed Mr. Grey to a narrow flat nestled beneath a massive pine. He had already hobbled the mules beneath it, where the tree's enormous lower branches stretched out six feet from the trunk, offering shelter.

"Bring the oxen under here," Mr. Grey called. "Hobble them. If the snow thickens, we can't risk them wandering."

He grabbed his axe and began trimming lower branches from nearby trees. "Tom, Daniel, help me gather wood before it's too wet. Cut what's near the trunks. It'll be the driest."

As he spoke, he threw a rubber tarp beneath the springboard wagon and strung another one between the branches above to create a covered space for cooking.

Then, the orders began in earnest.

"Throw dry branches under your wagons and wrap them in tarps. Prepare for a hard night. The sound of a grouse drumming is an omen. The Indians believe it signals a heavy snowfall. If they're right, we'd best be ready."

Rachael's memory stirred. Her father had once said the same thing during an unexpected spring blizzard. They had rushed home at the sound of that distant thump.

"Rachael, Hannah, and Camille organize the children's sleeping arrangements. No tents tonight; they'll collapse under snow. Unload what you can from the wagons and use the tents to cover it. Pad the wagon beds with as many blankets as you can find. Lay something underneath for insulation. We'll have to sleep close together for warmth. If it worsens, we may need to dig snow caves under the wagons, but only if it becomes dire."

"Rachael, check on Ann and the child. See that she's warm enough, and if not, take some of my blankets. I've got my buffalo coat and can manage. Work quickly now before everything is wet. It will freeze later."

Robert, Mrs. Dix, Rachael, Hannah, and the children worked together, unloading the wagons as best they could. They moved from wagon to wagon, hauling out trunks and supplies, laying them beside the wheels, and covering them with tents. It occurred to Rachael that each pile should be positioned in the same spot beside its wagon. If heavy snow buried everything, knowing what belonged where might help them find the essentials again.

She took Mr. Grey at his word and brought three blankets to cover Ann and the newborn Joseph. It was a good chance to give Ann the last of her medicine, this time with some Valerian to help her sleep. Ann's eyes looked unnaturally protruding, her skin parchment-thin. Rachael placed a hand on her forehead, though hers was so cold she couldn't tell whether Ann had a fever.

Ann looked at her and lifted the blanket to reveal the baby nursing.

He was so small. So impossibly small.

Then she heard the others calling her name.

"I'll check in on you again, Ann, as soon as I can," Rachael said gently. "Robert's helping to organize the camp. Are you warm enough? Do you need anything?"

"No, Rachael. Thank you. The children, are they safe?" Ann whispered.

"Yes, Ann. Hannah has them well in hand. Just worry about yourself and little Joseph now."

Rachael forced herself to stay calm, though her chest ached with the rush of panic. She knew the alarm wouldn't help. Mr. Grey had taken control, as he always did. But even his competence might not be enough this time.

The snow fell steadily, now piling on the branches of the pines around them. As dusk turned to night, only one glow remained visible: the small cookfire that Mr. Grey had started by clearing a ring of earth and carefully stacking kindling. Rachael warmed her hands beside it, studying its construction.

He had laid stripped branches in a tall square tower, one layer at a time, forming a platform of fire. As it collapsed into embers, the heat rose evenly. But the tarp stretched between a pine tree, and the wagon began to sag under the snow's weight. Mr. Grey stood and lowered the tarp's edge to the lower branches, hoping the snow would slide off.

Still, the tarp groaned with accumulating snow.

Rachael saw the tight set of his shoulders. If the tarp gave in, the fire would be extinguished. Their one comfort was lost.

"Rachael," he called, "bring me the pot, fill it with clean snow. We'll need something warm in everyone's belly before the night is over."

She filled the kettle and brought it to him.

"May I take some of the water once it's hot? I'd like to steep herbs for Ann."

He glanced up from tending the flame. "How are your patient and her son?"

Rachael hesitated. "To tell you the truth... I don't know. She seems weak. I'll ask Hannah what she thinks. I'd like to give her another dose of the medicine Mari gave me. It seemed to help."

Mr. Grey nodded and added some dried venison to the boiling pot. Rachael ladled some water into a cup and tucked her herb pouch against her chest for warmth.

Their conversation was cut short by Mrs. Dix's shrill voice.

"Daniel, you must go find James! I can't bear the thought of him alone in this weather with those wretched sheep. I don't trust Mr. Miller. Go now, right now!"

"Betsy, it's already dark. I'll never find their camp in this snow. They're far ahead, maybe already down the mountain. Don't worry. Mr. Miller's a smart man."

"What would you know?" she snapped. "You can't even yoke a pair of oxen! I should've known better than to trust you with James. You've never cared for him, not once, because he's not your son. I've always known that!"

Rachael and Mr. Grey shared a look of discomfort. The words were too intimate, too cruel, and too loud to ignore, but there was no avoiding them.

Soon, Camille's soft, steady voice cut through the air.

"Auntie, there's nothing we can do tonight. You're exhausted and becoming hysterical. We all care for James. Look, you're scaring Henry."

"I don't care! Daniel, I demand that you go after him. It'll kill me if something happens to him. I never should've come on this trip. Not with that fractious Mr. Grey and that Indian lover, Rachael, with her devil's medicine, why, I—"

"Hush," Daniel and Camille said in unison. "Hush now."

Mr. Grey gave Rachael an arched eyebrow, then called out, his voice hard with intention.

"Daniel, I could use your help setting out what little dinner we can manage tonight. Bring some of that excellent tea if Mrs. Dix still has any. It might help us all keep warm."

They heard rather than saw Daniel emerge from behind the wagon, rummaging through his family's tack box for the tea tin.

He brought it to the cookfire and handed it to Mr. Grey. "Mr. Grey," he said, "I'm sorry if you—"

"Don't worry about it, Daniel. I don't blame your wife for worrying about her son," Mr. Grey said, brushing soot off his gloves.

"But you can reassure her that Mr. Miller and his crew are likely down in the valley by now. They didn't have to contend with lowering wagons off cliffs. They'd have moved faster, even with the sheep."

"Well, still, sir, I would hate to think—"

"Let it go. And thank your wife for sharing her tea. I'm sure all our stomachs will appreciate some warmth."

"Frankly... I didn't tell her." Daniel looked sheepish.

He turned to watch Rachael as she carefully added more herbs to her small pot to steep.

"Mrs. Williams, how are Ann and the lad?"

"As I told Mr. Grey, I'm not entirely sure, Daniel, but I know she'll appreciate some of Mrs. Dixon's fine tea. It might help soften the bitterness of these herbs."

She patted his arm gently. "Tell her thank you from me as well."

Everyone huddled close to the fire, wrapped in whatever scraps of clothing and blankets they could find. They sipped Mrs. Dix's tea and a watery venison broth provided by Mr. Grey. Hands were rubbed together or tucked into armpits.

Mrs. Dix whimpered now and then, still anxious about James.

It was decided that everyone would try to sleep in the wagons.

Mr. Grey organized the men to build small snow caves beneath each wagon. Firewood was shifted to one side, and walls of snow were stacked to the height of the wagon beds. Tarps were stretched across the openings so wagon occupants could crawl underneath for warmth if needed. The snow caves, it was hoped, would insulate better against the night's cold than the wagons alone.

Rachael offered to sleep in the Godleys' wagon with Ann and the baby. Reverend Robert agreed to sleep with Mr. Grey beneath the springboard, where a snow cave lined with blankets had already been prepared.

Sara, Christopher, Tom, Hannah, and Roy would sleep together in the Evans' wagon. Crowded, but their body heat would help. The Dix family would do the same, swaddled in Mrs. Dix's treasured blankets.

Soon, all turned in.

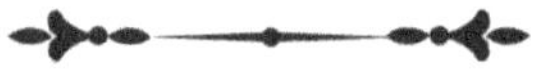

Before she left the fire, Mr. Grey pulled Rachael aside.

"It's going to be a cold one, Rachael. Do you have enough blankets? Will Ann and the baby be warm enough?"

Rachael was taken aback by his concern. And, to her surprise, something warmed inside her.

"We'll manage, Mr. Grey. Don't forget, I bought those buffalo robes in Laramie. I'll use one for myself and the other to cover Ann and the baby." She paused, then added with a teasing smile, "But I might ask you the same. Will *you* be warm enough? I doubt Robert offers much in the way of comfort."

In the dimming firelight, his expression softened. He reached out and, almost absently, tucked a lock of her hair behind her ear. His hand brushed her cheek for a heartbeat. Then he pulled it back quickly, almost as if startled by the impulse.

She looked up at him, still feeling the warmth of that small, unexpected gesture.

"If Ann gets worse, or you need help," he said, pointing, "I'll be under the wagon. Just call, and I'll come. Here, take the lantern and matches."

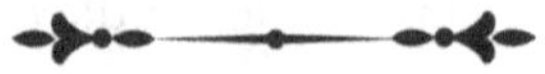

Rachael woke.

It was so cold it hurt to breathe.

She sat up shivering, pulling the buffalo robe tighter around her shoulders. Earlier, she'd tried to curl up beside Ann and the baby to offer warmth, but Ann had pushed her away. Rachael understood. Sometimes, when one is sick, the presence of another body, even a comforting one, can be simply too much.

Lifting the canvas she'd pinned up earlier to keep out the snow, she looked out into the night.

The snow had stopped. Above, the sky glittered with stars, so many that it seemed the heavens had descended. There was no moon, but starlight alone was enough to illuminate the wagons. The tracks between them, visible at dusk, had vanished beneath the snowfall.

She had never seen a sky like this. Not even in Geneva.

The silence was profound, so deep it rang in her ears.

She looked over at the quilted shape that was Ann and her infant, sleeping beside her. Rachael was relieved she had managed to brew Mari's remedy earlier and refill Ann's medicine bottle. She had used the last of the powdered root in boiling snow water, working by flickering firelight. Moments after she'd pulled her small pot off the flame, the canvas Mr. Grey had used to shelter the fire gave way beneath the snow's weight, extinguishing the flames.

It had been just in time.

The medicine had soothed both Ann and Sara, who had begun their first menstrual cycle earlier that day.

Sara had been shy and frightened, but Hannah and Rachael had comforted her, explaining the changes were natural. Later, Rachael returned to Sara's wagon with a spoonful of the herbal blend.

"Sleep now, sweet child," she had whispered, brushing a strand of hair from Sara's forehead. "Tomorrow, you can see your mother and your baby brother."

That memory made her smile.

How she cared for this child.

Rachael wondered how long she had slept and whether it was time to wake Ann to give her another draught.

She slid her arms into her coat, drew it tight around her, and reached for the lantern. But there were no matches. She swept her hand across the floor of the wagon bed—nothing. She would have to manage without it.

She crawled toward Ann. Reaching her, Rachael pulled back the blanket to rouse her. It was too dark to see her face clearly. As her hand slipped beneath the covers to check the baby, her fingers touched something sticky. She brought her hand to her nose.

It smells rusty. What's that… blood?

She threw back the blankets and shook Ann. "Ann? Ann!"

Frantic now, Rachael placed a hand on her chest, feeling movement. Shallow but present. She grasped Ann's hands. They were ice cold.

I need help. I need to see. Where is the baby?

Her fingers searched the tangled blankets, stiff with dried blood. Finally, she found the infant wrapped in Ann's shawl. She pulled him close, slipping him inside her coat.

A mewling sound.

"What can I do?" she whispered. "Help…" Then louder, more urgent, "Help! Someone help!"

Boots crunched in the snow. A lantern's glow broke the dark as Mr. Grey tore back the canvas.

"Rachael? What is it?"

"It's Ann. Something's wrong. She's been bleeding. I don't know what to do. I have the child in my coat."

"Listen to me. Hand me the child. I'll take him to Camille and come right back. Is Ann breathing?"

"Yes. A little, but—"

"Give him to me. I'll be back."

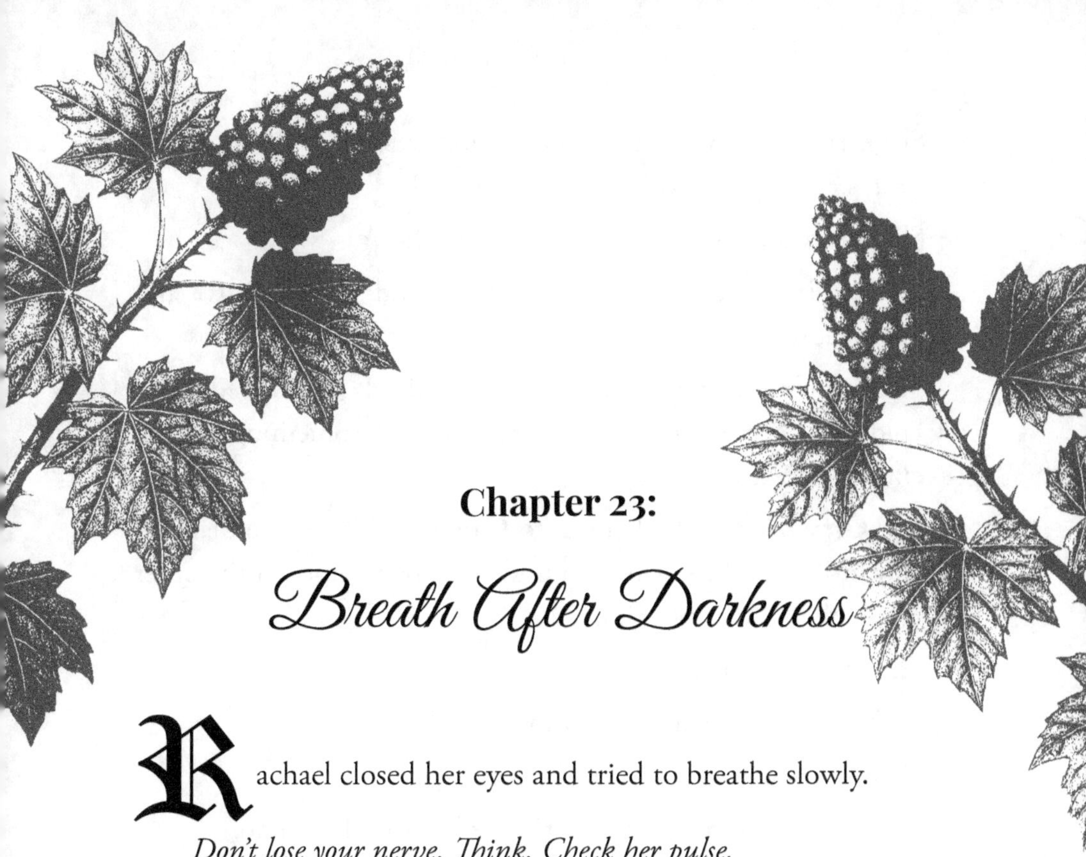

Chapter 23:

Breath After Darkness

Rachael closed her eyes and tried to breathe slowly.

Don't lose your nerve. Think. Check her pulse.

She pressed two fingers to Ann's neck, praying to feel movement beneath them. It was there, but faint. She tried to count the beats, but her mind raced too fast.

The canvas lifted again. Mr. Grey returned Camille just behind him. The wagon swayed as they climbed aboard, the lantern casting a pale glow over the scene.

Rachael had shifted toward Ann's legs to make space. Camille took Ann's left hand, rubbing it gently. Ann moaned.

"Mr. Grey, can you hold the lantern lower?" Rachael asked, her voice unfamiliar to her own ears.

With trembling hands, she reached for the blankets, steeling herself. Slowly, she drew them back. Ann's bedclothes were soaked with blood, some of it already frozen to the quilt.

Rachael closed her eyes and turned her face away. *You know what you'll see. You don't want to see it.*

"Rachael."

She met Mr. Grey's eyes. His expression was steady. "I know you can do this. You'll need to act quickly now."

She forced herself to look. *Is there fresh blood?*

Slowly, she lifted the quilt again. Her hands shook. But… no. No new bleeding.

"There's blood," she said quietly. "But I think it's stopped. She's very cold. We need warm clothes, clean blankets, something to raise her temperature fast."

Mr. Grey handed the lantern to Camille. "I'll get the blankets and inform Robert. See if you can find clean bedclothes. If the other side of the quilt is dry, turn it over."

Then he was gone.

Only then did Rachael remember the child.

"Where's the baby?" she asked Camille.

"My aunt has him. Don't worry. She knows what to do."

Rachael hesitated. "But—"

Camille cut her off gently. "Mrs. Dix probably knows more about babies than either of us."

"All right. Let's get Ann into something clean. Check that chest under the seat. And bring my blankets, too. We need to warm her quickly."

Camille dug through the chest and returned with a worn flannel nightgown. Cradling Ann's head, she guided her upright, letting her rest against her chest.

Ann moaned.

Rachael knelt and lifted her legs to remove the bloodied nightdress. It clung to her skin. As she peeled it away, Ann whimpered in pain.

Camille eased the clean nightgown down over her torso. Her hands brushed Ann's chest—another groan.

Looking down, Camille caught sight of her thighs. Still stained with blood.

"Oh, Ann..."

Her eyes brimmed with tears as she looked at Rachael.

Rachael broke the thin layer of ice in the bucket hanging at the wagon's rear. Dipping a piece of the old nightdress into the icy water, she returned and gently tried to sponge the dried blood from Ann's legs.

Was this making her colder? Rachael's brow furrowed in worry. Ann lay still.

"Quick now," she said. "I'll pull the nightgown down. Put my blankets on her, too."

The canvas lifted again. Mr. Grey returned with Robert.

He vaulted into the wagon. Camille scrambled out of the way.

"Where is my son?" he cried. "Where is my son?"

Rachael took the blankets from Mr. Grey, barely glancing at Robert. She met Mr. Grey's eyes and shook her head.

"We have to get her warm."

Camille looked directly at Robert, her eyes hard. "Ann is very ill. Can you not see that, Robert? The baby is with my aunt. He's safe for the moment."

Robert looked down at Ann, brushing her hair back from her damp forehead. He made the sign of the cross on her brow. "She is in God's hands now. May God bless you, wife. I commend you to our Lord. If it is His will, may He lead you to eternal rest. Amen."

"Not if I can help it," muttered Rachael.

The wagon shifted as Robert stepped out. The three women inside looked at one another. Mr. Grey was in the wagon with Rachael and Camille, and Ann was unconscious.

"How can we get her warm? Is there a chance of a fire?"

"No," said Mr. Grey, appearing beside them. "But I know a way to warm her. I thought to ask Robert, but..."

"Just tell me. Hurry," Rachael cut in.

"Is Ann cleaned and changed? I see you've used your blankets. Add mine, too. The only way to warm her is with body heat. Someone must get under the blankets and hold her. That's the only way."

"I can do that," said Rachael. "Camille, what about you? We can place her between us; that would be quickest."

Camille nodded.

Both women removed their boots. Rachael began to unfasten her coat, but Mr. Grey stopped her.

"No, keep it on. Open it and draw Ann next to you inside the coat. Here, Camille, take mine. It's large enough to cover you and her from behind."

Rachael hesitated. "But what will you wear, Mr. Grey?"

"Don't fuss, Rachael. I'll wrap up in one of the spare blankets until I can get my other coat. Hurry now. I'll pile the rest of the blankets on top of all three of you."

It was then that Rachael realized that together, they might be enough. They would be a team. They were needed.

Ann murmured faintly as the two women lay beside her, enclosing her in their arms.

She's so cold, Rachael thought. *Like a fish frozen in ice.*

The warmth, the exhaustion, the relief, it overcame her. Rachael drifted into sleep, surrounded by the hush of breathing bodies, the weight of coats and blankets, and the fragile thread of hope.

When she woke, she found her hand clasped in Camille's across Ann's sleeping form. She didn't move. Instead, she scooted closer to Ann, her eyes wide, seeking a sign.

And there it was, Ann's chest rising and falling in a soft, steady rhythm. She was breathing.

She was warm.

"Thank you, God," Rachael whispered. "Oh, thank you. Perhaps she will live. Perhaps we've saved her."

The canvas flap shifted, and Mrs. Dix climbed into the wagon with a grunt, managing to squeeze her solid frame through the opening.

Seeing that Rachael was awake, she asked, "So, how is she?"

"Better, I think," Rachael whispered. "She's not bleeding, and she's warmer. In fact… she feels hot."

"Hmph," said Mrs. Dix. "We must get that baby to her breast. He needs to eat, or he'll fade. I've had him wrapped against me for warmth, but I can't give him what he needs. I've done all I can for him, but he's weakening."

"Mrs. Dix… thank you—"

"Nonsense," she interrupted. "We've had our differences, but now's not the time. We must work together, or we may lose both mother and child. Enough talk. Help me get him to her breast."

Rachael took the infant, tiny, searching, his mouth already rooting, and gently loosened the laces of Ann's nightdress. She pressed him against her breast.

Ann shrieked. "It hurts! It hurts!"

Mrs. Dix was instantly beside her. She took the infant and passed him to Camille, who cradled him tightly inside Mr. Grey's coat.

Then she pulled back the blanket and exposed Ann's swollen breast. She examined it with quick, practiced hands.

"As I feared," she said grimly. "She's milk sore. Third child, her milk came in early, and it's backed up. We've got to get it flowing, or we'll lose her and the baby too."

"What should we do?" Rachael asked. "I don't know anything about this."

"I do. I had the same trouble. The milk's clogged. We need heat and hot towels to ease the swelling, and the baby must nurse, painful or not. There's a trick that helps with the pain, but she's too weak for that now."

She turned to Ann, speaking firmly. "Ann, you must listen. The child must nurse. It will hurt, God, yes, but you have to bear it. He'll die otherwise. Do you understand me?"

Ann's eyes fluttered open. She raised shaking arms. "Give him to me," she whispered.

The women exchanged a look. Camille gently placed the baby back on her chest.

Ann winced and stifled a scream as he latched. Her face went pale, her jaw clenched, but she endured it.

Rachael reached up and began stroking her temple in slow, rhythmic motions. Ann's breathing steadied under her touch.

Mrs. Dix nodded approvingly. "Good. If she can manage ten minutes, switch to the other side. That'll help clear it."

She stood and motioned to Camille. "Come. We'll find Mr. Grey and the Reverend. We'll need a fire to heat some cloth. That'll help, but it's the nursing that matters most."

Rachael felt the wagon bounce as it descended into the quiet light of dawn. She looked down at Ann and the child nestled beside her. Ann's eyes were open, luminous as they gazed upon her small son.

Rachael blinked, but tears escaped anyway. They had made it through the night.

Ann managed to nurse the baby on both sides before mother and child slipped into sleep. Rachael, warm beneath the blankets, began to nod off. She crawled deeper into the pile, drawing her robe tightly around them all. Comforted by the steady rhythm of Ann's breath and the tiny sounds of the baby, Rachael drifted into a deep, dreamless sleep.

It seemed only moments had passed when the canvas parted, and Mr. Grey and Robert peered inside at the bundled women and infant.

"Rachael," Mr. Grey hissed quietly. "Can you hear me? Wake up."

Reluctantly, she stirred. Her hand fumbled for the coat sleeve.

"Put your coat on and come with me," he said gently. "Let Robert tend now to his wife and son. We've got the fire going, and the rags are being soaked. I need your help."

Still half-asleep, Rachael slipped on her coat, found her boots, and crawled toward the wagon's opening just as Robert climbed in. They exchanged places without a word.

As she stepped outside, Mr. Grey's arms caught her and lifted her gently down. Her feet sank into the snow.

The cold bit through the air, but the landscape no longer seemed harsh. The world around her looked like the snowy painting that once hung above her family's hearth.

Then she saw Mr. Grey's face, red-eyed, lined with exhaustion.

"Come, Rachael," he said. "Come by the fire. It'll warm you. Here, take my arm. The snow is slick."

He had never offered her his arm before. She glanced at the hand resting on her sleeve.

"Rachael," he said softly. "I have something to tell you."

She met his gaze.

"Sara is gone."

Her brow furrowed. "Gone? Gone where?"

"We must find her. She'll freeze!"

Mr. Grey turned toward her and placed his hands gently on her shoulders.

"Oh, Rachael…" His voice broke. "What I'm trying to tell you is that Sara is dead."

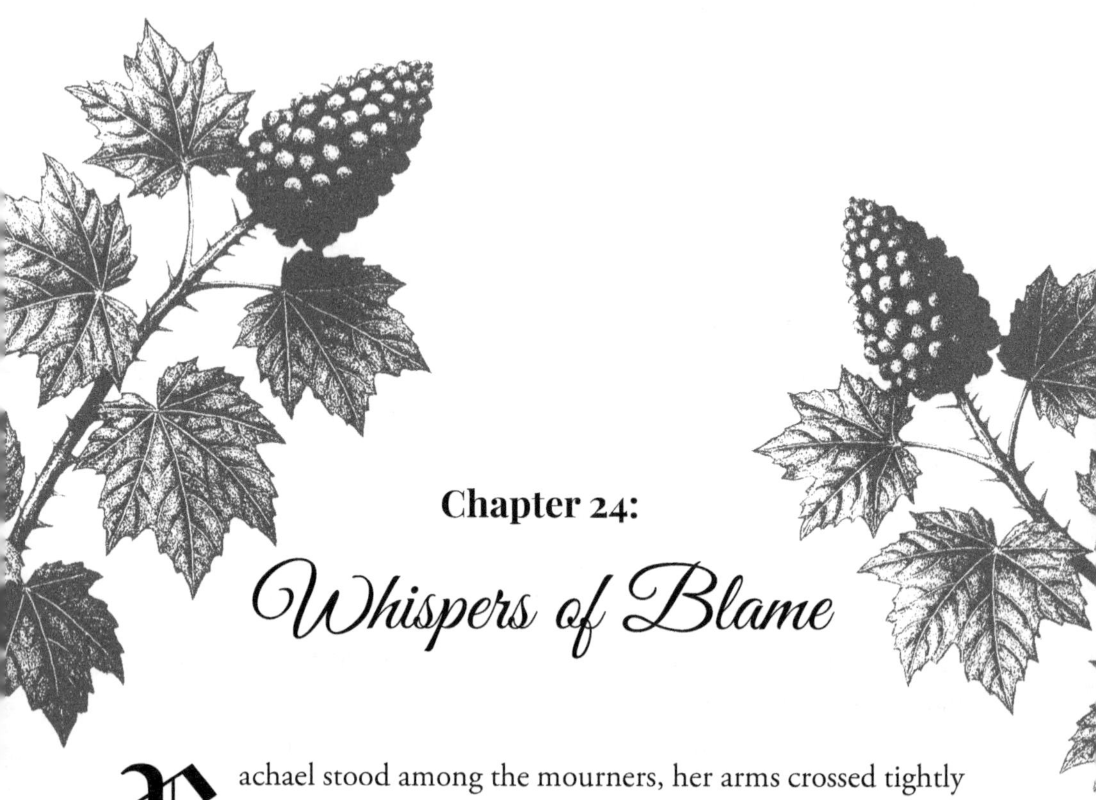

Chapter 24:

Whispers of Blame

Rachael stood among the mourners, her arms crossed tightly at her waist as though holding herself together. Her breath came in sharp, shallow pulls. She feared she might faint or scream.

The grief hollowed her out. It was jagged and physical, like a blow to the chest.

What had taken Sara? No one could say.

Still numb with shock, Rachael kept seeing her little face, smiling shyly as she had the day Rachael had called her the "daughter of my heart." It had been after Sara survived the grippe. That smile, soft and radiant, stabbed Rachael now like a blade to the heart.

She turned her eyes toward Ann, who stood silently at the graveside, her face lined with tears. Joseph, swaddled tightly, pressed against her chest. Camille held Ann up, an arm around her waist.

Robert and Mr. Grey lowered Sara's small, shrouded body into the shallow grave. Christopher stood beside his mother, clinging to her skirt. The rest of the party, Hannah, Tom, Roy, Mrs. Dix, Daniel, and Henry, circled the grave in silence.

Rachael lifted her eyes to the surrounding pine trees, their dark limbs towering over the clearing. Patches of snow still lingered on the ground, glinting under a gray sky. There was no time to carve a marker, but she and Camille had borrowed a knife and blazed a notch into one of the trees above the grave. Later, they would cover the mound with stones to keep animals away.

Oh, Sara…

Reverend Robert began to pray over the body wrapped in white linen.

Rachael felt the sob building in her chest and swallowed hard against it. She remembered skipping hand-in-hand with Sara after the dance.

Stop it, she told herself. *You have no right to this grief. You are not her mother.*

But the tears came anyway.

She turned away as Ann reached for a handful of earth and let it fall onto the linen. The soft thud of dirt against cloth was too much to bear.

A raw cry built inside her. She couldn't stop it. *Maybe it was my fault. What if what I gave her caused this?*

The guilt surged. *No, no… I can't think that… I mustn't lose control…* But she already was.

Before she realized it, her legs were moving. She fled.

She scrambled up the mountain trail, slipping on the wet snow, gasping for air. As she climbed, the snow deepened. Finally, she collapsed face-first into the drift, feeling its cold bite on her skin.

She clawed her way forward, then simply gave in and curled up, the pain overtaking her.

She wept into the snow, her sobs swallowed by the white silence around her.

Unseen behind her, Mr. Grey stood silently, bearing witness to the full weight of her grief.

The next day, the party headed down the mountain. The sun had melted the snow on that side, making the track treacherous, slushy in shaded areas, icy in others. Progress was slow, and the incline steep. Mr. Grey ordered the back wagon wheels to be chained together to prevent them from overtaking the animals. The chains clanked and rattled as the wagons slid down the slope.

Rachael walked behind the wagons, as did most of the women and children. It was the least they could do to ease the burden on the struggling beasts.

Christopher slipped his small hand into hers, looking up with wide, uncertain eyes. Barely able to contain her grief, Rachael gave his hand a squeeze, trying to steady him and herself.

She could see the questions forming behind his eyes.

"Rachael," he asked softly, "why did God take Sara? My father said He did. What happened? Why did she die? Did she do something that made God mad?"

Rachael's throat tightened. "Oh, Christopher… I don't think God took her. She was a fine person, a good one. She was always kind to you. She loved you very much."

"Then… if God didn't take her, why did she die? Was she sick? Can I catch it?"

"No, darling. I don't think so. If it were something you could catch, you'd be sick already. I don't know why she died. If I'd known she was ill, I would have done everything I could to help her feel better."

"Hannah said you did give her something the night she died. Why didn't it work?"

Rachael froze, the words catching in her chest. "I don't know, child. I only gave her something to help with something normal for a girl her age."

Christopher's voice rushed out in a guilty tumble. "Some say it's what you gave her that caused it. You… you wouldn't have done that, would you?"

Rachael stopped walking. "Oh, Christopher. Of course not." Then, gently, "Who told you that?"

"I can't tell. I promised," he said, his eyes fixed on the trail.

The words struck her like a blow. Her deepest, most unspoken fear, uttered now by a child.

Had she caused Sara's death?

She'd dismissed the thought again and again. But now, hearing it voiced aloud, it clawed back into her mind. She replayed that night yet again: the dark, the cold, the hurried medicine over the fire, the slippery packet in her hand, and her frantic rush to help both Ann and Sara. What if she had grabbed the wrong packet?

She had been too afraid to look. But now she knew she must. She had to.

If she had made a mistake, if she had caused this—

The dread swelled up in her, her stomach twisting. She looked down the rutted, icy trail and at the people walking ahead. No one had met her eye in days.

They must believe that she was the reason.

Even Mr. Grey.

Her shoulders were hunched under the weight of it.

Oh God… please. Help me. If this is true, I can't live with myself. I can't. And I won't.

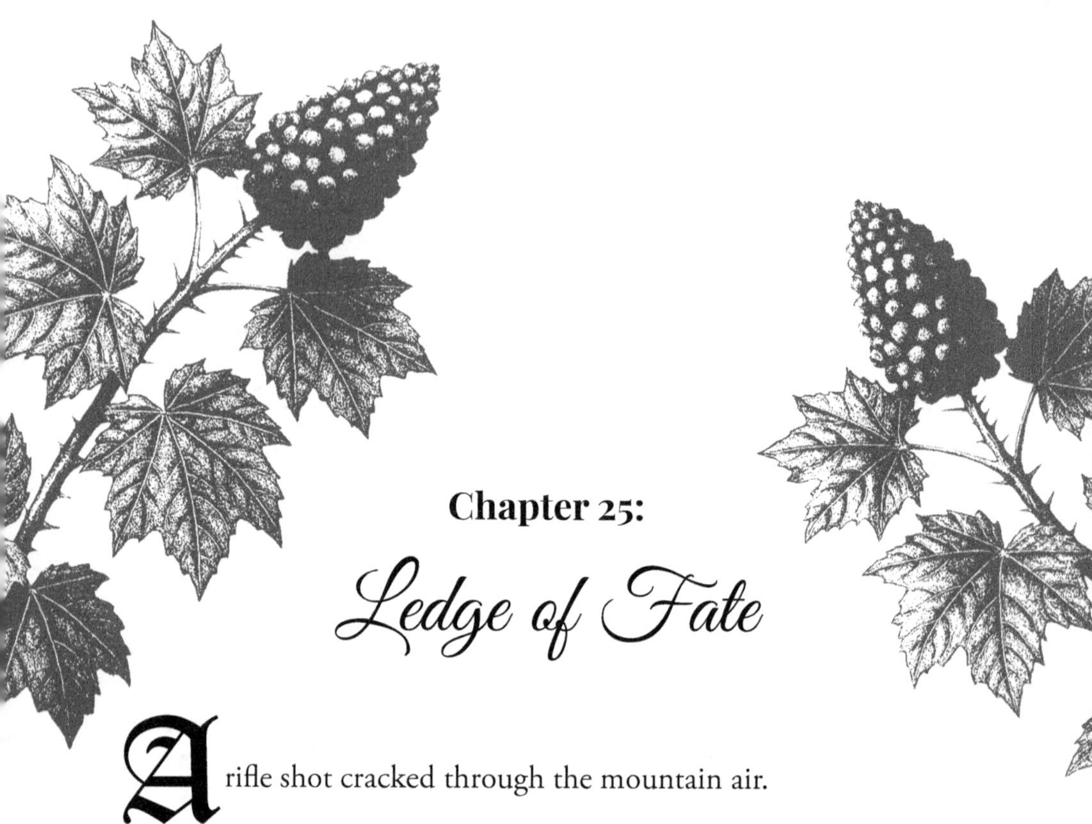

Chapter 25:

Ledge of Fate

A rifle shot cracked through the mountain air.

Mr. Grey responded immediately, firing two shots in return. He called a halt.

They had reached a small clearing before the next descent.

Leaping from the springboard wagon, he unhitched his mules quickly, leaving their harnesses on. He pulled off his hat and wiped his brow.

"Pull your wagons in here," he called out, gesturing with his chin. "Unchain the wheels. Hobble the animals; they've done enough work this morning. Let them graze. We'll make noon here. Children start gathering wood. Let's get a fire going. Looks like dry tinder nearby."

Christopher let go of Rachael's hand but gave it a final squeeze, glancing up at her. "It's all right, Rachael. I know you'd never do nothing to hurt Sara."

He ran off to join the boys gathering wood.

Rachael watched him go, shaking her head slowly. *If only that were true.*

The morning's descent had left everyone famished. Hannah and Mrs. Dix began to unload the tucker boxes. Camille tended to the mother and child still resting in the back of their wagon. It had been too risky for Ann to attempt the icy slope on foot. Some of their supplies had been shifted to the Dixes' wagon to lighten the oxen's load.

Rachael walked over to help with the noon meal preparations. Hannah reached out and gently patted her hand.

"Are you all right? I know this has been terribly hard for you. Well, hard for all of us. We all knew how you felt about Sara."

"Hannah," Rachael said, her voice trembling, "could we talk later about that morning, how you found Sara, and what you remember?"

"There's really not much to say," Hannah replied, her eyes fixed ahead. "Sara had vomited earlier in the evening before you came. She seemed comforted by your presence when you arrived. Later, her stomach pains woke her up. She was warm and restless, so I gave her the little medicine in the cup. It appeared to settle her. She slept after that. It was only in the morning, when I tried to wake her, that I realized… she was gone."

"You know I would have done everything I could to save her?"

"Yes, Rachael." Hannah met her eyes. "I believe you would. But you couldn't. That's the simple truth."

She turned away, stepping toward a squabble between Henry and Roy, leaving Rachael with the weight of those words.

Out of habit, Rachael scanned the camp, expecting to see Sara or Christopher nearby. Her heart seized when she remembered there would be no more sightings of Sara.

She was suddenly transported to another moment: arriving home with her father after a long day of collecting, calling out, *"Mother, guess what?"*—throwing open the studio door, only to find the room empty, her mother's easel covered. Her father had flinched. She had flushed with guilt, realizing too late how deeply it must have cut him. It had seemed so natural then, calling out to someone who was no longer there.

A sharp crack rang out, another shot. A shout followed. A familiar voice.

Mr. Grey whistled, the sharp, urgent signal they had all come to recognize.

Rachael usually obeyed immediately unless she was a mid-specimen gathering. In those moments, time seemed to slow. But that was another life. She didn't collect anymore. She couldn't… not if she—

A horse thundered into the clearing, breaking her reverie. George Miller was in the saddle, the horse streaked with sweat. It had clearly come by a separate path.

Mr. Grey rushed to meet him, catching the reins as George dismounted.

"And the sheep?" he asked, breathless.

Always the sheep, Rachael thought.

"How are the sheep? Tell me now."

"They're fine, sir. Fattening up some in the valley. Beautiful place. Fine land to raise a family."

Mrs. Dix bustled toward them.

"And my son? Is James all right? Tell me he is."

"He was when I left. We've been in the valley for four days waiting for you. There's a trading post there, though they sell too much liquor to the Indians for my liking."

"Indians? Oh, my God. Is he safe?"

"He's safe from the Indians, ma'am. Just not from his own temptation to drink."

"Hmph." Mrs. Dix's shoulders rose and fell, but it was clear to everyone she was relieved.

"I heard there was snow in the mountains," George added. "Thought I should come back and check on you."

His eyes swept the camp.

Rachael knew who he was looking for. She searched, too, but Camille was not in sight.

Then Camille rounded the wagon, having just finished tending to Ann. The moment she saw Mr. Miller, her hand flew to her mouth.

"Oh," she said softly, flushing pink.

All eyes turned to George Miller. His expression said everything.

"Why… why, Miss Camille?" he stammered, stepping forward. "There's something I'd like to talk to you about. In private."

"You will not speak to my niece in private!" Mrs. Dix barked. "That is inappropriate. Improper."

"Danielle," said her husband, stepping in. "Now, Mrs. Dix, come with me. We have more important things to tend to." He took her arm and gently steered her toward the rear of their wagon. "Let the young folks talk."

As the others began to settle and eat, Rachael took the opportunity to retrieve her bag from the back of the Godleys' wagon and to check on Ann. They had barely spoken since Sara's passing. Rachael wasn't sure she was ready, but the need to access her supplies was stronger than her dread.

She drew back the canvas. Inside, Ann sat propped against the wagon box, a pillow behind her, blankets draped across her legs. Baby Joseph nursed at her breast.

"Oh, Rachael, I'm glad to see you. This has been… a horrible time. My poor Sara…" Her eyes filled with tears.

"Ann, I'm so sorry, I—"

"I meant to thank you," Ann interrupted. "For helping Joseph and me. Without you, I'm not sure we would have survived."

She gazed down at her infant.

"God is strange, isn't he? He takes one and leaves another. I do not understand it. But Robert says it's part of His plan, and we must accept it."

Accept it? Rachael's thoughts roiled. *How could anyone believe that God would take one child and leave another by design?*

"I don't know if I can believe in a God like that," she blurted.

"Rachael!" Ann's eyes widened. "Don't say that. You can't mean it. That's blasphemy. We're all protected and subject to His will."

Rachael knew then that she had to be quiet. Their grief was different. She understood that Ann believed what she said because it comforted her. But Rachael found no comfort. Her heart had hardened. *If God had taken a child as sweet as Sara, then I would be done with Him.*

"We all know how much Sara admired you and even loved you. I also need to thank you for that. She could always count on you to take her part. I'm afraid I wasn't much of a mother to her in the last few months of pregnancy. You were more of a mother to her than I was."

Ann looked up, her eyes flooded with gratitude.

At those words, an arrow of grief pierced Rachael's chest. She clutched at it as though trying to rip the pain away with her bare hands.

"Why, Rachael, are you all right? Should I call for someone?" Ann asked, alarmed.

"No. I'm fine, Ann. Really." Rachael forced a breath and added, "Do you know where my medicine bag is? I need it."

"Why, it's here beside me," Ann replied, sliding her hand across the blanket.

Rachael stared at the bag as if it were a coiled snake. For a moment, she imagined it *was* a snake. Her hand trembled as she reached for it.

"Thank you, Ann. I'm glad you're better. And the child, too," she said, forcing a smile.

The wagon swayed slightly as Rachael climbed out and bumped into Mrs. Dix, who was arriving with a bowl of food for the mother.

"Why, Rachael, are you all right? You look odd."

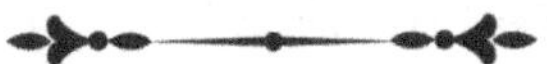

"I'm fine, Mrs. Dix. Really."

She couldn't bear anyone's concern. *If only they'd leave me alone.*

Rachael wandered off into the woods, clutching the medicine bag. Once she turned to glance back, only Mr. Grey had noticed. He rubbed his chin and said something to Mr. Miller, then turned away.

The ground still held patches of snow, though rays of sunlight filtered through the pine boughs. Normally, she would've paused to enjoy the light, but not today. The bag felt heavier with every step. She switched it to her other hand, gripping it tightly. Whatever it revealed now held her fate.

At last, well out of sight, she came to a cliff overlooking a deep ravine. The valley below stretched far in the distance. She sat on a flat boulder, sighed, and opened the bag.

One by one, she laid out the contents, small pouches tied with careful knots. She had done it just as Mari taught her. At least that much she had done right.

But one pouch, she remembered, had been empty and untied. She lifted it now and brought it to her nose. It smelled of dirt... and something else. A scent she couldn't name.

She remembered Mari pounding a root to stop bleeding and ease cramps. *Was that the one I used?* Her mind scrambled for clarity.

She retied the empty pouch and closed her eyes. Reaching into the bag again, she tried to feel what she had chosen before. Her hand closed around one. She withdrew it and opened her eyes.

No...

She smelled it. A strong, sharp bark, medicine she'd traded for at Fort Laramie. It had a scent almost identical to the one she had used. Mari had warned her: only for emergencies. It had anesthetic-like properties.

Could I have given this to Sara by mistake?

Ann had slept deeply, but Sara, smaller than her mother, took the same dose. And hadn't Hannah said there was some left in the cup? That she gave Sara a little more?

Rachael jumped to her feet. *I can't bear this. I can't. I'll throw the bag off this cliff and never give another remedy again.*

Perhaps Mrs. Dix was right. Perhaps these are the Devil's medicines.

She stormed to the cliff's edge. The valley lay below, the last mountains of their journey behind them. She looked down. The wind tugged at her skirt.

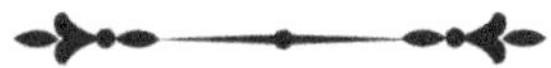

"Rachael, don't! Don't move!"

Mr. Grey's voice rang out. He lunged for her, grabbing her arm and yanking her backward just as the bag flew from her grasp into the air.

As he reached for it, his foot caught a loose rock.

He slipped.

He tumbled over the edge.

Rachael screamed.

She dropped to her stomach, inching forward to the brink, pressing herself against the earth, terrified of what she might see.

His body. Broken. Mangled. Gone.

Could I possibly be responsible for the deaths of the only two people I had ever loved?

Realization thrummed through her, but when she dared open her eyes, Mr. Grey was looking up at her, cradling his left arm, perched on a ledge about twenty feet below.

"Rachael, get help. I've hurt my arm."

"Oh, Mr. Grey, I'm so sorry." She began to weep.

"For God's sake, stop sobbing and get help!"

"Yes, yes, I will…"

She scrambled backward on all fours, heart pounding with relief and fear. Her medicine bag lay forgotten as she leaped down the hill, dodging branches and rocks. She heard voices ahead, "Camp!" but her lungs burned too fiercely to call out. At last, startled faces turned toward her as she burst into the clearing, gasping.

Tom and Mr. Miller rushed to her side.

Tom placed a steadying hand on her back. "Catch your breath, then speak," he said gently.

"It's Mr. Grey. He fell off a cliff. He's hurt his arm. We have to help him!" she panted.

Tom didn't hesitate. He grabbed a coiled rope and bridled a mule. "Come on, Rachael, show me the way." He swung onto the mule and pulled her up behind him.

"I'm coming too," said Mr. Miller. "We might need both of us."

The two men kicked the mules into motion, galloping up the trail. Branches whipped past them, hooves thudding on packed soil. At last, they reached the cliff. Rachael's bag still lay beside the boulder.

Too breathless to speak, she pointed.

The men crawled to the cliff's edge and peered over. Mr. Grey was slumped against the rocky wall below, unmoving.

They called to him. No response.

Back with Rachael, who chewed her knuckle, Tom asked, "What happened? How did he fall?"

"I, I don't know. He slipped on a rock. I was just, then he was." Her voice faded.

"Did he speak to you afterward?"

"Yes. He said to get help. His arm hurt."

The men exchanged grim looks.

"He probably hurt more than his arm," muttered George. "He's out cold now."

Tom nodded. "One of us needs to go down."

"You tie the rope around my waist," said George. "Wrap it around that tree and hook it to the mule's harness. Start the mule back about thirty feet. I'll yell when I'm ready for Slack."

"Wait," Tom interrupted. "I'll go. You've got a wife, a son, and another on the way."

"And you just got engaged."

Rachael snapped, "Stop arguing, or I'll go myself."

"You're not strong enough to carry him, Mrs."

"I'm not going to carry him. I'm going down first. There's room for two on that ledge. I can assess his injuries before you haul him up. You might make it worse otherwise. I'm light, and I've done this before. My father taught me in Maine." She paused. "Tie the rope on me. It's getting colder, and those clouds, there's no time."

They looked at each other and nodded.

"Good. Tie my medicine bag on, too. Mr. Grey won't like it, but I've got bitter herbs that'll knock him out if needed. And let me borrow your gloves, holding the rope burns."

Reluctantly, the men secured the rope around her waist and another loop under her arms. They double-checked each knot.

Rachael stepped to the edge, faced the mule, and gripped the rope. She gave a nod. The mule moved forward steadily, and Tom braced the rope as she went over the edge.

Her descent was cautious but confident—knees bent, feet flat, every breath measured. She could feel her father's voice in her head: *steady now, don't lock your knees.* The rock face scraped her skirt, but she didn't care.

Her boots touched the ledge.

"Stop!" she called up. The rope slackened.

She untied the loop beneath her arms but kept the waist rope secured. Then, crawling on her knees, she approached Mr. Grey.

He was slumped against the rock, unconscious but breathing. His left arm hung at an unnatural angle, and a gash above his eye had already begun to swell. She reached for his pulse.

Even through her shaken thoughts and grief for Sara, she found the presence to pray. *God, please... help him.*

She sat beside him, leaning against the rock wall, and opened her medicine bag. Pulling him up, though carefully, was going to hurt no matter what. A small dose of bitter bark might ease the pain.

She rubbed some on her palm and opened his mouth, pressing it against his gums.

He sputtered and groaned.

"Lie still now, Mr. Grey. You're hurt. Don't move or try to talk. Your arm is injured, and you've got a cut on your eye. We've got to get you up the cliff. Let me look at that cut now."

She gently brushed his hair away from his forehead.

"Hold still. Just hold still."

The cut wasn't deep, and it had stopped bleeding. His eye was swollen but open, watching her.

Trying to steady her own shaking hands, she said, "First, I'm going to secure your arm so it won't move. Then I'll tie the rope around your waist. I've given you something to take the edge off, but as Mr. Miller and Tom pull you up, it's going to hurt. Try to push with your feet, and use your good hand to hold the rope. Do you think you can do that?"

He nodded. She noticed his pupils were dilated but said nothing.

"Ready?" she asked.

Another nod.

She looked up the cliff face, forcing herself not to glance down at the sheer drop. *Don't look. Just don't.*

Tom's face appeared over the ledge. He was lying flat, peering down.

"Ready?" he called.

"One moment, checking the rope again."

She ran it firmly around Mr. Grey's waist and twisted it into his belt. She owed another debt to the Indian trader woman at Fort Laramie, who had taught her how to tie this kind of knot. She knew it would hold.

He was pale but lucid. She helped him turn, guiding his face toward the cliff.

"Ready, William?"

"Yes," he croaked.

"Okay, Tom. Steady, pull."

Tom gripped the rope as Mr. Miller backed the mule slowly. Inch by inch, Mr. Grey rose.

Rachael cringed as one of his boots slipped. He slammed into the cliff face, and she clapped her hand over her mouth to keep from crying out.

What felt like an eternity took only a few minutes. Then—

"Got him," Tom called, and the rope came sailing back down to her.

Rachael tied it under her arms, making sure it was still connected to the one around her waist.

"Ready?" Tom's voice called down.

She began her ascent.

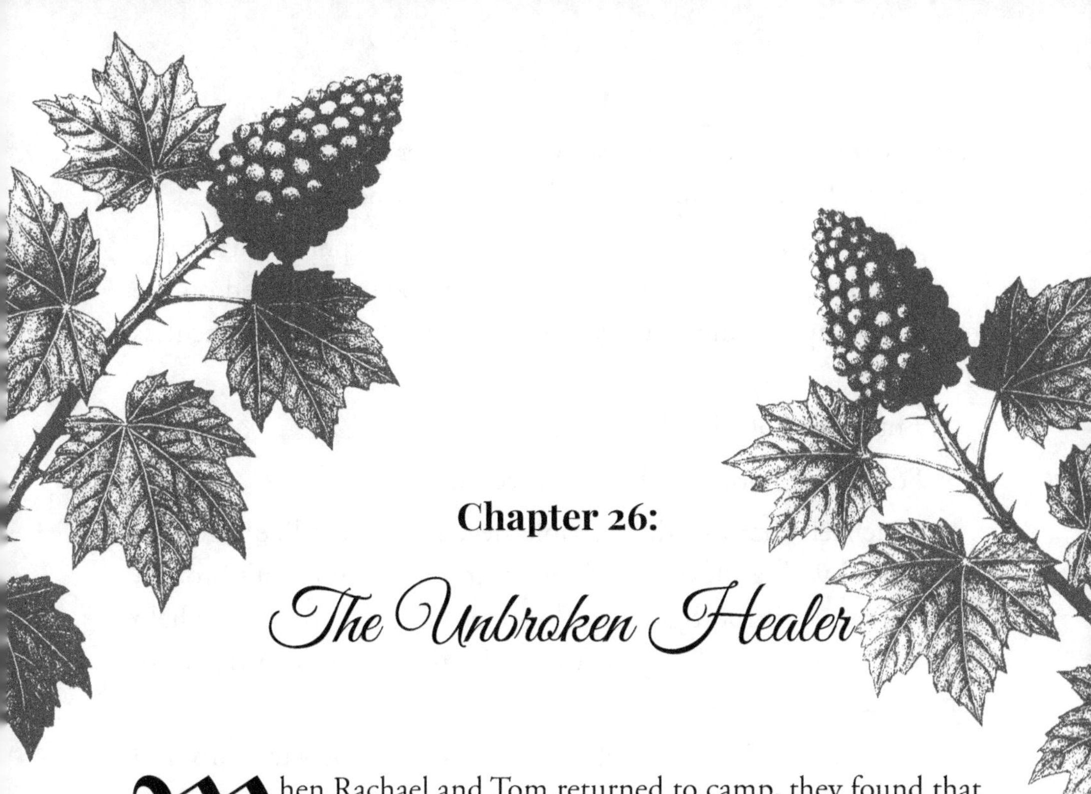

Chapter 26:

The Unbroken Healer

When Rachael and Tom returned to camp, they found that Hannah, Camille, and Mrs. Dix had everything under control. Tents were pitched, a fire blazed, and wood was stacked in a tidy pile. The air promised a cold night, but at least there would be no descent into the valley in the dark.

Mr. Miller had already arrived with Mr. Grey and helped him into the back of the springboard wagon. Rachael glanced at Mr. Miller, searching his expression.

"He's tough," he told her with a small smile. "Go see for yourself. He's already complaining about lost time and, naturally, the sheep."

Tom helped her down from the mule and handed her the medicine bag. "Best go check on him now, Rachael."

She nodded, glad that the others were busy preparing supper. Her eyes met Hannah's across the fire. Hannah lifted her eyebrows in a silent question.

Rachael only shook her head. She didn't know.

She stepped on the axle and climbed over the backboard of the wagon. Mr. Grey leaned against the front seat, his arm bound tightly across his chest, his right eye swollen shut. Her face flushed, and she looked quickly away. He watched her with his one open eye.

Turning away to collect herself, she was overcome with strange dizziness, relief, perhaps, or pure exhaustion. A quip danced on the tip of her tongue about how pleased he must be to see her speechless for once.

But instead of a laugh, a sob escaped.

Still, he said nothing. Just watched her.

"Rachael," he rasped. "Terrible headache. Feels like I got hit in the head with a shovel. Arm's pounding. Don't think it's broken, but you've tied it too tight, and I can't undo the knot. Come help me. What were you doing on that cliff, anyway? I keep trying to remember what happened, but I can't."

Relieved by the sound of his voice, she crawled forward and squatted beside him.

"Hold still," she said, pushing gently on the area around his swollen eye. It was inflamed but clean. She'd have to watch it closely.

"Rachael, my arm—"

"Don't fuss," she snapped in her most authoritative tone. "I'm just going to loosen it a little. I need to look at your hand first. Don't forget, I watched what you did with Christopher."

He scowled. "Just hurry."

He winced as the knot came loose, and his arm dropped slightly.

"Hurts."

Carefully, she supported it against his chest, then slid the sling further down his shoulder to ease the weight on his neck.

"Rachael, give me something for the pain."

She was checking the circulation in his hand, pressing the nail beds to observe the blood return. She didn't look at him.

"I can't give you anything," she said flatly.

"Why ever not?"

"I... I—" Rachael looked up at him, still holding his bruised hand. "I'm afraid."

"Whatever for?"

"I might have hurt Sara."

"What?" His voice rose, confused. "For goodness' sake, speak up."

"I'm afraid I killed Sara," she burst out. "I gave her something for the cramps. Maybe I gave her too much. Maybe it was the wrong medicine. It was my fault."

He blinked at her in disbelief.

"Oh, Rachael. That's ridiculous. You take too much on yourself. It could've been appendicitis. It could've been anything. We'll never know. You can't carry the burden of something no one can truly know. That's not one of your better traits."

"I can't. I won't give you anything."

"Rachael, look at me."

She looked. His face was bruised and bloodied but still somehow composed.

"I need that medicine. Whatever happened is in the past. I need your help now. I *trust* you. Please, go and concoct one of your remedies."

"But—"

"Now," he bellowed, then winced at the pain it caused.

"No, William, I can't. And I won't."

"Rachael, you must."

Just as he had done to her so many times, she ignored him and left.

Behind the wagon, Rachael leaned against the frame and put her face in her hands. She would not risk harming someone again. She had fooled herself into thinking she possessed true knowledge of herbal remedies.

No more.

She shook her head and made a vow: she would never use the medicine again, no matter the consequences. She couldn't erase what she'd learned, but she could silence it.

Instead of throwing the medicine bag away where someone might find it, she buried it under woolen blankets at the back of the springboard wagon. Out of sight, out of reach.

She would forget it. All of it.

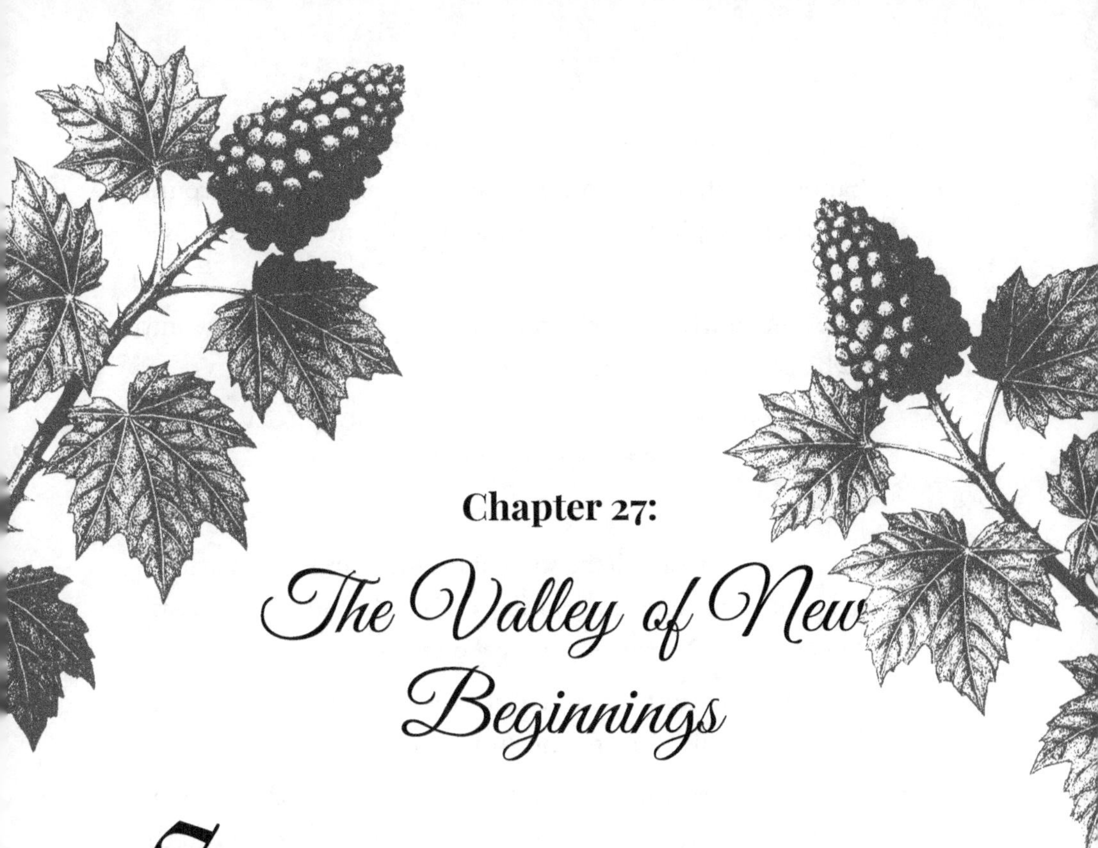

Chapter 27:
The Valley of New Beginnings

Several days later, it was time to move on.

Mr. Grey, still cranky and aching, insisted on inspecting his sheep. Footsore and weary of heart, the company began its slow descent into the valley.

The slope was steep, so steep that all four wagon wheels had to be chained: front wheels to the front, back to the rear. Under Grey's supervision, the men tied themselves with ropes behind the wagons to help slow their descent with their own weight.

Everyone else walked, carrying goods to lighten the wagons.

Ann and her newborn rode in the springboard wagon, Mr. Grey using his good arm to work the brake. Watching them, Rachael worried the wagon might tip. She decided not to look.

Instead, she took Christopher's hand and invented games to distract him. Since his baby brother's birth and Sara's death, he had become especially attached to her. Mischievous and bright, he was the kind of child who always needed a watchful eye or a firm hand.

When they finally reached the valley at dusk, all were stained with mud and too exhausted to notice the stunning beauty around them. They built fires, pitched tents, ate a small dinner, and collapsed into sleep.

All except the newly engaged couple, who sat by the fire late into the night, whispering about their future.

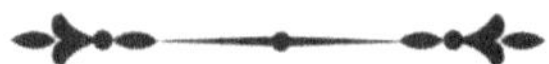

At dawn, Rachael woke to the song of meadowlarks and sparrows. Light spilled gently through the tent flaps. Camille and Mrs. Dix still slept beside her, Mrs. Dix snoring a ragged saw-song.

Careful not to wake them, Rachael crawled out of the tent and stretched her aching limbs in the morning chill.

The valley was beautiful. A slender river twisted lazily through its center. Rich soil, dark from rain, promised new life. And far in the distance, she could just make out the blue shadow of the Cascades.

Soon, this journey would end.

She wasn't sure how she felt.

She would miss Mr. Grey, though he was married, and there could never be anything between them. And then there were Hannah and Camille. Women who had become, in their own quiet ways, sisters.

Hannah had told her she was pregnant again. This time, she had told Tom.

Rachael would've liked to stay to see the new baby. But...

She turned to see the men gathered around the fire, clasping tin cups in their hands. The smell of real coffee wafted toward her. Mr. Miller must have bought some at the last post.

Drawn by the scent, she laced her boots and made her way toward them.

As she arrived, Mr. Grey held out a steaming cup, offered with his good right arm.

"How's the arm, Mr. Grey?" she asked.

"It hurts, Rachael. I've put up with it for four days. That's enough suffering. It'd be better if—"

"No," she cut him off, turning away. But not before she noticed the cut on his forehead was beginning to heal.

The men continued their talk, mostly about the health of the sheep. The delay in the mountains had given them a chance to graze in the valley and regain weight. Mr. Grey had inspected them the day before and counted them. His losses upset him, but Rachael thought losing one hundred out of four hundred seemed a small price for having come this far.

Today, he and Mr. Miller were going out again to check on the flock. Mr. Grey wanted each animal marked with a bright red dye, easy to spot when they encountered other herds. It would take all day, which meant a rest day for the rest of the company. Rachael looked forward to it. She desperately wanted to wash her clothes and what she could of her body. Everyone was filthy.

Then Tom said something that caught her attention.

"Yeah, Mr. Grey, I'm concerned about him. Seems James has a bit of a drinking problem. Mean drunk, too. Got into a fight last night, just fists, but too many men with knives for that to end well. I talked to him. Maybe someone else can get through."

"If he starts another fight, I'll dismiss him," said Mr. Grey. "I'm short on drovers. Need every man I can get to get these sheep to my ranch. Where'd he sleep last night?"

"As far as I know, he passed out on the post porch."

"I'll stop by and set him straight," Mr. Grey said grimly. "Used the whip on him before. Might have to again."

"His mother won't like that," Tom muttered.

"So be it. Better she sees that than see him bleeding from a knife wound. She didn't like it last time, either, but he has to learn."

Mr. Grey wiped his hands on his pants.

"George, I need you, the boy, John, and James to mark the sheep. It's a full day's job. We'll get the dye at the post when we find James."

But James wasn't at the post. No one had seen him that morning. Mr. Grey scowled but went out to work with the others anyway.

Rachael noticed Camille was now dressed and tending the cookfire. She joined her, pleased to have a moment to talk and relax. She looked forward to clean clothes and a bath. She had seen a pretty little stream nearby, perfect for washing.

She sighed, content for the moment, and began to plan her day.

Suddenly, a shriek pierced the morning calm. Then another. Camille dropped the spoon she was using to stir the ever-present beans and bolted toward the Dix wagon.

Rachael followed and stopped short at what she saw behind the wagon.

Mrs. Dix was kneeling over James, sobbing and screaming, shaking him as if trying to will him awake. Daniel was beside her, trying to calm her, but she pushed him away, crying out for her son.

Rachael felt the familiar drop in her stomach. She ran forward to help Camille and Daniel. James's shirt was soaked in dark, dried blood.

As always, Rachael forced herself to pause, assess, observe, and analyze.

Camille helped Mrs. Dix cradle James's head in her lap. That seemed to calm them both a little.

Rachael knelt beside them and gently laid her hand on Mrs. Dix's arm.

"May I look at him?"

"Yes, please," said Daniel quickly.

Mrs. Dix turned to Rachael, her face a mask of pain.

"Do something. Please. Will he die? I couldn't bear it."

"Let me look first," Rachael said gently.

She reached for the blood-soaked shirt but didn't pull it back yet. From the pool of dried blood beneath him, James had lost a lot. The bleeding had stopped for now.

"Camille, bring blankets, rags, a knife, and water," she said without raising her voice. "We need to see what we're dealing with."

Camille nodded and ran.

"Daniel, help me lift him just enough to get the blanket underneath. Then please go to the post and ask if there's a doctor."

He obeyed at once.

Camille returned, arms full. She laid everything beside Rachael, who nodded.

"Mrs. Dix, hold him. Talk to him. Keep him calm."

Tears streaming, the older woman did as asked.

Rachael cut away the shirt carefully. Part of it stuck to the wound, and she poured water over the area to loosen the fabric. As the bloody cloth pulled away, the wound came into view.

Mrs. Dix covered her mouth. It was a horrible sight: a ragged wound turning crimson as it swelled. Rachael looked away for a moment, then forced herself to look back. It was a knife wound about two inches across. She had no idea how deep.

She continued to pour water over it. *Where was Daniel with the doctor?* What should she do? Then, she remembered Fort Laramie, how the Indian woman Jacob had arranged for her to meet had treated a young soldier's ax wound.

Rachael closed her eyes to recall: *Yes, yes, she had poured water over it again and again, then packed it… right with mallow and yarrow.*

She kept washing James's wound, willing the water to clear away the dirt. Next, she needed her bag. She had to pack the wound with mallow and yarrow.

Rachael reached beside her. The bag wasn't there. *Where was it?*

Then she remembered: she had left it in the springboard wagon.

She stood up, her heart pounding.

She shouldn't be doing this. She wasn't ready. She might do more harm than good. She could kill James, too.

She backed away from the wound, breathing hard. "I'm sorry, Betsy. I don't know what to do."

Mrs. Dix turned to her, pleading. "But Rachael, you must. I've seen you with Ann, with her baby, and with Christopher. You knew what to do, and it helped. Help him, Rachael."

Rachael placed a hand on her chest, still backing away. "I'm sorry. I can't."

Suddenly, Camille's arms were around her waist, steadying her, anchoring her.

"Rachael," she whispered, her voice calm and certain in Rachael's ear. "There's no one else. You must help James. Surely you know that."

"I know you think you hurt Sara, but you don't know that. No one does. Without you, he might die. You can't let that happen. I know you, Rachael. Now, where's your bag?"

"I can't," Rachael choked.

Mrs. Dix stared at her, eyes burning. "If you don't do this and he dies, then you will be responsible for his death. The Lord will never forgive you. Neither will I."

"Indeed, He would not," added Reverend Robert, who had joined the circle. Ann stood beside him, her tiny baby in a sling, Hannah at her side.

Rachael looked at the people around her, people she had come to know so intimately over these long weeks. She saw the fear in Mrs. Dix's eyes and remembered the storm and the fierce love for James. She thought of her own helpless grief when Sara had died. She thought of Hannah, terrified of her pregnancy.

They needed her.

"The bag is in the back of the springboard wagon," she said, her voice hoarse. "Bring it to me. I'll try my best, but I may fail. Are you willing to risk that?"

"Yes," came the chorus of voices.

Camille returned minutes later, breathless, the bag clutched in her hands.

Rachael's fingers shook as she opened it, rummaging through the pouches until she found the mallow and the yarrow. Carefully, she packed the dried leaves and flowers into James's wound as gently as she could. She covered it with a clean cloth, wound it around his back, and tied it firmly.

Rising from the ground, her knees unsteady, she felt faint. Her vision swam.

"Ánimo, ánimo, dear heart."

Her father's voice. She blinked. He wasn't there, of course, but the words steadied her.

At that moment, Daniel returned with a man in a brown coat carrying a black bag. His red-rimmed eyes and the sour smell of tobacco and sweat gave Rachael pause. She looked at his blackened fingernails.

Was this really the doctor?

Out of breath, Daniel explained, "There is no doctor here, but Frank's the barber and serves as their only doctor."

Rachael and Frank regarded each other. She realized how ragged she must look: her hair loose, her dress stained, her hands filthy.

She shouldn't judge.

"Tell me, little lady, what'd you do?" the man asked.

For once, she ignored the condescension in his tone. *There was something to learn here, and she wanted to learn.*

Quietly, she told him about washing the wound and packing it with mallow and yarrow. "I also used some of a root that Mari, a native healer, gave me. She said it was strong medicine. Only for serious cases. I've kept it wrapped in a pouch with a purple string."

"Let me see it."

He held out his hand. "I've heard a tale of a powerful root found in the Blue Mountains. Prized by all the Indian healers in this valley. Only seen it once."

Rachael handed him the pouch, her breath shallow. *Could it be?*

He turned it over in his hands and brought it to his nose. "Yes. I think this is it."

"Do you know its name?" she asked. Her voice barely audible.

"Devil's something. Can't remember, but I can find out for you. I'd be glad to."

Rachael's heart skipped. *Could it be her plant? Could she have had it all along?*

Her mind raced. She didn't know, but she would find out. Her hands trembled as she returned the root to her bag.

Frank placed a hand lightly on her shoulder and turned to examine James's bandage.

"Well, don't think I could've done better by him myself. Best to get him off the ground and onto a pallet. He's goin' to be mighty sore if he survives, but thanks to your quick thinking, he has a chance."

Rachael looked around at the small company of souls who had toiled so long together. Each one gazed back at her with gratitude. Mrs. Dix embraced her, as did Daniel, Camille, and Hannah. Even Reverend Robert offered a solemn blessing.

She didn't know who had changed more, her or them. She supposed it didn't matter now. For the first time, she felt a genuine part of the group. She would learn all she could. She would find the name of the root and of all the others she had used. She would go to Oregon and become a healer. And if the root she found wasn't Devil's Club, then she would keep searching. She knew that now.

When Mr. Grey returned with George and the two extra hires to help mark the sheep, he learned what had happened to James. Rachael watched him enter the small room at the back of the barber's establishment, where the boy now lay under care. James was asleep, and his mother sat beside him in a rocking chair.

Grey stepped forward, lifted the sheet, and looked at the boy's chest. Rachael, on the other side of the bed, watched him closely. The swelling had gone down. There was no fresh blood on the bandages.

This would change everything.

Rachael understood that. The Dixes would not leave their son behind. Camille was now engaged to Mr. Miller. And Miller, though contracted to deliver the sheep to Grey's ranch, wanted to stay in the valley. She couldn't blame him; it was a lovely place.

What would Mr. Grey do?

To her surprise, he asked to speak with her after supper. She wondered if this was the moment he would tell her that he had known all along she had lied and that now, she would have to stay behind. Rachael reasoned that she could be left in worse places. At least she'd have Camille's company for the winter. She could cross the Cascades into Oregon City in the spring.

But the one thing she could not say aloud, not to anyone, was that she didn't want to leave him.

Admitting her feelings for him had changed everything. She struggled not to lean into him when they rode together in the springboard wagon. When she did, even by accident, a thrill passed through her body, and her heart began to pound. She was used to his gruffness, but beneath that crust was a steady, reliable strength. A kind man.

She would never forget the look on his face when he told her that Sara was dead or the way he had held her arm. She realized now that she would not feel safe crossing the mountains without him.

That mattered more than she dared admit.

Quietly, she slipped the wedding ring off her finger and placed it in her apron pocket. A pale band of skin marked where it had long been.

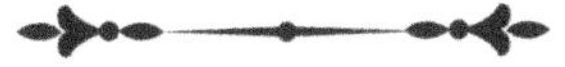

After supper, Rachael and Mr. Grey walked together up a small rise that overlooked the town and the valley beyond. They sat together on a flat boulder, waiting in silence for one or the other to speak.

Below them, the river meandered. Stove pipes poked from rooftops, sending lazy plumes of smoke into the dusk. The grass beneath their boots gleamed with dew. A single star appeared above them, just beside a silver crescent moon.

Rachael broke the silence. "How's your arm? The bruise on your forehead is almost gone now. I can just see the outline of what'll be a scar. Do you still get headaches?"

"I don't want to talk about my health," he said. "I want to talk about something else, and maybe, God help me, ask your advice."

He moved his foot slowly back and forth, scraping the dirt in front of them.

Rachael didn't dare look at him. Her advice?

"As I'm sure you know, George would rather stay here in this valley and marry Camille as soon as possible. He told me as much while we were marking the sheep. I understand how he feels, but I can hardly spare him. I know you've always thought my sheep matter more to me than the people in this company. That's not true, but they're important to my future. I mortgaged my ranch to buy them. If I don't get them to Oregon on time, I'll lose everything."

"Oh," she said quietly. That was news to her.

"Could you hire someone from town?" she asked. "One of the drivers who helped with marking? Surely someone would be willing."

"I've thought of that."

She hesitated. "If you lost the ranch… what would happen to your wife and children?"

He turned to look out over the valley. "Do you remember when you jumped into the river to save Roy? Do you remember my reaction?"

She turned to meet his eyes, chin lifted. "I do. I'll never forget it. I never understood it."

"My wife and two boys drowned in that river. When I saw you in the water holding that child, I… I went a little crazy. It was such a stupid thing to do. But now I know it's exactly the kind of thing you'd do."

Rachael lowered her gaze, emotion flooding her chest: sorrow for his loss, fear of her own feelings, and a sudden flash of joy she didn't quite understand.

"I'm so sorry," she whispered.

Mari. The signs she'd made before they left for the Blue Mountains. That's what she was trying to say—*wife, children, dead.* Had Mari seen her feelings for Mr. Grey before even she did?

"I didn't tell you this for sympathy," he said. "I'm telling you because, despite all my intentions, I've developed an affection for you over this journey. I've even gotten used to your questions. When we danced at the feast, when we walked back to camp, when I carried Christopher on my shoulders… I felt something I hadn't felt in a long time. I felt… happy."

He paused, then added, "And I'll also say this, as a man should. I've known you weren't married for quite some time. Suspected it before Mrs. Dix confirmed it. But by then, well…"

He turned to her fully now.

"I need to ask you something plainly. If you don't feel the same way, I ask that you stay here and let me go on alone. I can't bear the tension any longer."

Rachael took a breath. Her heart was beating fast.

"Oh, Mr. Grey, William, it's all so tangled. I wanted to tell you the truth so many times. I knew you suspected. But it should've come from me. I'm ashamed."

She looked out at the moonlit land below.

"I did lie. It was the only way I could go. I needed to find my plant to prove myself and earn a place at the university. It all feels so long ago now. So unimportant now. You *must* know I have feelings for you. Surely, you must."

She reached for his hand.

He smiled faintly, one eyebrow raised. "So then we're both liars."

"Yes. I suppose we are."

"Will you always question my judgment? Wander off looking for plants?"

"Yes. Probably. And you'll be irritated. But I won't change."

"Nor probably will I."

She smiled. "So… it's settled then."

He put his arm around her waist. She leaned her head against his shoulder.

"Yes," she said softly. "I guess it is."